The Lost Romans

History and Controversy on the Origin of the Romanians

Published by CreateSpace
Illustrations from the public domain (Wikipedia Commons)
Cover photograph of Tudor Tulok (Wikipedia Commons)
Cover design by CreateSpace

Library of Congress Catalog Number: 2013914373

ISBN 978-1-490-53253-0

Printed in the United States of America

\

Dedicated to my grandfather and grandmother, George and Elena Ulieru, who taught me the value of history and humor.

Table of Contents

PART 1: THE HISTORY

1. THE ROMANIANS IN TEN PAGES OR LESS

Romania has always been on the fringes of "Europe", whether we consider the Europe of the Roman Empire in antiquity, the "Christian Europe" of the Middle Ages, or even the modern European Union. Entire books could be written and indeed have been written, on Romania's special position in European history. Romania has somehow both been part of Europe and apart from Europe for almost two thousand years.

The Romanians are consequently perhaps the most misunderstood people in Eastern Europe. How are around 20 million people all but invisible to the modern world? For many in the Western world, Romania is (wrongly) thought of as one of those "Slavic-speaking" countries, its province of Transylvania is believed to exist only in fiction, while Bucharest (capital of Romania) and Budapest (capital of Hungary) are considered essentially synonymous. It is perhaps fitting that Vlad Dracula has become the poster boy for Romania. He is likewise misunderstood, most Western audiences only knowing of him from a 19th century novel by Bram Stoker about the fictional vampire. Much in the same way, Romanians and Romania are, in the minds of Western observers, a product of nineteenth century Orientalism and mystification.

In order to gain a better understanding of what the Romanians are, and of what they are not, we must look at the beginnings of Romanian history. What the Romanians are (and whether they might be edible) is best clarified by knowing the ingredients that went into making them. The nineteenth century Romanian historian Mihai Kogălniceanu was keenly aware that modern people are a product of history, which "contributed to the preservation of our nationality. For what can better preserve it than its history, which shows us what we were, from whence we came, what we are, and … what we will become."(Kogălniceanu, 1967, p. 107)

If the history of the Romanians were a simple and clear-cut affair then perhaps this question could be solved by one Wikipedia article; unfortunately, this is not the case. The origin of the Romanians has been shrouded in controversy for at least 150 years. To this day arguments continue on not only what contributed to the formation of the Romanians, but also on where the Romanians formed and even what they are today. Some of these arguments were started out of a genuine curiosity for clarifying this issue that perhaps has never been clear at all. Romanian history itself is mysterious enough, regarded by prominent historians as the most obscure corner of European history.(Seton-Watson, 1934, p. 16) Consider that almost a century after the death of Richard the Lionhearted, Romanian history was still confined only to legends of a yet-unidentified hero called "Radu the Black" (*Radu Negru*) or "the Black Warlord" (*Negru Vodă*).(Stoicescu, 1980, p. 153)

While some genuinely wished to resolve the historical identity of the Romanians, others purposefully propagated the mystery for political purposes. Indeed, rather than hoping to clarify the issue, many who have raised the topic of the origin of the Romanians have only contributed to its mystification, manipulating facts and figures to fit pre-conceived and politically-expedient theories. The reasons for this are not hard to fathom: Romania more than doubled in size at the end of World War One,[Turnock, 2007, p. 17] when territories that were formerly parts of the Austro-Hungarian and Russian Empires, but which were overwhelmingly Romanian in ethnic composition, were united with Romania under the principle of self-determination.[a] Sadly, historians from the countries on the losing end of this territorial exchange sought to discredit Romania's sovereignty over her new-found territories by turning Romanian history itself into the battlefield where they hoped (and still hope) to reclaim their lost territories.

These controversies however originate even before the end of World War One, most dating to the nineteenth century, a time when millions of Romanians in Austro-Hungary and Tsarist Russia were clamoring for self-determination, and when the governors and historians of these countries could see the inevitable end. Hungarians were worried about losing their province of Transylvania where Romanians were the uncontested ethnic majority. Seeing that modern circumstances supported Romanian ownership, Hungarian historians began to dig up the dead, sometimes literally. They argued that though Romanians were the majority of the population, the Hungarians were the first inhabitants of Transylvania, predating the Romanians in the region, and therefore it is "rightfully" theirs. To the Hungarians, the Romanians only came to Transylvania centuries after the Magyars were already settled, and the Romanians grew to their majority only through constant immigration. As such, from the Hungarian point-of-view, the Romanians usurped Transylvania from its "rightful owner."

The controversy has remained alive to this day, in spite of its loss of any political relevance. It is hard to imagine another war between Romania and Hungary, both members of NATO and the European Union, let alone one where the deciding factor for territorial claims would be childish arguments of "I was here first." Still, the polemic has gained a life of its own, and some Hungarians still argue for Hungary's enlargement on historic grounds at the expense of pretty much all of its neighbors (some of which, such as Slovakia, would be annexed whole). Thus, in many ways, there are still parties interested in continuing the confusion over the history and identity of the Romanians.

In order to clarify the origin of the Romanians one must become familiar with the defining features of the Romanian people and nation; after all, it is always better to know what to explain before one starts explaining. The story of the Romanians (or to your great grandfather: "Rumanians") begins with their name. The term "Romanian" as well as "Romania" is derived from the ancient Romans, who in their native Latin called themselves *Romanus*. This makes the Romanians, along with the Romansch of Switzerland, the sole keepers of the ancient Roman name.[Posner, 1996, p. 105] In Romanian itself this name takes the form of *român*. There is substantial evidence that the

---

[a] The idea that ethnic groups should be allowed to live in their own countries and govern themselves, perhaps at a revolutionary notion at a time when much of the world was part of one empire or another.

5

Romanians called themselves by such a name in the Middle Ages, provided not only in the accounts of numerous travelers to the region, but also in Romanian documents themselves. Francesco della Valle for instance noted in 1534 that the Romanians spoke a language very similar to Italian, and that they referred to themselves by a name derived from *Roman*.(Armbruster, 1972, p. 79) The very first document in the Romanian language, a letter by a Romanian merchant, records the name of the author's country as "*Țeara Rumânească*" ("Romanian country/land").(Cioban, 1989, p. 80) The name is the most evident reminder of a Roman origin of the Romanians, who must descend from Roman colonists in southeastern Europe, and it seems likely the ancestors of the Romanians took up the Roman name when they were still in the Roman Empire. Though the empire collapsed, the Romanians must have preserved the name to distinguish themselves from the surrounding non-Latin "barbarians."

The term *Romania* has an extensive history. It first appeared in the fourth century, during the reign of Constantine the Great, as the name of the entire Roman Empire.(Curtius & Trask, 1990, p. 31) Its appearance came as a result of two developments. Firstly, for much of the Roman Empire's history the term "Romans" (*Romani* in Latin) was reserved only for the ruling upper class of Roman society; most of the inhabitants of the empire were called *perigrini* instead. However, in 212 the emperor Caracalla had bestowed Roman citizenship on all free inhabitants of the Roman Empire, thereby granting them the right to call themselves "Roman."(Burdrick, 2003, p. 204; Burger, 2008, p. 181) Secondly, a more defined frontier emerged in the second and third century, separating the barbarians (*Barbari*) from the Romans (*Romani*). Thus, the Roman Empire came to be known as *Romania*, while the *Barbaricum* came to denote anything beyond Roman authority. It seems evident that the Romanians must have been within the Roman Empire at least until Caracalla's proclamation in order for them to adopt the Roman name as a general ethnonym.

Romania was for a long time only loosely, if at all, associated with the Romanians. For centuries it continued to be associated with the Eastern Roman (Byzantine) Empire, many Greeks referring to themselves as "Romans" (*Rhomaioi*) up until the nineteenth century.(Kaldellis, 2007, p. 47) Even after the Byzantine Empire had ceased to exist, the term Romania had continued to be used for Ottoman possessions in the Balkans, often bastardized as *Rumelia*. In fact, the first reference to *Romania* as being the lands populated by the Romanians did not happen until 1816, when it appeared in the works of the Greek scholar Daniil Philippides.(Drace-Francis, 2006, p. 9) So while the Romanians continued to refer to themselves by Roman name, and continued to call their country "land of Romans" – *Țara Românească* – no one else followed suit.

Most foreign authors preferred to use the term "Wallachian" or "Vlach" when referring to the Romanians. Though the medieval and renaissance authors were aware of the Latin character of the Romanians, and would easily have found an explanation for the term "Romanian" had it been used, they had no ready explanation for the name "Vlach", and thus had to invent one. Among the first erroneous theories of Romanian history was one which suggested that their name derived a mythical Roman general named *Flaccus*, who lead the Romanians into their present homeland. It is telling that the leader of the Vlachs was explicitly stated to be a Roman general, a tacit acknowledgement of the Roman origin of the Romanians.(Armbruster, 1972, p. 51) Aside from indicating that historical writers were aware of the Latin character of the Romanians, today we know that the entire *Flaccus* legend is nonsense.

It may be surprising to learn that the word "Vlach" *does* mean Roman, but only in another form. It can be traced back to a Celtic tribe called *Volcae* that inhabited Central Europe. The *Volcae* had become associates of the Roman Empire, acting as an intermediary of Roman civilization to their Germanic neighbors. The name *Volcae* was transferred (and mangled) in the Germanic languages as *walh* (pronounced "valh"), where it gained the meaning of "foreigner" or "Latin speaker", being introduced into the Balkans by the Goths – a Germanic tribe – in the fourth century.(Friedman, 2001) The Germans used the term *walh* as a synonym for "stranger, Celt, Roman" and had over time morphed from *walha*, to *walh*, and finally to *walah*.(Kunstmann, 1996, pp. 177-178) The Slavs then borrowed the word *walh* and in turn produced the terms *Vlach* or *Vloch*.(Rankin, 1996, p. 19) Thus, *Vlach* is a Germanic word used by Slavs to refer to Latin-speaking people.

The term "Vlach" was and still is not used exclusively for the Romanians but rather has been used, in various forms, for Latinate and Celtic people all over Europe. Some of them are familiar to English speakers, for instance the Welsh of Britain or the Walloons of the Low Countries. Others are more specific to other languages: the Germans refer to the French Swiss as *Welschschweizer* (Welsh Swiss), the Polish use the word *Włosi* for the Italians and had up until recently used the term *Wołosi* for the Romanians, and Hungarians refer to the Romanians as *Oláh* (believe it or not, also derived from "Vlach") and Italians as *Olasz*.(Armbruster, 1972, p. 227) The name Vlach is thus not a divider between the Romanians and the rest of the Latin world, but rather a unifier. It evidences that the Germans, Slavs, and even Hungarians had, since the earliest days, always associated the Romanians with the other Latin people of Europe.(Arvinte, 1983, p. 184)

Of course, the Romanians did not just become Roman in name alone. Their second defining feature is the Romanian language which, surprising as it is to some people, is a Romance language more closely related to Italian and French than it is to the Slavic languages spoken in Romania's neighboring countries. The Romanians are first and foremost a Latin people, this being evident to anyone who has not only seen how they drive but also has heard them speak. This makes Romanian related to Italian, French, Spanish, Portuguese, and all the other smaller Romance languages in-between. Some even went so far as to call it a "dialect of Latin."(Drummond & Nelson, 1994, p. 30) Unfortunately, while all of the other Romance languages are adjoining each other (Spain being next to France, France being next to Italy), Romanian is today isolated from its linguistic kin. There used to be a Romance language spoken in the region of Croatia – Dalmatian – that bridged the gap between Romania and Italy, but that language is today considered extinct.(Posner, 1996, p. 195)

The Romanians have therefore often been described as an "island of Latinity" in a largely Slavic sea.(Boia, 2001b, p. 28; Gallagher, 2001, p. 41) There are a few relatives of Romanian in the Balkans, namely Aromanian and Meglenoromanian in the southern Balkans and Istroromanian in Croatia. As their names imply, all of these languages are strongly related to Romanian. These dialects of Romanian must have separated in the sixth and seventh centuries due to Slavic settlement in the Balkans.(Gönczöl-Davies & Deletant, 2002, p. ix) The question remains of how these languages relate to each other: did Aromanian branch off of Romanian, was it the other way around, or were the two groups separated before either language formed, with both languages descending directly from Latin?

The Latinity of Romanian does come with a few caveats. Though Latin forms the core of the Romanian language, this core does not encompass the majority of the vocabulary. Latin words in Romanian comprise about 30-35% percent of the lexicon,(Chiţoran, 2001, p. 27) though by adding "internal formations" (i.e. Romanian words originating from other Romanian words) the total percentage of Latin words can be brought to roughly 60%.(Bulei, 2005, p. 25) While the words of Latin origin are the single largest group, this still leaves 40% of the vocabulary as being non-Latin in nature. These words are mostly of Slavic or Turkish origin, with a smaller number derived from Hungarian and Greek. Many of these often dominate certain categories and spaces in the Romanian vocabulary. Words of Slavic origin abound in the religious vocabulary as well as terms for (mostly medieval) political institutions. Meanwhile words of Hungarian origin are found for articles of clothing and urban life, including the word for city (oraş). There is also an enigmatic group of roughly 100 words believed to derive from the pre-Roman populations of the region, namely the Dacians and Thracians. Unfortunately, this theory cannot be verified as almost nothing has survived of the Dacian and Thracian languages, and so the words are officially considered as being of "unknown origin." In addition, many of these words are strikingly similar to words found in Albanian. This has pressed the question of whether such words were preserved in Romanian from the ancient populations, which were Romanized/Latinized by the conquering Romans, or whether they are borrowed directly from Albanian as loanwords.(Schulte, 2009, pp. 234-239)

This leads us to the third aspect of the Romanians: where did they form as a people? Given that "The Roman Empire" could mean anything from Britain to Egypt, this can be a daunting question. Where the Romanians are today provides some hints. Historian A.D. Xenopol gave a simplified but accurate picture of their geographical extent: the Romanians are situated around a triangle formed by the Carpathian Mountains that surround Transylvania like a crown... a very angular and uncomfortable crown, but a crown nonetheless. From this center, the native Romanian population stretches out for some distance and is bound by a triangle of three rivers: the Tisa to the west, the Dniester/Nistru in the east, and the Danube to the South.(Xenopol, 1913, p. 18) "Triangulating" the position of the Romanians like this is not entirely accurate – the Romanians in fact barely reach the Tisa and extend well beyond the Dniester(Boia, 2001b, p. 224) – but the geographical simplification is basically true. Any attempt at explaining the origin of the Romanians must explain how the Romanians wound up in such a place.

As mentioned earlier, Balkan Latinity is not restricted only to the Romanians. Today the Balkan Peninsula contains several populations that speak languages related closely to Romanian. The verdict is still out on whether these are distinct languages or only dialects of each other,[Price, 2000, p. 383] but the distinction between "dialect" and "language" has sometimes been more political than substantial.[Roca, 1999, p. 661]Linguists refer to Romanian itself as "Daco-Romanian", the name deriving from the Roman province of Dacia that was located in modern Romania. The Aromanians and Meglenoromanians inhabit Macedonia, Serbia, Bulgaria, Greece, and Albania. Depending on whom you ask they number anywhere between 200,000 and 300,000 speakers.[Kahl, 2002, p. 53] The Istroromanians are located in the Istrian Peninsula in Croatia but their language is critically endangered; less than a thousand speakers remain. The Balkan Latins thus occupy each of the corners of the triangular Balkan Peninsula, separated from each other by a large body of Slavs in the center.

With so many different flavors of Romanian to go around, two very obvious questions have been raised: first, where did they all come from, and secondly, how do these different types of Romanians relate to each other? Judging by the linguistic evidence, Balkan Latinity can be divided into two groups: the northern group of Istroromanian and Daco-Romanian, and the southern group of Aromanian and Meglenoromanian.[Ruhlen, 1991, p. 59] Generally it is believed that Meglenoromanian broke off from Aromanian and Istroromanian broke off from Daco-Romanian,[Friedman, 2001, p. 27; Price, 2000, p. 383] but how do Aromanians and (Daco-)Romanians relate to each other? One possibility is that there had originally been one massive body of Latin Romans stretching from one part of the Balkans to the other, which was broken into separate populations by the Slavic settlement in the Balkan center during the seventh century.[Nandriș, 1939, p. 152] Greek scholars are keen to support this view as it distances the Aromanians from the Romanians and turns the Aromanians into "Romanized Hellenes."[Schwandner-Sievers, 2004, pp. 123-124] Another possibility supported by some scholars, notably Romanians and Aromanians, have proposed that the smaller Aromanian broke off from the much larger Daco-Romanian core and migrated south with the Slavic invasion of the Balkans.[Schwandner-Sievers, 2004, p. 122] The opposite scenario has also been proposed, notably by Hungarian scholars, who claim that the home of all Balkan Latin people was somewhere in the southern Balkans. Though the details (or major points, for that matter) are unclear, at the very least we can say these populations have lived apart from each other for more than one thousand years.[Bryant, Filimon, & Gray, 2005, p. 81] This leaves their point of separation somewhere in the "Dark Ages," and like many events in that era, there is a great deal of speculation as to how it happened.

The last defining aspect of the Romanians is their religion. Most Romanians profess to belong to the Orthodox Church of Christianity, something which has been a historical constant for several centuries. The Romanian Orthodox Church today has its own patriarch but for much of medieval history it was subject to the Byzantine Church in Constantinople. Some might be surprised that a Latin people belong to the Orthodox Church, long associated with Slavic-Byzantine culture, rather than the Roman Catholic Church associated with Latinity. Even Romanian authors, especially converts to Greek or Roman Catholicism, have considered that Orthodoxy had something "non-Latin" and therefore "un-Romanian" about it.[Hitchins, 2001, pp. 89-91] All other Romance people of Europe are historically Catholics, so this religious divergence needs some explanation.

Why the Romanians became Orthodox Christians has a lot to do with when they were Christianized, which is a conundrum in its own right. In fact, there is no concrete date for when the Romanians became Christians. Once this is resolved, we can ask why the Romanians became Orthodox Christians; surely it was not just because leavened bread tasted better. A variety of factors need to be taken into account. For instance, why is it that terms fundamental to Christianity in Romanian come directly from Latin (e.g. *Dumnezeu* (God), *biserica* (church), *cruce* (cross), *etc.*) while those relating to church hierarchy and structure come mostly from Slavonic and Greek (e.g. *popă* (priest), *blagoslovire* (blessing), *călugăr* (monk), and *tetravanghel* (four gospels))?[Georgescu, 1991, pp. 10-11] Where and when the Romanians originated will have a huge impact on the discussion of their Christianization, and vice versa.

The last aspect of the Romanians that requires some explanation is how the Romanians, among oldest inhabitants of the European continent, were also among the last people of Europe to form their own independent states. The Principality of Wallachia in southern Romania, the first state of the Romanians, only gained independence in 1330, and was shortly followed up by the independence of the Principality of Moldova in the East in 1359, close to three hundred years after England's foundation. The late foundation of the Romanian states can be explained by a combination of factors, not the least of which being that the territory of the future Romania hosted numerous invasions throughout Late Antiquity and the Early Middle Ages. While in Western Europe the barbarian migrations largely ended in the seventh century, Eastern Europe and Romania would remain a trampling ground for nomadic invaders up until the Mongol invasion of the 1241.

However, the Romanians were delayed in establishing their own countries even relative to their neighbors such as the Hungarians and Bulgarians, and this requires a particular explanation. The delay may be explained by considering who established Europe's new kingdoms after the collapse of the Roman Empire: the barbarians. The Franks were responsible for the creation of France, the Visigoths set the foundations in Spain, the Anglo-Saxons and later the Normans filled this position in Britain; even in Italy it was the Lombards in the north and the Normans in the south that formed the post-Roman kingdoms. The locals were often subjects of these foreign aristocracies and slowly assimilated their overlords. On the other hand, in Romania, the locals did not live under a foreign aristocracy. Certainly one had been imposed on them by the many barbarian tribes that passed through Romania, but none of these regimes survived the test of time. The founders of Wallachia and Moldova instead were ethnically Romanian, and this may be the key to explaining why it had taken so long for the Romanians to form their own state. In essence, the barbarians needed to be driven out before such a thing became possible.

An aside must be made on a topic not normally delved into by historians, but which requires clarification, namely the relation between Roma (Gypsy) people and the Romanians. Western audiences, even those well-educated, are repeatedly confused as to the relation between these two people. The problem stems from a deceptive word association between "Roma", "Romania", and "Romanians", causing some to wonder if there is a relation between these two different people. The confusion has been exacerbated by the fact that Romania is home to arguably the largest Roma population in Europe. The blunt answer however, is no, the Romanians and Roma are not ethnically related. The Romanians are a Latin people related to the Italians, Spanish, and French, and the names "Romania" and "Romanian" are derived from the name "Roman" and their capital, Rome (called *Roma* in Latin, Italian, and Romanian). The origin of the ethnic term "Roma" for the Gypsies, though still unresolved, is unrelated to that of the word "Romanian." The Roma Gypsies are believed to have originated in the Punjab region of India and their name, *Rom*, is believed to derive from the *Dom* ("slave") caste in Indian society.(Bakker & Kiuchkov, 2000, p. 57) They arrived in Europe, and Romania, only in the late fourteenth century. In Romania and much of Europe they are known by the (pejorative) name of *ţigani*, *cigany*, or *zingaro*, derived from the Greek *atinganoi*, "untouchable." Though the names may be deceptive, believing Roma and Romanians are related is no better than suggesting the same thing about Austrians and Australians.

The Romanians are thus in many ways a walking contradiction. Though Romanians are among the most ancient people of Europe, they were among the last to achieve independence. Though they are more numerous than most of their individual neighbors, they still remain stranded behind an impregnable "Slavic Sea." Though they are a Latin people by language, by faith they belong to the Slavonic Orthodox world. Though the Romanians have always referred to themselves as *român*, with its obvious historical implications, the rest of the world had called them *vlachs* until very recently. Yet perhaps the greatest contradiction of all is that even though they bear the ethnonym *român*, even though their language is Latin-based, and even though it is well-known by historians that the Roman Empire had heavily colonized the region of modern-day Romania, there are still some who – often in bad faith – deny and mystify the origin of the Romanian people. The next few chapters will thus establish and summarize the facts of the early history of the Romanians, and how the Romanians came to be what they are today.

Works Cited

Armbruster, A. (1972). *Romanitatea Românilor: Istoria Unei Idei [The Romanity of the Romanians: the History of an Idea]*. Bucharest, Romania: Editura Academiei Republicii Socialiste România.

Arvinte, V. (1983). *Român, Românesc, România [Romanian people, Romanian, Romania]*. Bucharest, Romania: Editura Ştiinţifică şi Enciclopedică.

Bakker, P., & Kiuchkov, K. (2000). *What is the Romani Language*. Hatfield, UK; Paris, France: University of Hertfordshire Press Centre de recherches tsiganes.

Boia, L. (2001). *Romania: Borderland of Europe*. London, UK: Reaktion.

Bryant, D., Filimon, F., & Gray, R. D. (2005). Untangling our past: Languages, Trees, Splits and Networks.

Bulei, I. (2005). *A Short History of Romania*. Bucharest, Romania: Meronia.

Burdrick, W. L. (2003). *The Principles of Roman Law and Their Relation to Modern Law*. Clark, NJ: Lawbook Exchange.

Burger, M. (2008). *The Shaping of Western Civilization: From Antiquity to the Enlightenment*. Peterborough, ON: Broadview Press.

Chiţoran, I. (2001). *The Phonology of Romanian: a constraint-based approach*. Hawthorne, NY: Mouton de Gruyter.

Cioban, Ş. (1989). *Istoria literaturii române vechi [The History of Old Romanian Literature]*. Bucharest, Romania: Editura Eminescu.

Curtius, E. R., & Trask, W. R. (1990). *European Literature and the Latin Middle Ages*. Princeton, NJ: Princeton University Press.

Drace-Francis, A. (2006). *The making of modern Romanian culture: literacy and the development of national identity*. London, UK: Tauris.

Drummond, S. K., & Nelson, L. H. (1994). *The Western Frontiers of Imperial Rome*. Armonk, NY; London, UK: Sharpe.

Friedman, V. A. (2001). *The Vlah Minority in Macedonia: Language, Identity, Dialectology, and Standardization*. Helsinki, Finland: University of Helsinki Press.

Gallagher, T. (2001). *Outcast Europe: the Balkans, 1789-1989, from the Ottomans to Milošević*. London, UK; New York, NY: Routledge.

Georgescu, V. (1991). *The Romanians: a history* (A. Bley-Vroman, Trans.). Columbus, OH: Ohio State University Press.

Gönczöl-Davies, R., & Deletant, D. (2002). *Colloquial Romanian: the complete course for beginners*. London, UK; New York, NY: Routledge.

Hitchins, K. (2001). *The Idea of Nation among the Romanians of Transylvania, 1700-1849*. Paper presented at the Nation and National Ideology: Past, Present, and PRospects, Bucharest, Romania.

Kahl, T. (2002). The Ethnicity of the Aromanians after 1990: the Identity of a Minority that BEhaves like a Majority. *Ethnologia Balkanica, 6*, 145-169.

Kaldellis, A. (2007). *Hellenism in Byzantium: the transformations of Greek identity and the reception of the classical tradition*. Cambridge, UK: Cambridge University Press.

Kogălniceanu, M. (1967). *Texte social-politice alese*. Bucharest, Romania: Editura Politică.

Kunstmann, H. (1996). *Die Slaven : ihr Name, ihre Wanderung nach Europa und die Anfänge der russischen Geschichte in historisch-onomastischer Sicht*. Stuttgart, Germany: Steiner.

Nandriş, G. (1939). The Earliest Contacts between Slavs and Roumanians. *The Slavonic and East European Review, 18*(52), 142-154.

Posner, R. (1996). *The Romance Languages*. Cambridge, UK; New York, NY: Cambridge University Press.

Price, G. (2000). *Encyclopedia of the Languages of Europe*. Malden, MA: Blackwell.

Rankin, D. (1996). *Celts and the Classical World*. New York, NY: Routledge.

Roca, I. M. (1999). Stress in the Romance Languages. In H. v. d. Hulst (Ed.), *Word Prosodic Systems in the Languages of Europe*. Berlin: Mouton de Gruyter.

Ruhlen, M. (1991). *A Guide to the World's Languages: Classification*. Stanford, CA: Stanford University Press.

Schulte, K. (2009). Loandowrds in Romanian. In M. Haspelmath & U. Tadmor (Eds.), *Loanwords in the World's Languages: A Comparative Handbook*. Berlin: De Gruyter Mouton.

Schwandner-Sievers, S. (2004). Times Past: References for the Construction of Local Order in Present-Day Albania. In M. Todorova (Ed.), *Balkan Identities: nation and memory*. New York, NY: New York University Press.

Seton-Watson, R. (1934). *A History of the Roumanians*. Cambridge, UK: Cambridge University Press.

Stoicescu, N. (1980). *Constituirea Statelor Feudale Românesti*. Bucharest, Romania: Editura Academiei Republicii Socialiste România.

Turnock, D. (2007). *Aspects of Independent Romania's Economic History with Particular Reference to the Transition for EU Accession*. Burlington, VT: Ashgate.

Wright, R. (2008). Romance Languages. In K. Brown & S. Ogilvie (Eds.), *Concise Encyclopedia of Languages of the World*. Oxford, UK: Elsevier Science.

Xenopol, A. D. (1913). *Istoria Românilor din Dacia Traiană [The History of the Romanians from Trajan's Dacia]* (Vol. I). Bucharest, Romania: Librariei Şcoalelor.

2. IN THE DAYS OF THE DACIANS

Where does one begin discussing the origins of the Romanians? Romania has arguably the oldest evidence of human habitation in Europe, with *Homo sapiens* fossils discovered at Peștera cu Oase (Romanian: "Cave with Bones") dating from well over 32,000 years ago.(B. Lewis, Jurmain, & Kilgore, 2010, p. 295) It is however grossly inappropriate to consider these cavemen as the cultural ancestors of modern Romanians. While many Romanians bear genetic markers that came to Europe immediately after the Ice Age, the same is true for the rest of the Balkans, showing that the genetic landscape of this corner of the world was formed long before the cultures began to take shape,(Varzari et al., 2007) and though national pride may wish to deny it, the people of the Balkans are essentially the same genetically.(Bosch et al., 2006, pp. 459-487)

Romanian cavemen aside, the first evidence of what we could call "culture" in Romania appeared around 8,000 years ago. Named after regions where they were discovered, the cultures of Hamangia, Cucuteni, and many others present in what is now Romania had refined the arts of metal-working, agriculture, animal domestication, as well as pottery and weaving. Some artwork produced by these cultures, such as the *Thinker of Hamangia*, clearly deal with higher expressions of human thought. Much of it was also centered on the female figure, some having taken these works as evidence of a matriarchal society.(Marler, 2003, pp. 8-9) Who really wore the pants (that had yet to be invented) in such societies is up for discussion,(Macko & Blair, 1999, p. 36) but what is clear is that the Cucuteni settlements had achieved a considerable level of civilization, perhaps comparable even to early societies in Mesopotamia.(Haarmann, 1996, p. 15)

Unfortunately, the Cucuteni civilization and their relatives were not ancestors of the Romanians since their cultures ended in around 2000 BC. There were two fundamental reasons for this. Firstly, the Cucuteni people had an odd and wasteful practice of cremating their dead with all of their belongings, including houses, rapidly depleting nearby forests.(Kohl, 2007, p. 45) Unsurprisingly, several villages perished by fire.(MacKendrick, 1975, p. 15) The second problem came with the arrival of the Indo-Europeans, the ancestors of most modern European people. The Indo-Europeans, pretty much wandering barbarians, began moving into Europe around the beginning of the second millennium BC. Though some have argued that the homeland of these people was in Anatolia or the Balkans, most scholars believe they originated in Ukraine.(Mallory, 1997, p. 557) Whatever the case, their arrival brought a sudden collapse of most of the civilizations in the area.

As disastrous as their arrival was for the former cultures, the arrival of the Indo-Europeans in Romania kicked off the Bronze Age and created the first ancestors of the Romanians. These settlers, present over the entire landscape of the Balkans, began to split into two groups by 1800 BC: the Illyrians in the west and the Thracians in the east. This split became more defined through time, and a definitive "Thracian" identity had formed by the sixth century BC, when they were first mentioned by the ancient Greeks.(Georgescu, 1991, p. 2) The Romanian lands fell under their control, though "Thrace" to classical authors was mostly in Bulgaria.

14

Herodotus, the father of history, described the population of Thrace as being "the largest in the world, after the Indians, of course." Herodotus, of course, probably never heard of China. Still, it is clear that the Thracians formed a substantial (and menacing) people to the city-dwelling Greeks. They were however fractured into numerous small tribes, Herodotus himself added that "if they were ruled by a single person, or had a common purpose, they would be invincible and would be by far the most powerful nation in the world"... but of course, for Herodotus, these were dumb barbarians, and therefore "there is no way that this will ever happen – and that is why they are weak." (Herodotus, 1998, V, 3)

By the fifth century Herodotus' prediction still seemed correct, as the Thracians had divided themselves into two camps, the border between them situated roughly on the Danube. While to the south most of the tribes were known as Thracians, a whole new civilization was developing in the north: the Getae and Dacians, often shortened to Geto-Dacian. The Dacians were situated mostly in Transylvania and along the Carpathians, and the Getae were found south and east of the Carpathians. The separation between the Thracians and Geto-Dacians is best noted in the different endings of town names north and south of the Danube. While the Thracians of Bulgaria generally ended their city names with –para, the Geto-Dacians typically used –dava, much like German use of stadt and English use of ton. Some believed this is evidence that the Dacians had their own language as well, distinct from Thracian.(Georgiev, 1966)

What was the relation between the Dacians and Getae? Authors from antiquity unanimously suggested the two people were essentially the same. The Roman geographer Strabo noted that "The language of the Daci is the same as that of the Getae" and claimed the only difference was one of names: "some of the people are called Daci, whereas others are called Getae."(Strabo, 1924, VII, 3, 13) This assertion is backed by several other Roman writers. Cassius Dio asserted that the only difference between the Dacians and the Getae was that the former name was used by the Romans and the latter by the Greeks; Cassius Dio of course claimed the Roman version was more correct and closer to what the Dacians called themselves.(Dio, 2004, LXVII, 6, 2) The Roman historian Justin added that "the Dacians are descendants of the Getae"(Justinus, XXXII, 3, 16), though whether he meant this in an ethnic or a political sense is debatable. The ancients in general had a pretty clear idea that the Getae and Dacians were the same people.

Romanian historians during the Communist era took the Roman authors at face value, perhaps out of a desire to promote national unity between Romania's different provinces. More recently this conclusion has come under fire,(Niculescu, 2007, pp. 139-141) the chief complaints being that it makes no sense for the Romans and Greeks use different names for the same people and that the primary sources are unreliable. Strabo for instance, was not a linguist and it is hard if he ever heard either Getic or Dacian.(Boia, 2001b, p. 43) Still, there is a very small chance that all of the primary authors mentioned were wrong. Even if Strabo was linguistically inept, what should one say of Cassius Dio or Justin? Furthermore, archaeology in ancient Romania presents a homogenous cultural landscape; if these people were different they did a good job hiding the fact. There is no compelling reason to believe that the *Getae* and *Dacii* were different people.[Price, 2000, p. 120] As the two people are largely the same, we will use "Dacian" for all of the Geto-Dacian tribes in order to avoid the cumbersome nomenclature.

The Dacians separated from the Thracians due a variety of external influences on their culture. Even ancient Romania was a frontier of cultures and the Dacians appear to have been very utilitarian in adopting good ideas from their neighbors. The "civilized" and "barbarian" influences around them made Dacia the most dynamic barbarian culture of antiquity, a hybrid between northern European, Steppe, and classical civilization. Strabo hints that the Dacians gradually separated from the Thracians due to these influences. While Herodotus clearly threw the Getae in with the Thracians, Strabo wrote four centuries later that "the Greeks used to suppose that the Getae were Thracians"[Strabo, 1924, VII, 3, 2], indicating – perhaps – that Greek opinion had changed in four centuries, and that the Dacians had become their own people.

The first of these influences came from the Scythians, horsemen from the Caucasus and Ukraine who attacked and temporarily subdued the Dacian tribes in eastern Romania. Many Dacians were driven away from the plains near the Danube and into the fastness of the Carpathian Mountains and Transylvania. Other Dacians, lacking the fortress of the Carpathians, opted to make their own, leaving behind many fortresses in Romania, more than twenty of which have been discovered.[Georgescu, 1991, p. 3] The Dacians and Scythians coexisted on the Dniester river in modern Dobrogea, but little cultural mixing occurred. Scythian culture – with its "cannibals, transvestite shamans, and head-hunters who drank from skulls"[Taylor, 2001, p. 373] – was as barbaric to the Dacians as Dacian culture appeared to the Greeks.

Even though their cultural patronage was undoubtedly lacking, the Scythians certainly left their mark on warfare in the region. The composite bow, a staple weapon of steppe nomads, became revered among the Dacians. The Greek historian Thucydides remarked that the Getae "border on the Scythians and are armed in the same manner, being all mounted archers."[Thucydides, II, 96] Some have even pondered whether cataphracts[b] portrayed on Trajan's Column depicting the Roman-Dacian war belong to the Scythian or Sarmatian allies of the Dacians, who were known for employing such heavy cavalry, or if they are actually Dacians themselves. This style of warfare continued north of the Danube for centuries, as in the first century BC Ovid wrote of them "every one of them carrying bow and quiver and poisoned arrows, yellow with viper's gall."[Ovidius, 2005, V, 7, 15] Strangely, mention of poisoned arrows used by the Romanians can even be found in the fourteenth century,[Breza & Pascu, 1977, p. 155] indicating perhaps that the Scythians left a long-lived impression.

As the Scythians were encroaching on Dacian territory from the East, an equal but different barbarian influence was coming from the West: the Celts. Traditionally

---

[b] Heavily armored horsemen known for encasing themselves and their horses in armor. Armed with long lances and relying on a devastating charge, cataphracts have been referred to as the knights of antiquity.

associated with Gaul, Britain, and the rest of Western Europe, the Celts had expanded into Dacia in the third century BC. Their arrival set new trends in ancient Dacia, as fashion, jewelry, and metalworking all began to imitate Celtic designs. Anyone familiar with Romania's emulation of French culture in the nineteenth century, when Bucharest was known abroad as the "Little Paris," will find subtle irony in the proto-Romanians imitating the proto-French in antiquity. This Celtic-influenced culture in Dacia is known as "La Tène", and Dacian metal-working techniques find their origins in Celtic methods adopted in this time.(Schmitz, 2005, p. 29) The extensive use of Dacian goods in centers of Celtic culture(MacKendrick, 1975, pp. 50-51) and vice-versa suggests a great deal of contact between the two people.(Ferencz, 2006, pp. 140-141)

Soon the Dacians began to best the Celts at their own game. The Dacians organized themselves into the first true barbarian kingdom of Europe, and with this, were able to take Celtic metal-working to an industrial scale of production. The results are perhaps more evident on the battlefield than anywhere else: most Dacian warriors were armed with expensive swords as opposed to the Celts, where the cheap spears remained the mainstay of the armies. The clear military advantage over the spear-armed Celts became evident when the Celts were both literally and figuratively cut down to size and driven out of Transylvania.(Schmitz, 2005, p. 30)

One Dacian blade stands for particular attention, becoming almost iconic of the Dacian people and feared by both barbarian and classical enemies alike: the *falx*. A long two-handed scythe-like blade attached to a sword hilt, it had a habit of opening up Roman armor like tin cans. The bas reliefs from both Trajan's Column and the Adamklissi memorial monument in Romania depicts the Romans with reinforced helmets and armors, even adopting what was considered dishonorable segmented arm guards associated with gladiators, to deal with the new deadly weapon. The scar this weapon inflicted on the psyche of Roman soldiers is cleanly captured by the writer Fronto: when Trajan marched his armies against the Parthians in Iran after fighting the Dacians, the soldiers were "making light of the impact of their [Parthian] arrows compared with the gaping wounds inflicted by the scythes of the Dacians."(Fronto, 1988, II, 9) Dacian soldiers were even recruited into the Roman army with their native weapons.(Ruscu, 2004, pp. 82-83) Much like Germany in the Industrial Revolution, the Dacians began the Iron Age playing catch-up only to surpass their "mentors." The Celts came to a Dacia of bows and arrows, and left a Dacia armed with the most frightening blades of the barbarian world.

The "barbarian" nature of Dacian society is only half of the story. The Dacians were also a peripheral part of the classical world, being influenced by the ancient Greeks. These were not influences from the Greece of Athens and Sparta, but rather from nearby Greek colonies on the Black Sea. The ancient Greeks, like modern tourists, tended to monopolize the beachfront property wherever they went, and the Black Sea was no exception. Greek colonies along the Black Sea stretched from Trebizond, in modern Turkey, all the way to Chersonesos on the Crimean peninsula. Greek colonies on the Dacian coastline included Tomis (modern-day Constanţa), Histria, Tyras,

Callatis, and Dionysopolis. The lands of Romania thus became a part, if only a fringe part, of Mediterranean culture.

The story of how the Greeks settled in Romania is interesting and convoluted. The Greeks originally called the Black Sea *Pontus Axinus*, the "Inhospitable Sea." This was, however, just an unfortunate transliteration of the original Scythian name for the sea, *Akhshaina* (meaning "Dark Sea"), but the name stuck for some time for a number of reasons. Firstly, news of the violent Scythians that menaced the Greek colonies must have dissuaded many would-be colonists. Secondly, the Black Sea's absence of islands which could serve as rest-stops for navigating merchants made crossing the Black Sea was a perilous journey. Thirdly, Greek myths identified the Black Sea with various calamities. Nevertheless, one cannot dismiss the possibility of deliberate manipulation given the wealth of the Black Sea colonies. Much in the same way the Viking Erik the Red tried to attract settlers to a desolate frozen land by calling it "Greenland", the Greeks already living on the sea's coast may have tried to dissuade new settlers from the Greek mainland and deliberately used false advertising to keep them away. The secret could not be kept for long however, as news of the wealth of the Black Sea colonies spread, and by the sixth century BC *Pontus Axinus* had become *Pontus Euxinus*, the "Hospitable Sea."(Djakonov, 1991, p. 361)

Though the Greeks had a tendency of walling themselves off in their *polis* cities, nevertheless their influence through trade was substantial. Greek influence on the Dacians could fill entire books.(Glodariu, 1976) Greek luxury goods reached the Dacians, and the tombs of wealthy Thracian and Dacian kings show many fine Greek furnishings.(MacKendrick, 1975, pp. 25-29) In exchange the Greeks received certain commodities considered by them to be essential for civilization, particularly slaves. Greek trade also brought coinage to the Dacians, who began to imitate Mediterranean coins, the most famous of which are a series of coins that bear the inscription "Koson", likely the name of a local tribal leader, in Greek letters. The Dacians had an appreciation for coins beyond a simple love for shiny objects, and understood the value of currency beyond bullion value. The imitation of currencies continued with Roman coins in the first century BC.(Rodewald, 1976, pp. 39-42)

But perhaps where the Greeks contributed most to Dacian culture was in designing the impressive Dacian fortresses in Transylvania, which are today considered a UNESCO site. The unique walls earned a particular title of "the Dacian wall" (*murus Dacicus*) to classical authors. The exterior was made of large, uniformly sized blocks, sometimes brought from quarries many kilometers away. The two faces of the walls were then connected laterally by dove-tailed wooden beams that, fitting into openings on the blocks, prevented this whole shell from falling apart. With all of the beams in place, the two or three meter wide hollow was filled with dirt and rubble.(Oltean, 2007, p. 61) The result was a durable wall with a hard exterior capable of resisting fire and a soft core capable of absorbing the shock of catapults and battering rams. The Dacians appear to have had foreign architects help in construction as Greek letters incised on some of the blocks indicate the pride its architects placed in their work.(Lockyear, 2004, p. 61) Large towers, capable of mounting siege engines, also show Greek influence. When such fortresses were situated on top of a ravine, as they often were, they would be a daunting obstacle for any invader.

The Dacians thus appear to be at odds with their classification as "barbarians." It is hard to imagine how the Dacians fit the caricature of half-naked brutes conjured up by such a polarizing word. True, they were not fully part of the Mediterranean world, which has so tinted our definition of what "civilization" is, but they clearly possessed their own version of civilization. They were definitely a step closer to the Greeks than their neighbors, be they the egalitarian societies of the Germans, the tribal confederations of the Celts, or the Scythian steppe nomads. The Dacians enjoyed a standard of living which far surpassed the barbarians in Western Europe.(Everitt, 2009, p. 105) Dacian culture was vibrant, taking the best influences from their neighbors (save for Greek alcoholism) and forged a flourishing society out of them.(Rossi, 1971, pp. 20-21)

Certainly expert archers armed with finely crafted swords and occupying a sophisticated network of forts would be a formidable enough force, but the most considerable weapon the Dacians wielded was their home-grown organization. Their social stratification, religion, and government gave the Dacians an unrivaled edge in the barbarian world. The nobility, the church, and the state were to prove essential to the rapidly emerging Dacian powerhouse in Eastern Europe.

In spite of communist historiography's insistence on "egalitarianism" in Dacian society, it is clear that the Dacians did not live in a classless utopia. Roman sources attest the existence of at least two social strata: the *tarabostes* (or *pileati*) who were the nobility of Dacian society, easily identified by the Phrygian caps ("liberty caps") that they wore and the *comati* warrior-class, meaning "long-haired ones", noted for the absence of the aforementioned caps. Like any people skilled in war, the Dacians did enslave their prisoners, but it is interesting that the Dacians rarely kept slaves for themselves.(Oltean, 2007, p. 114) The practice of slavery was driven by Rome's thirst for slaves. For the Romans a slave was seen as an essential element of any self-respecting household. For the Dacians and much of "barbarian Europe", slaves were only worth as much as Rome was willing to pay for them. From a modern perspective, this is a rather ironic contrast between "civilization" and "barbarity."

The Dacian religion was also something in a world of its own. Unlike their neighbors, Dacian religion evolved into a monotheistic faith centered on a prophet-god: Zalmoxis. A man of outstanding philosophical teachings, Zalmoxis would be deified by the Dacians and became renowned even in classical civilizations. Diodorus Siculus listed Zalmoxis among the three great non-Greek lawgivers and philosophers (the other two being Moses and Zoroaster).(Diodorus, 2004, I, 94) While the other two might be common names today, most people undoubtedly have never heard of Zalmoxis. Nevertheless, in antiquity Zalmoxis was considered a true revolutionary.

But who exactly was Zalmoxis? So little is known of the man even the spelling of his name has been brought into question. What does seem clear is that his teachings appear rather similar to those of Jesus. Like Jesus, Zalmoxis spoke of the immortality of the soul, and claimed that those who believed in him would never die but only join him in the afterlife.(Herodotus, 1998, V, 94) The similarities do not stop there. Herodotus claimed Zalmoxis said "neither he nor those who drank with him nor any of their descendants would die", in a manner somewhat similar to the Christian communion. Zalmoxis also decided to prove this immortality, like Jesus, through a first-hand example. Zalmoxis however, was not just going to die for three days – apparently not enough to convince his Dacian skeptics – but rather died for three years! He sealed himself in a cave with no food and water, and only emerged three years later, to the amazement of his Dacian subjects that began to revere him as a god.(Herodotus, 1998, V, 95)

This gave the Dacians a certain fanaticism in battle unmatched by their enemies. Julian the Apostate satirical portrayal of Emperor Trajan envisioned the emperor reflecting on how the Dacians perceived Zalmoxis' teachings:

"I subdued the Getae, the most warlike race that ever existed, which is due partly to their physical courage, partly to the doctrines that they have adopted from their admired Zamolxis. For they believe that they do not die but only change their place of abode, and they meet death more readily than other men undertake a journey."(Julian, 1913-1923, 327)

Zalmoxis also provided other lessons to his followers, ranging from astronomy and the movement of celestial bodies(Jordanes, 1960, XI, 69) to curative knowledge on healing the soul and the body, being even recounted by Plato.(Plato, 1964, 157) The cult of Zalmoxis did come with some habits not found today in the modern church, namely human sacrifice. Furthermore, Christians today hardly have to "threaten their god by shooting arrows up into the sky at thunder and lightning." Zalmoxis however, still remains an interesting case of parallelism to Christianity, especially given that Zalmoxis lived centuries before Jesus.

Unfortunately Zalmoxis shared another trait with Jesus: he didn't bother writing any of his teachings down. Zalmoxis, unlike Jesus, also had no literate followers either. Everything written on the man, and indeed on the Dacians in general, comes from Roman and Greek sources. This presents a problem since we have no way of confirming if the information we have is not even factually accurate. The few sacred sanctuaries at Dacian archaeological sites reveal little in terms of ritual or theology.

But learning of a religion from foreign sources presents a more serious problem since to non-believers, the Dacians were irrevocably foolish. Learning of Zalmoxis from the Greeks is about the same as learning of Jesus from Richard Dawkins. Herodotus himself presents an account which may be the first case of nationalism in historiography on the (proto-)Romanians. Herodotus stated that Greeks on the shores of the Hellespont believed Zalmoxis to have been a slave of Pythagoras, and that the Thracians, "a poor ignorant race", were duped by Zalmoxis who "by his commerce with the Greeks... was acquainted with the Ionic [Greek] mode of life and with manners more refined than those current among his countrymen." Zalmoxis tricked the Thracians into believing he had died, when in fact he had only stowed himself away safely in a secret "underground apartment" and only later "came forth from his concealment."[(Herodotus, 1998, V, 95)] This not only showed the barbarians were stupid but that Zalmoxis was only so wise because he had lived among Greeks. Herodotus however disregarded these stories with fitting behavior as the world's first historian. In regard to such propaganda he stated "I believe Zalmoxis to have lived long before the time of Pythagoras"[(Herodotus, 1998, V, 96)] which was the most tactful way of saying that the Greek stories were rubbish.

The Dacians still lacked one aspect needed to take their civilization to the next level: good government. As Herodotus remarked, the Dacians remained divisive and weak, and thus spent their early history mostly on the losing end of various engagements. The Persian Empire under Darius I invaded the Getic lands in 514BC. It is in this context that Greek writers remarked of the Dacians, the only Thracians to have resisted Darius, were "the noblest as well as the most just of all the Thracian tribes"[(Herodotus, 1998, IV, 93)] though this might have been simple propaganda produced as a result of the Dacians fighting on the right [i.e. Greek] side of the war. One man's barbarian is another man's noble savage. In any case Darius was unable to establish his rule over the Dacians and later withdrew, being the first Dacian victory on written record.

The Dacians bravely but unsuccessfully attempted to resist another great general, Alexander the Great, in 335BC. Alexander made short work of a local Dacian army, but his victory is attributed more to Alexander's own brilliance rather than any superiority of the Macedonian army. Furthermore, his victory did not produce any lasting results. The Macedonians looted a city (or village) before retreating back south.

In any case, the Dacians would be better prepared for their next encounter with the Macedonians, this much was proven when one of Alexander's governors, Zopyrion, attempted invasion of Getia in 331; he feared that he had gained a reputation of indolence and thought that a cakewalk of a war against the northern barbarians would improve his reputation. He crossed the Danube with a massive force of 30,000 men, but was unable to take the coastal cities and his retreat across the Danube was blocked by a great storm. The Getae, by now experimenting with ways of crushing the Macedonian armies,[(Muşat & Ardeleanu, 1985, p. 23)] took this opportunity to pay back their defeat at the hands of Alexander with interest: Zopyrion and his army was encircled and annihilated.[(Justinus, XII, 2)] Zopyrion himself went down in history as not only an indolent governor, but an incompetent one as well.

Whether they had not learned their lesson or they simply decided to go for the best two out of three, the Macedonians invaded Getia once more in 294BC under Lysimachus, the governors of Thrace (modern Bulgaria). Even if his army did not number the 100,000 men claimed by ancient writers, it is clear Lysimachus was not just going for an evening stroll; this must have been a substantial force.[(Polyaenus, VII, 25)] He soon discovered the error of his decision as he found himself completely outmatched by the Dacians, "men not unversed in warfare and far his superiors in number."[(Pausanias, I, 9, 5)] Pressed by the Dacian leader Dromichaetes, Lysimachus did the only honorable thing he could think of and ran for his life, but he, his son, and army were captured by the

Dacians. The "punishment" received by the Macedonian captives was something quite unlike what we think of as barbarian: the Dacian king wined and dined his "guests" on fine silver, held them in the highest manner of hospitality, and even crowned Lysimachus before sending him home... but not before convincing him that he had nothing to gain from warfare against the Dacians.[Diodorus, 2004, XXI, 11-12] The subtle irony of a barbarian king teaching "civilized Greeks" to live in peace with their neighbors was clearly lost on the classical authors.

The Dacians had no sooner relieved their southern frontier with the Greeks that they suddenly found themselves pressed with a Celtic invasion from the West after 300 BC. True, the Celts made great additions to Dacian culture, but with this cultural borrowing came a decline in political importance. Put it simply: one cannot be both the student and the master at the same time. Chieftain burials overtly Celtic in nature, with ample weaponry to boot, leaves little doubt as to who constituted the new political elite in Dacia.[Koch, 2006, p. 549]

But the Celts found some trouble establishing any firm footing across the Carpathians, and as the Scythians had almost simultaneously withdrawn from eastern Romania, it left the field wide open for a Dacian resurgence. Inscriptions from the Greek colonies on the coast attest of the need to pay tribute (i.e. "protection money") to a variety of Dacian kings Zalmogedikos, Rhemaxos, and Oroles.[Murgescu, 2001, pp. 36-37] Complete control over the Danubian plains is one overt fact the inscriptions indicate, but that these small-time chiefs were indicated by name shows a certain level of centralization was already underway. The Dacian chiefs were no longer simply the men with the biggest houses and the most jewelry, but became true rulers in their societies. Dacian power had become formalized and organized and there was no bigger worry for "civilized people" than an organized barbarian.

Dacian power culminated in the retaking of Transylvania under the reign of Rubobostes around 150 BC.[Justinus, XXXI, 4] Some historians argue that Rubobostes was just a misspelling of another Dacian king's name, Burebista,[Vékony, 2000, p. 38] but as Burebista died in in 44 BC, Rubobostes would have reigned for an impressive 106 years of his life, putting even Queen Victoria to shame. The other possibility, that the dating by the Roman authors of Rubobostes' reign is incorrect and needs to be pushed forward to the time of Burebista, does not stand up to archaeological scrutiny. The retreat of the Celtic La Tène culture around 150 BC, eerily close to the dating given by the Roman authors for Rubobostes' reign, would be very mysterious without a Dacian resurgence.[Pop, Barbulescu, & Nägler, 2005, p. 75] Today it acknowledged that Rubobostes reigned significantly earlier than the Burebista and was responsible for the ascendancy of Dacian power in Transylvania.

Rubobostes may have softened the ground, but it was only under the leadership of Burebista, in the second and first centuries BC, that the Dacians begin to muscle their way to the top of the barbarian food chain. Burebista did this by breaking the curse of disunity among the Thracians that Herodotus had noted. Whether by force or by diplomacy, his reign transformed the Dacian state beyond mere tribal allegiances and into a vast barbarian kingdom as Europe had not seen before. Burebista made sure his followers knew that his right to rule was divinely ordained by making the chief priest of the Zalmoxis cult his right-hand man, a practice that proved so convenient it continued to the end of Dacian civilization.(Pop et al., 2005)

Burebista's chief priest, the interlocutor between Zalmoxis and the common man, was called Deceneus, and it is with his help that the last few "barbarian" stereotypes on the Dacians break down. Even the Romans took note that "through training, sobriety, and obedience to his [Burebista's] commands", the Dacians had become a true powerhouse. Dacian discipline went to lengths the Romans could hardly comprehend, even going so far as to cut down their vines and "live without wine."(Strabo, 1924, VII, 3, 5-11) A sober mind was needed to lead the barbarian world.

The contrast in organization between the Celts and Dacians is perhaps best shown in the layout of their strongholds. Dacian fortresses, unlike Celtic fortresses, were only large enough to house a military garrison, keeping civilians strictly outside the walls. Rather than being walled settlements ruled by an independent chief, Dacian fortresses were commanded by a subordinate noble and were intended to be stumbling blocks for any invading army, part of a large network designed to provide early warning of an invasion that gave time to the king to gather an army and repel the invaders. The very existence of such a network implies a highly coordinated military apparatus and organization around a centralized authority.

Burebista used his fanatical followers as a formidable weapon, and this Dacian force wasted little time in crushing all of its neighbors. If the Celts were not in a world of hurt before, they certainly were in for a ride now, being pushed back as far as the modern Czech Republic. It is no coincidence that in this same time we see the appearance of a slave trade between Dacia and the Roman Empire. The Romans needed slaves and the Dacians could provide them with Celtic and German prisoners in great numbers, some estimating 30,000 slaves a year. To the East and South, the Dacian state expanded up to the Black Sea, subduing all of the Greek colonies nearby and conquering northern Thrace up to the Balkan Mountains. The fall of the Greek colonies came as a surprise to the Greeks who believed a strong wall was all that was needed to keep out the barbarians, who the Greeks assumed did not know siege warfare. The port-city of Olbia, surrounded by strong walls that had centuries before resisted the siege by Zopyrion's Macedonian war machine, fell to a clearly more competent Dacian force.(Krapivina, 2005, p. 256) Burebista, with his army of 200,000 men, was now the most powerful barbarian in all of Europe.

Dacia's meteoric rise did not go unnoticed by the other important power in the region: the Roman Empire. Dacia had previously been little more than a source for slaves and a topic for the musings of geographers, but in Burebista's time it became a very serious threat to the Romans. The Dacians were already raiding into Roman provinces without fear of the seemingly-impotent Roman forces. No peace could last between a Rome that saw itself as the mother of the world and a barbarian kingdom that had just gained its place in the imperial sun. Another war was brewing for the Balkans.

Works Cited

Boia, L. (2001). *Romania: Borderland of Europe*. London, UK: Reaktion.

Bosch, E., Calafell, F., González-Neira, A., Flaiz, C., Mateu, E., Scheil, H.-G., . . . Comas, D. (2006). Paternal and maternal lineages in the Balkans show a homogeneous landscape over linguistic barriers, except for the isolated Aromuns. *Annals of Human Genetics, 70*(4), 459-487.

Breza, M., & Pascu, Ş. (1977). *Documenta Romaniae Historica*. Bucharest, Romania: Academia de Ştiinţe Sociale şi Politice a Republicii Socialiste România.

Dio, C. (2004). *Roman History* (E. Cary, Trans. Vol. LXVII). Cambridge, MA: Harvard University Press.

Diodorus. (2004). *Library of History* (Vol. I). Cambridge, MA; London, UK: Harvard University Press.

Djakonov, I. M. (1991). *Early Antiquity*. Chicago, IL: University of Chicago.

Everitt, A. (2009). *Hadrian and the Triumph of Rome*. New York, NY: Random House.

Ferencz, I. V. (2006). Settlements and Necropoles: few considerations on the archaeological discoveries on the middle course of the Mureş River belonging to the La Tene B2-C1. *Acta Terrae Septemcastrensis, V*(1).

Fronto, C. (1988). *Principia Historiae* (C. R. Haines, Trans. Vol. II). Cambridge, MA: Harvard University Press.

Georgescu, V. (1991). *The Romanians: a history* (A. Bley-Vroman, Trans.). Columbus, OH: Ohio State University Press.

Georgiev, V. (1966). The Genesis of the Balkan Peoples. *The Slavonic and East European Review, 44*(103), 285-297.

Glodariu, I. (1976). *Dacian Trade with the Hellenistic and Roman World*. Oxford, UK: British Archaeological Reports.

Haarmann, H. (1996). *Early civilization and literacy in Europe: an inquiry into the cultural continuity in the Mediterranean world*. Berlin: Mouton de Gruyter.

Herodotus. *The Histories*.

Jordanes. *Getica* (Vol. XI).

Julian. *The works of the emperor Julian* (W. C. Wright, Trans. Vol. II).

Justinus. *Epitome of the Philippic history of Pompeius Trogus* (Vol. XXXII; XXXI; XXXII).

Koch, J. (2006). *Celticu Culture: a Historical Encyclopedia*. Santa Barbara, CA; Oxford, UK: ABC-CLIO.

Kohl, P. L. (2007). *The Making of Bronze Age Eurasia*. Cambridge, UK: Cambridge University Press.

Krapivina, V. (2005). Problems of the Chronology of the Late Hellenistic Strata of Olbia. In V. Stolba & L. Hannestad (Eds.), *Black Sea Studies: Chronologies of the Black Sea Area in the Period c. 400-100 BC*. Aarhus, Denmark: Aarhus University Press.

Lewis, B., Jurmain, R., & Kilgore, L. (2010). *Understanding Humans: an introduction to physical anthropology and archaeology*. Belmont, CA: Wadsworth Cengage Learning.

Lockyear, K. (2004). *The Late Iron Age Background to Roman Dacia*. Portsmouth: Journal for Roman Archaeology.

MacKendrick, P. (1975). *The Dacian Stones Speak*. Chapel Hill, NC: University of North Carolina Press.

Macko, N., & Blair, J. (1999). Glimpsing Romania. *Frontiers: A Journal of Women Studies, 20*(3), 36-41.

Mallory, J. P. (1997). *Encyclopedia of Indo-European Culture*. Chicago, IL: Fitzroy Dearborn.

Marler, J. (2003). *The Iconography and Social Structure of Old Europe: The Archaeomythological Research of Marija Gimbutas*. Paper presented at the World Congress on Matriarchal Studies, Luxemburg.

Murgescu, B. (2001). *Istoria României în Texte*. Bucharest, Romania: Corint.

Muşat, M., & Ardeleanu, I. (1985). *From Ancient Dacia to Modern Romania*. Bucharest, Romania: Editura Ştiinţifică şi Enciclopedică.

Niculescu, G. (2007). Archaeology and Nationalism in the History of the Romanians. In P. L. Kohl (Ed.), *Selective Remembrances: archaeology in the construction, commemoration, and consecration of national pasts* (pp. 139-141). Chicaco, IL: Chicago University Press.

Oltean, I. (2007). *Dacia: Landscape, Colonisation and Romanisation*. New York, NY: Routledge.

Ovidius. (2005). *Tristia* (P. Green, Trans. Vol. V). Berkeley, CA: University of California Press.

Pausanias. *Description of Greece* (Vol. I).

Plato. *Charmides*.

Polyaenus. Stratagems.

Pop, I.-A. e. a. (2005). *The History of Transylvania, I (up to 1541)*. Cluj-Napoca: CTS, Romanian Cultural Institute.

Price, G. (2000). *Encyclopedia of the Languages of Europe*. Malden, MA: Blackwell.

Rodewald, C. (1976). *Money in the Age of Tiberius*. Totowa, NJ: Rowman and Littlefield.

Rossi, L. (1971). *Trajan's Column and the Dacian wars*. Ithica, NY: Cornell University Press.

Ruscu, D. (2004). The Supposed Extermination of the Dacians: the literary tradition. In W. S. Hanson & I. P. Haynes (Eds.), *Roman Dacia: the making of a provincial society*. Portsmouth: Journal for Roman Archaeology.

Schmitz, M. (2005). *The Dacian Threat: 101-106 AD*. Armidale, Australia: Caeros Publishing.

Strabo. (1924). *The Geography* (J. R. S. Sterrett & H. L. Jones, Trans. Vol. VII).

Taylor, T. (2001). Thracians, Scythians, and Dacians, 800BC-AD 300. In B. Cunliffe (Ed.), *The Oxford Illustrated History of Prehistoric Europe*. Oxford, UK; New York, NY: Oxford University Press.

Thucydides. *The Landmark of Thucydides: a comprehensive guide to the Peloponnesian War* (R. B. Strassler, Trans. Vol. II).

Varzari, A., Stephan, W., Stepanov, V., Raicu, F., Cojocaru, R., Roschin, Y., . . . Weiss, E. (2007). Population history of the Dniester-Carpathians: evidence from Alu markers. *Journal of Human Genetics, 52*(4), 308-316.

Vekony, G. (2000). *Dacians, Romans, Romanians*. Budapest, Hungary: Corvinus Library.

3. I CAME, I SAW, I STAYED: DACIA AND THE ROMANS

The story of the Romanians is inseparable from the Romans. As a Latin people who also appear to have kept the imperial brand name, the Romanians are undoubtedly the product of Romanization, a gradual adoption of Roman culture and identity. As the reader might guess from the previous chapter, this Romanization has something to do with the Roman conquest of Dacia. There is a not-so-small problem however with Dacia's Romanization: Roman control of Dacia was relatively short-lived. Annexed in 106 AD and held only until 271, Dacia was the last region Rome conquered and the first it abandoned. Whether Romanization could occur in such a short time, especially when provinces held for a much longer time (like Britain) were not lastingly Romanized, is a fundamental question for Romanian history.

The Romans were never a humble people. They believed that their culture was not just different from other cultures but better. To them Rome was "the mother of the world", destined "to give mankind civilization."[Pliny, III, 5, 38-40] Other people were just "barbarians" who needed Rome's guiding hand (or sword). This is not to say that Rome pursued a policy of making everyone Roman; it was more or less an unintended consequence of Roman occupation wherever they went. Dacia was to be in some ways same as other provinces, and in other ways drastically different.

Rome's success at forcing its will upon its neighbors came largely from its superior armies. Though Cicero believed Rome's hegemony over other people was due to divine intervention,[Cicero, IX, 19] A more realistic explanation came from the historian Vegetius several centuries later: Rome won because it had the best organization and army.[Vegetius, I, 1] The Romans were aware of the individual strength of barbarian warriors, but they knew that individuals or entire tribes could be overcome by the old motto *divide et impera*: "divide and conquer." The Romans slowly but surely ate away at barbarian Europe, always sure to not bite off more than they could chew.

Rome was however faced with a different kind of problem in Dacia. Burebista's veritable barbarian empire was the only force in Europe capable of rivaling Rome itself,[Bennett, 1997, p. 87] and the old maxim of Roman strategy had no ground to gain with the fanatically loyal Dacians. Dacia was not another Gaul, where one barbarian tribe could be used as allies against another. On the eve of the Dacian-Roman confrontation, it ironically appeared as though the Dacians were trying to divide the Romans! Burebista was no Machiavelli, but he knew that the Roman civil war from 49-44 BC presented an unequaled opportunity to intervene in Roman affairs. Upon hearing of the start of the war, he quickly sent his ambassador – a Greek of course,[Murgescu, 2001, p. 38] what better way to seem civilized – to ally with Pompey, but Pompey was dead by 48 BC and Caesar proved victorious in Rome soon after.

Caesar was slow to forget his enemies, and Burebista soon appeared on his hit-list. He had already planned an invasion of Dacia in 58 BC,[Goldsworthy, 2006, p. 197] but had been sidetracked by his Gallic wars. Now he had every reason to go after Burebista, not only because Burebista had been an ally of Pompey, but because a war against barbarians (like in the "good old days" before the civil war) would be a sure way to unite the Romans under his banner. Caesar's ambitions were however cut short by Roman swords in 44 BC when he was assassinated and it seems Burebista's rule depended on there being a perceived threat from the Romans as Burebista himself was assassinated less than a year later.[Crişan, 1978, p. 243]

The breakup of the Dacian kingdom presented a golden opportunity for the Romans to employ their strategy of pitting one chief against another and collecting the remains of both. Rome's interference became especially noted between 31 and 27 BC. The man left in charge of dealing with the Dacians by Octavian was the unimaginatively-named Marcus Licinius Crassus, son of Marcus Licinius Crassus, grandson of Marcus Licinius Crassus.[Lica, 2000, pp. 93-120] After driving Cotiso from his southern lands due to alleged betrayal, he allied with the Dacian chief Rholes who became a "friend of Rome" against the rival chief Dapyx. Dapyx was soon defeated, and Crassus began another war against the Dacian chief Zyraxes.[Dio, 2004, LI, 26, 1-6] It was Roman diplomacy at its finest. *Divide et impera* was once again working, due more to the divisive nature of the Dacians than anything else.

The Dacians and Romans soon realized they had better things to do than kill each other. The Dacian chief Scorilo, probably aware that his kingdom's chances of victory against Rome was slim, convinced his subjects to no longer intervene in Roman civil wars through allegory: he pitted two dogs against one another "and when they became engaged in a desperate encounter, exhibited a wolf to them. The dogs straight away abandoned their fury against each other and attacked the wolf."[Frontinus, X, 4] The message was clear: let the Roman dogs scrap among themselves. Scorilo's wisdom aside, a barbarian still had to make a living, and the Dacians raided into Roman territory in 10 BC and again in 6 AD. The Romans for their part negotiated with the Dacians, though Roman propaganda insisted that this equality was actually triumph. Augustus claimed that the Dacians had been subjected to Roman rule,[Res gestae divi Augusti, 1967, 30] a specious claim at best, and an inscription dedicated to Nero dated around 60 AD claimed he had made the Dacians subjects of Roman rule. The Roman emperor did indeed have Dacian subjects... but these subjects were Dacians that had moved (or been moved) inside of the empire. About 50,000 Dacian refugees were transferred south of the Danube during Augustus' reign[Strabo, 1924, VII, 3, 10] and an additional 100,000 were settled in Moesia[c] by Nero.[Braund, 1984, pp. 136-137] A Dacian society was starting to form south of the Danube if Roman epigraphic sources are anything to go by. The Dacians south of the Danube were thus already experiencing Romanization by the late first century AD.

Peace could be maintained on the frontier provided the barbarians remained divided and the Romans remained satisfied with their territorial possessions, something easier said than done. Diodorus Siculus had noted a century prior that the Romans "rule practically the entire inhabited world"[Dio, 2004, LXVIII, 9] but "practically" was hardly enough for the emperor. The new emperor Domitian, a man renowned for his greed and

---

[c] The northern half of modern Bulgaria.

megalomania, was keen on adding to his prestige with a military triumph. His attack on Caledonia, Rome's first offensive beyond the Empire's European frontiers in nearly four decades, left many barbarians wondering whether the Romans would ever leave them alone.

The Dacians, unified once again by the threat of Rome, quickly took on the role of defenders of barbarian freedom against Roman aggression. Though the reunified Dacia was small when compared to the Roman Empire or even Burebista's kingdom, Dacia and her allies could still muster an army numbering around 250,000 men.[Schmitz, 2005, pp. 7-13] Of course, 250,000 armed men do not remain idle for long and in 85 AD the Dacians raided and plundered the province of Moesia, killing its governor and annihilating its army. Though it may be tempting mark the Dacians as typical bellicose barbarians, at least one source presented the actions as defensive in nature.[Jordanes, 1960, XXIII, 76] The Dacians could see where Rome was heading if left unchecked and opted for a "pre-emptive strike" to weaken a possible Roman offensive.[Vékony, 2000, p. 58]

Whatever the case may be, the Romans decided to retaliate with overwhelming force. Domitian arrived on scene to undertake what he thought would be another triumph, but what followed was a debacle that stained Roman honor for nearly twenty years. The initially successful counter-attack by Domitian in Moesia prompted Dacia's king to resign his throne to Decebal, a man "shrewd in his understanding of warfare and shrewd also in the waging of war" who "showed himself a worthy antagonist of the Romans for a long time."[Dio, 2004, XLVII, 6] Decebal sued for peace, possibly to paint himself as the good guy and convince his allies that he was trying to avoid war. He knew however that the terms he offered, which had every citizen of the Roman Empire paying taxes to him, was something the emperor was sure to refuse. On the other hand, Domitian desired a military victory in order to please his over-taxed aristocracy[Bennett, 1997, pp. 29-30] – a way to show that the money he had confiscated had been well-spent – so he would have refused the peace even if it had been on fair terms. Instead, he sent the Praetorian prefect Cornelius Fuscus (who even according to other Romans was not the sharpest gladius in the Roman army)[Juvenal, IV, 111-112] off to press the advantage. Confident in victory, Domitian left for Rome.

The news of Fuscus' defeat hit the Roman Emperor like a slap in the face. Not only was Fuscus' force annihilated by Decebal in a cunning ambush at Tapae, near the modern "Iron Gates" on the Danube in southwestern Romania, but Fuscus himself was killed and his baggage train looted.[Jordanes, 1960, XIII, 78] Domitian organized a second expedition against the Dacians, led by Tettius Julianus, resulting in a second confrontation at Tapae that left the Romans indecisively victorious. Reversals of military fortunes elsewhere on the Roman frontier prompted Domitian to send peace envoys to Decebal, where it is said the emperor had "given large sums of money to Decebal on the spot as well as artisans of every trade pertaining to both peace and war, and had promised to keep on giving large sums in the future."[Dio, 2004, XLVII, 7] Decebal in turn did his best to show who had won the war: not only did he refuse to meet the emperor, sending instead his brother Diegis, but Roman sources also agree that Decebal did not honor the return of captured equipment and prisoners. The emperor did his best to make a show of victory, even going so far as to forge a letter of submission from Decebal and parade his own furniture as spoils of war, but most Romans could see quite well through the pitiable charade.

More importantly, Domitian's war against the Dacians did not resolve any of the frontier issues. It had in fact made the situation even worse, as the Dacians became the saviours of the barbarian free world against "the evil empire."(Bennett, 1997, pp. 29-30) Decebal's army gained considerable strength due to his treaty with Domitian, adding valuable siege engines to their formidable arsenal, and becoming a force unmatched in the barbarian world.(Rossi, 1971, p. 22) Rome was humiliated, the barbarians were strengthened and rallied around Decebal, and Decebal's satisfaction with the lopsided peace made him complacent, giving Rome no justifiable opening to start a new war and rectify Domitian's diplomatic disaster.

Following the reign of Emperor Nerva – which lasted an impressive fifteen months – the Roman throne was passed on to possibly the best emperor it ever had: Marcus Ulpius Traianus, better known to us as Trajan. Ambitious, charismatic, and militarily brilliant – or according to some: "an alcoholic homosexual megalomaniac with a desire for glory"(McLynn, 2009, p. 319) – Trajan was just the man to deal with the Dacians. Before even going to Rome to honor his election, Trajan headed off to the Moesian Danube to get a grasp of the situation. Trajan undoubtedly sought to secure the Roman frontier,(Bennett, 1997, p. 53) and one Greek traveler put the means by which he intended to do so in no uncertain terms:

> "one could see swords everywhere, and cuirasses, and spears, and there were so many horses, so many weapons, so many armed men [...] all about to contend for power against opponents who fought for freedom and their native land"(Chrysostom, 1946, 16-20)

"Securing the frontier", in Roman terms, usually meant extending it. Trajan knew however, that one did not simply walk into Dacia. Three years passed in which Trajan organized his forces and the logistics for what was to become the biggest military operation in Roman history.

The motives for invading Trajan's Dacia have been repeatedly evaluated by historians. Some view Trajan as a naturally bellicose military man. Others argue that it was Dacia's goldmines that motivated the war. It is not hard to imagine a political thought spreading through Rome that essentially posed the question "what is our gold doing under their mountains?" Nevertheless, it seems that the strategic threat which Dacia posed was the primary motive for the offensive. The Dacians were the most important threat along the long Danube frontier, threatening six provinces. Their central government, very rare for people in the area, made them a far greater danger than any Germanic or Celtic tribal confederation of comparable size.(Luttwak, 1979, p. 97) Then again, maybe a singular motive is too simplistic. Certainly the Romans were dealing with a threat... but they did not mind helping themselves to Dacia's gold reserves in the process.

Trajan was aware that this conquest would immortalize him as a great emperor, and he tried to make sure his campaign would be the best recorded in history. Not only did Trajan write a journal of the war, *Dacica*, but his doctor Crito also wrote a first-hand account titled *Getica* (perhaps more proof that the Dacians and Getae were the same people), and accounts were also written by Dio Chrysostom and Appian; there was even a poem written about the campaign! Ironically and unfortunately, none of these primary records have survived.[(Bennett, 1997, p. 92)] Something which has survived however, is an incredibly-detailed bas-relief column in Rome: Trajan's Column. It effectively narrates the Dacian war in an almost comic book fashion, with a continuous "film" of scenes spiraling their way to the top of the column. Without the historical works to explain the events portrayed however, the column the scenes look more like the Bayeux Tapestry without the writing: historians have to make guess-work of where and when everything takes place based on later authors like Cassius Dio or Eutropius.

Trajan finally launched his major campaign against the Dacians in 101 AD. The army he had assembled over three years, numbering well over 100,000 soldiers, was easily the largest single Roman army to that date.[(Bennett, 1997, p. 91)] He was well aware that the war against the Dacians would be hard to execute, given that the enemy was not only familiar with Roman tactics but also well-equipped. The Dacians were not stereotypical "dumb barbarians" as depicted as on Trajan's column, where they are seen going to battle without armor or even so much as a helmet. While some have taken the column's portrayal at face-value, it is more realistic to believe that the Dacians were well-armored warriors who were carved on the column in plain shirts out of convention. Had the column depicted the Dacians in their full battle kit, the Roman onlooker would have had a hard time distinguishing just who on the column was civilized and who was not, especially given the frequent portrayal of headhunting by Roman auxiliaries. The Roman sculptors decided to make things simple for their viewers: armor for the civilized and shirts for the barbarians. We know the column does not give a truthful representation because there are numerous barbarian armors and coifs at the base of the column in a large heap, *sans* warriors, of course.[(Rossi, 1971, p. 122)] Thus, Trajan's Column in fact argues for the opposite interpretation on Dacian warfare: the Dacians were so well-equipped that in a pitched battle it would have been difficult to tell friend from foe! The Romanization that had taken place in the Dacian army, possibility to the point of creating a Dacian professional force, leads to the conclusion that the Dacians were not going to be primitive push-overs.[(Schmitz, 2005, pp. 33-36)]

Though it only lasted two years, the war was hardly a cakewalk for the Romans. Trajan's Column presents the campaign as one long string of effortless victories, but such is the nature of propaganda. The reality on the ground was very different. The Romans had to arduously take Dacia's fortresses one at a time, at such great cost that the Romans had to upgrade and change their armors to prevent excessive casualties. At the third battle of Tapae, the only significant field battle of the entire war, the Romans were victorious but received such a bruising that Trajan had to stop his campaign and even sacrifice his own clothes to make bandages![(Bennett, 1997, p. 95)] Any doubts that remain as to the true cost of this war can be quickly erased when one considers that even the governor of distant Britannia had to send some of his personal bodyguard to fill the gaps in Trajan's army.[Everitt, 2009, p. 114] Decebal for his part tried to wage the war on Roman soil in the winter, fighting a pitched battle that he lost but left nearly 4,000 Romans dead as part of a costly Roman victory. It was however not enough and the renewed Roman onslaught in the summer of 102 came near the Dacian capital of Sarmizegetusa, causing Decebal sued for peace.

Trajan's terms were so humiliating that it made a second Dacian war, one to put an end to the Dacians, inevitable. Decebal was forced to surrender all of his Roman helpers, demolish his fortresses, leave a Roman garrison in Sarmizegetusa and let Rome dictate Dacia's foreign policy. Decebal however, was not the kind of man to sit quietly in his Roman cage. According to the Romans, Decebal broke the terms of this treaty by refusing to demolish his defenses and reforming his army,[Dio, 2004, XLVIII, 10] and in 105 AD the second Dacian War erupted. Trajan was surprised by Decebal's hostility.[Bennett, 1997, p. 99] With an even bigger army, Trajan chose to crush the Dacians once and for all and turn Dacia into a Roman province. He built the world's largest bridge – over a kilometer in length – to connect his future province across the Danube with the rest of the empire. While resistance was fierce, soon the Dacian capital fell into Roman hands. Decebal fled but, being surrounded by Roman pursuers, chose suicide over decorating Trajan's victory parade in Rome. Dacia was finally subdued, and to top it all off, a Dacian traitor had shown the Romans where Decebal had hidden his treasury of nearly 165 tons of gold and 330 tons of silver. The conquest had returned Rome to the good old days of expansionism and imperialism, but it was to be the last acquisition the empire would make in Europe.

Why the Romans decided to keep Dacia, a province whose borders appear as though they were drawn by a slightly inebriated man, has been considered and reconsidered repeatedly. The simple motive is that most of Dacia's gold was still stuck in the ground, and the Romans were not the type to just leave it alone there. Of course, there was a matter of the dangers such an oblong protrusion into the barbarian world presented, but in actuality Dacia's existence greatly increased the security of the empire. This jagged, irregular Roman intrusion into the *barbaricum* made sense in light of Roman priorities: eliminate the Dacian threat and divide the other barbarians. Not only did it separate the barbarians diplomatically but it acted as a physical divide between the nomads in Sarmatia and the barbarians near Pannonia, and thus kept the southern Balkan provinces safe. Dacia would require an extensive military presence in order to survive, but manning Dacia as a military colony would be less expensive than having to defend the entire Roman Danube. In isolation Dacia would not have been worth having, but in the grand scheme of things Dacia was a complete payoff.[Husar, 2002, p. 18; Luttwak, 1979, p. 18] Rome's fist was lodged right into the gut of the barbarian world.

Before we turn the page on Dacia's history it is important that we consider the fate of the locals. What happened to the Dacians has been an element of intense debate since the Italian Renaissance. Trajan's column, full of portrayals of Romans head-hunting Dacians, burning Dacian villages, and torturing Dacian prisoners,[d] certainly presents a gruesome picture of their fate. This image is reinforced by three primary sources which claim the Dacians were wiped out; Trajan's doctor Crito even claimed that the Dacians had been reduced to only 40 men![Ruscu, 2004, pp. 75-77] Dacian names are almost completely absent from Roman inscriptions in the province hereafter. The Zalmoxis cult likewise entirely disappeared after 106 and Dacian temples were demolished all across the land. No Dacian collaborators are noted as aiding Rome in governing the region and almost all of the Roman cities in Dacia were started *de novo* rather than being built on former native foundations. The native fortresses were mostly dismantled.[Chappell, 2005, p. 221; Oltean, 2007, p. 226; Wanner, 2010, pp. 23-25] A few historians have used this to conclude that Trajan's Dacian Wars were wars of extermination, a position particularly popular among Hungarian scholars.[Jones & Ereira, 2007, pp. 112-113; McLynn, 2009, p. 320]

In spite of this bleak picture, claiming extermination is jumping the gun. The primary sources on the war were good for stroking the emperor's ego but little else. Numerous other cases exist where the Romans "exterminate" certain tribes only to have to fight them again a few years later. Rome did not control all of Burebista's or even Decebal's former kingdom, and "free Dacians" existed outside of the province such as the *Costoboci* and the *Carpi*; their existence would have been largely unaffected by the wars. Many Dacians were recruited in new military units in the Roman army *(e.g. ala I Ulpia Dacorum, cohors I Aelia Dacorum, Cohors III Dacorum, etc.)*, which to the chagrin of Crito must have numbered more than 40 individuals. It is true that these military units were stationed far from Dacia, but their mere existence confirms a Dacian recruiting pool. Archaeological evidence also confirms the continuation of Dacian settlements, funerary rituals and pottery. At least some settlements in Eastern Dacia have been attributed to the natives and Ptolemy's *Geography*, written decades the Dacian wars, listed twelve Dacian tribes in existence.[Ellis, 1998; Wanner, 2010, p. 25]

When all of the evidence above is considered we are left with the conclusion that it was not the Dacian populace as a whole which was exterminated, but rather the Dacian elite.[Bennett, 1997, p. 174; Chappell, 2005, pp. 222-223; Ruscu, 2004, p. 82; Wanner, 2010, p. 25] The elite would have been the most likely to record themselves officially and the elite formed the nucleus of the Zalmoxis cult. The fortresses of Dacia were similarly designed to house the fighting forces of the nobles and were not meant for civilians. It is therefore not surprising that the disappearance of the elite would result in the disappearance of their religion, their fortresses, and also their names, while the rest of Dacian life could still be noted archaeologically.

As for why the Dacian lower class is not noticeably present: this is in part due to their diminished numbers and in part due to their adoption of Roman culture. That local names are absent in epigraphy is rather indicative of successful Romanization rather

---

[d] One scene in particular, showing a dishevelled man being tortured by torch-wielding women, was originally thought to represent a Roman being tortured by Dacians (because only "barbarians" could torture, or so it was thought).. This original conclusion has been turned on its head by the fact that the scene seems to take place south of the Danube! In all likelihood, it represents Roman women having a little "fun" with Dacian prisoners.[Dillon, 2006, p. 267]

than extermination.(Oltean, 2007, p. 2225) Trajan had made it clear to the locals that it was the Roman way or the highway and the Dacians that remained joined the Roman way of life, while those who resisted left to join their free brothers across the Carpathians. However, even among the free Dacians one sees evidence of trade adoption of Roman customs,(Ellis, 1998) so it is unsurprising if the Dacians within the province became, in effect, Romans.

Dacia witnessed substantial Roman colonization, one that completely changed the landscape of the province. Trajan knew mountains do not mine themselves, so he brought in workers and colonists "from all over the Roman world."(Eutropius, VIII, 6) Some have compared Dacia's colonization to the California Gold Rush,(MacKendrick, 1975, p. 132) but this is not doing the event justice. It was not a matter of people coming into Dacia searching for wealth by themselves, but rather state-sponsored colonization, making Dacia unique in Roman history.(Burns, 1991, p. 3) Trajan probably colonized the province out of necessity: his wars simply got rid of too much of the local workforce. Clearly Dacia witnessed a substantial loss of life in order to warrant such a colonization effort. (Ruscu, 2004, pp. 83-84)

Though some Romanian nationalists of the 19th century hoped that all the colonists were from Rome (or at least Italy), the true nature of the colonization made Dacia an ethnic melting pot of the entire empire. Names recorded on inscriptions attest to large communities of Greeks, Illyrians, Celts, Germans, and even Northern Africans; less than five percent of the names are Italian. A large garrison of 27,000 soldiers was stationed as surety for the provincials, eventually consisting of two legions (*XIII Gemina* and *V Macedonica*) as well as a substantial multi-ethnic auxiliaries.(Bejan, 1998, pp. 90-91) Of particular note is the large representation of Thracian and Moesian units stationed in the province, since these soldiers would were ethnically related to their northern kin. Combined with the substantially diminished number of natives, the colonization program made Dacia the most cosmopolitan province of the empire. Dacia became a place where residents could choose food, customs, and even gods in a buffet-like fashion.(Chappell, 2005, p. 335)

Some historians, mostly Hungarian, assert that the multiethnic character of the province implies that no real "Roman" culture existed in the region, and therefore Romanization could not occur.(Sozan, 1997, p. 18) In actuality, the polyglot nature of the province is what allowed for Roman culture to predominate. The new settlers only had Latin as a common language and, being displaced from their homelands, only had Roman imperial culture to fall back on, a fact well-attested in the evidence. Around 75% of the names found on inscriptions within Dacia are generic Imperial Roman names as opposed to more specific ethnic names, over 3,000 inscriptions discovered in Dacia are written in Latin (Greek is a very distant runner-up with only 40 inscriptions)(Bejan, 1998, pp. 91-92) and Dacia was the only province outside of Italy where Latin was spoken by almost the entire population.(Vékony, 2000, pp. 124-125)

The great number of settlers that arrived in Dacia in its first years of occupation must have been exceptionally large given the actions of Trajan's successor, the Emperor

Hadrian. Having taken to the throne in 117 AD, a mere 11 years after the conquest of Dacia, Hadrian believed that Trajan had overextended the empire and quickly evacuated and abandoned all of Trajan's former conquests in the Eastern Empire. When it came to Dacia however, Hadrian was struck by a particular problem: evacuating the already-substantial population of colonists proved completely impractical. He convinced himself not to abandon Dacia for fear that "lest many Roman citizens should be left in the hands of the barbarians."(Eutropius, VIII, 6) The number of cities in Dacia grew over time from one to eleven, with each city gradually advancing in legal status (8 reaching the highest rank of *coloniae*), and Rome's substantial investment in the region resulted in its increasing prosperity. Dacia was also highly particular in its urban development in another sense: all but one of these cities were founded by retiring Roman soldiers – veterans – who set up their homes where they had formerly set up camp.(Bennett, 1997, p. 173) Many of these had undoubtedly fought in the Dacian wars and had thus, literally fought for their own piece of land.

Some explanation needs to be made on how the Roman retirement package worked as it was vital for Romanization. The Roman Empire was big, and soldiers taken from one corner of the empire were often stationed in another. This was simply a matter of security, since training and arming the people you had just conquered and then leaving them in their original homeland posed some obvious hazards. Service abroad could get a little boring and though the Roman army officially forbade Roman soldiers from marrying while on service, many of them frequently took local, unofficial wives; this is attested both by Roman authors like Tacitus (*Histories*, IV, 64) and also the soldiers' own funerary stelae.[e] For the wife the attraction to this was easy to understand, and it was not just the uniform: veterans of the Roman army would have been relatively wealthy, were granted land to settle, and would gain Roman citizenship for their families as well. The children of such marriages were not considered illegitimate.(Phang, 2001, pp. 60-69; 198-199)

Though the image of Roman veterans taking Dacian wives was beaten to death in Romania during Communist times, it nevertheless is an image based on a real phenomenon. The evidence that such unions occurred is literally carved in stone, as shown on funerary portraits of Roman veterans with their Dacian wives.(MacKenzie, 1986, p. 106) The current evidence suggests that around 82,500 veterans settled in Dacia during the roughly century and a half of Roman occupation, and the vast majority of these veterans came from the garrison of the province. At a modest family size of four individuals, this easily entails over 300,000 Roman inhabitants added by this method alone.(Bejan, 1998, p. 93) It is no coincidence that the word in Romanian for an old man, *bătrân*, derives from the Latin *veteranus*.

Whether a city was created by army veterans or by the natives of the land had a drastic impact on the region's Romanization. The neighboring province of Scythia Minor (today Romania's Dobrogea) on the Black Sea coast provides an ideal

---

[e] A fancy word for tombstone.

comparison to Dacia, and allows us to fill in the gaps of Dacia's urban history. Scythia Minor presents a very divided landscape, consisting of Greek cities crammed along the Black Sea coast and Roman army's garrisons stationed on the opposite side along the Danube.(Petculescu, 2006, pp. 32-33) Interestingly, the garrison forts bore Dacian names (*Capidava*, *Sacidava* etc.) suggesting that the locals were of Dacian origin. Like in Dacia, very few of the original native sites survived in Scythia Minor. Scythia Minor's two different founder populations (veterans along the Danube, Greeks along the sea coast) resulted in a highly divided landscape: the towns that formed around the Roman army forts were all Romanized while the Greek cities maintained their Greek identity throughout the empire's existence. The contrast is striking: all of the inscriptions along the Danube are in Latin while all but one of the inscriptions from the Greek cities are in Greek!(Petculescu, 2006, p. 36) What's more, the entire countryside appears to have been Romanized by the forts, or more specifically by the veterans of the garrison who settled nearby after their retirement. The Romanization of the region happened regardless of whether the garrison was composed of Roman legions or provincial auxiliaries; even the least Romanized soldier at the outset of his career became a Roman by the end of it.(Petculescu, 2006, p. 34) This is especially relevant since it turns Dacia's substantially international garrison into a potent force for Romanization. Thus, the military origin of cities in Dacia, similar to those cities on the Scythian Danube coast, undoubtedly aided in the province's Romanization.

The length of time the Romans spent in a region had an impact on Romanization, though it varied tremendously from province to province. The duration of Roman rule in Dacia was admittedly short, lasting only 165 years, and Hungarian historians who deny the Romanization of the province state that this was "too short a time for cultural assimilation."(Tóth, 2002, p. 115) This is usually followed by citing Roman Britain as a counterexample to Dacia, where Romanization did not occur in spite of over four centuries of Roman rule. However, the relation between length of stay and Romanization is not so cut-and-dry. A comparison of Dacia to the more pertinent Scythia Minor (a province with which Dacia shares many more similarities, not the least being their Dacian population) shows that Romanization could happen rapidly under the right conditions. Scythia Minor, a region much more similar than Britain to Dacia, was thoroughly Romanized by the mid-second century AD even though the region – with the exception of the Greek cities that were annexed earlier – had only been annexed in 46 AD; Romanization was complete within 100 years. It should be remembered that the Romanization of Scythia Minor also occurred in spite of the extra "inconvenience" of not having removed some of the locals.

The spread of Roman citizenship is also important, though for a reason which may seem trivial: the granting of citizenship allowed a resident of the empire to refer to oneself as Roman. In Dacia, as elsewhere, citizenship spread in several ways. One way was out of marriages with Roman soldiers. Another way for citizenship to spread was when a town was promoted to the rank of *municipium* which resulted in the universal granting of citizenship to all of its inhabitants. This occurred in all 11 cities in Roman Dacia.(Husar, 2002, p. 161) Clearly not all of the inhabitants could get Roman citizenship through these means; not everyone could find a convenient Roman soldier to marry.

This all changed in 212 AD when the Emperor Caracalla granted citizenship to all free males in the empire, an event which occurred during Roman control of Dacia. All of the men in Dacia thus became citizens, and with it they were allowed to call themselves Romans, explaining how the Romanians gained their ethnic name.

To what extent was Romanization a matter affecting the natives and not just the new colonists? Some have argued that the Dacians were aloof and rural and could not have been Romanized,(Chappell, 2005, pp. 332-333) adding that for the locals Roman rule was "a landscape of disenfranchisement."(Wanner, 2010, p. 310) The lack of Dacian names in inscriptions shows that Dacians were absent from cities, the nuclei for Romanization. Similarly, Rome made no official attempt to reach out to the Dacians other than through enlisting Dacians in military units. No evidence exists for the locals taking part in the Roman administration of the province. It is easy to imagine the Dacians as unaffected by Roman culture that surrounded them given the Romans did not actively pursue Romanization and the Dacians were not just going to learn Latin for fun.

However, political disenfranchisement does not always mean lack of assimilation. Rome's policies were not equally harsh to the locals, noteworthy being the Dacian women and young children. Even on Trajan's Column, a monument to Roman brutality, one sees the emperor frequently extending his mercy to the locals, especially women.(Bennett, 1997, p. 95) After the wars, needless to say, Dacia would have been lacking in men in a very literal sense. Many women were likely taken up by Roman soldiers as wives. The presence of Dacian hand-made goods in Roman settlements, especially at military bases, is easy to explain if Dacians became part of the soldiers' families. Though women were largely invisible in the official record because, as is typical for this time, history often became a matter of "his-story", they nevertheless left their mark in archaeology. The hard evidence for Dacian-Roman marriages and the existence of a Romanized Daco-Roman community is undeniable.(Wanner, 2010, p. 333)

A brief mention must be made on what we mean by "Romanization" when we refer to Dacia. Romanization is typically defined as an adoption of Roman culture and the use of the term for Dacia's cultural development – or that of any frontier province for that matter – has come under fire. Some argue that "Romanization is not a good method of interpretation for the development either of imperial provinces at large or for Dacia in particular."(Chappell, 2005, p. 327) This is however, only if one defines Romanization as adopting the full gamut of Roman culture, including belief in the Roman gods and observation of public festivities like gladiator games or chariot races. In this sense it is correct to criticize Romanization in Dacia, since no city in the province had chariot racing and public baths only existed around military camps. Similarly, classical deities fared much worse in Dacia when compared to exotic gods like the Persian Mithras.(Chappell, 2005, pp. 328-330) In this sense Romanization in Dacia did not follow traditional models.

We should not use this however to argue against a Daco-Roman origin of the Romanians. Dacia would require a fundamental Romanization, namely the adoption of Latin as a native language and some aspects of Roman identity (e.g. the Roman name), for the Romanians to originate within it. The rest of the bells and whistles are superfluous, and nitpicking on whether the average resident of Dacia went to gladiatorial games or not is irrelevant to the subject of Romanian origins. Modern Romanians do not watch gladiatorial games or chariot races, nor do they worship Jupiter or the other Roman gods. The relationship between the Romanians and Romans is their language and their name. It is only important to prove the adoption of these aspects in Dacia in order to make a Daco-Roman origin tenable, and this has been proven beyond doubt. While in Britain the lower classes still spoke Celtic, Latin remaining an aloof and formal language, in Dacia the Latin tongue quickly replaced Dacian and developed vigorously.(Bennett, 1997, p. 175) The very names of Dacia's inhabitants attest a willingness to adopt Roman culture and identity.(Varga, 2008, pp. 244-245) It is for this reason that today Romania is Romania and not Dacia.

Today it can safely be concluded that Dacia was fundamentally Romanized, at least in language and legal status. Trajan started the process – both north and south of the Danube. Rome exerted its influence in the region at the peak of the empire's power, allowing the Romans to use heavy-handed policies towards the natives that they could not afford implementing in other provinces such as Britain. The Dacians were given a choice: become Roman "or else." Dacian culture was mostly wiped out as a result (though not the Dacian people) and the greatest colonization effort in ancient history replaced it. The result speaks for itself: "by the end of the second century and within two generations of the conquest, a recognizably Roman provincial culture had developed in a long arc across what is now modern Romania."(Kulikowski, 2007, p. 40) The rapid Romanization of Dacia is a testament to Roman power in second and third centuries.

If Roman history, especially its later parts, were all sunshine and lollipops then the discussion of Romanian origins could end at the Romanization of Dacia: the Romans arrived, the Dacian survivors assimilated their new culture, and a new people were born. Unfortunately things are not that simple. The Roman Empire eventually collapsed, and what followed was centuries of barbarism that are colloquially known as the Dark Ages. It was the end of the world, and yet, it was this breakdown of the Roman Empire that allowed all of the new Latin people of Europe like the French, the Italians, and the Romanians to emerge. You cannot make an omelette without breaking a few eggs, and it was time for the barbarians to get cooking.

Works Cited

Augustus. Res Gestae.

Bejan, A. (1998). *Dacia Felix: Istoria Daciei Romane*. Timisoara, Romania: Editura Eurobit.

Bennett, J. (1997). *Trajan Optimus Princeps: A Life and Times*. London, UK New York, NY: Routledge.

Braund, D. (1984). *Augusts to Nero: a sourcebook on Roman history, 31 BC-AD 68*. London, UK: Croom Helm.

Burns, T. S. (1991). *A History of the Ostrogoths*. Bloomington, IN: Indiana University Press.

Chappell, L. S. (2005). *Romanization in Dacia*. Los Angeles, CA: University of California Los Angeles.

Chrysostom, D. *Oratores*.

Cicero. *De Haruspicum responsis*.

Crişan, I. H. (1978). *Burebista and His Time*. Bucharest, Romania: Editura Academiei Republicii Socialiste România.

Dillon, S. (2006). Women on the Column of Trajan and Marcus Aurelius. In S. Dillon & K. Welch (Eds.), *Representations of War in Ancient Rome*. New York, NY: Cambridge University Press.

Dio, C. (2004). *Roman History* (E. Cary, Trans. Vol. LXVII). Cambridge, MA: Harvard University Press.

Ellis, L. (1998). Dacia Terra Deserta: Populations, Politics, and the [de]colonization of Dacia. *World Archaeology, 30*(2).

Eutropius. *Breviary*.

Everitt, A. (2009). *Hadrian and the Triumph of Rome*. New York, NY: Random House.

Frontinus, S. J. *Stratagems*.

Goldsworthy, A. (2006). *Caesar: Life of a Colossus*. New Haven, CT: Yale University PRess.

Husar, A. (2002). *Din Istoria Daciei Romane*. Cluj-Napoca, Romania: Presa Universitară Clujeană.

Jones, T., & Ereira, A. (2007). *Barbarians: an Alternative Roman History*. London, UK: BBC Books.

Jordanes. *Getica* (Vol. XI).

Juvenal. *The Satires*.

Kulikowski, M. (2007). *Rome's Gothic Wars*. Cambridge, UK: Cambridge University Press.

Lica, V. (2000). *The Coming of Rome in the Dacian World*. Konstanz: University of Konstanz Press.

Luttwak, E. N. (1979). *The Grand Strategy of the Roman Empire from the First Century A.D. to the Third*. Baltimore, MD: John Hopkins University Press.

MacKendrick, P. (1975). *The Dacian Stones Speak*. Chapel Hill, NC: University of North Carolina Press.

MacKenzie, A. (1986). *Archaeology in Romania: the mystery of the Roman occupation*. London, UK: Hale.

McLynn, F. (2009). *Marcus Aurelius: A Life.* Boston, MA: Da Capo Press.

Murgescu, B. (2001). *Istoria României în Texte.* Bucharest, Romania: Corint.

Oltean, I. (2007). *Dacia: Landscape, Colonisation and Romanisation.* New York, NY: Routledge.

Petculescu, L. (2006). The Roman Army as a Factor of Romanisation in the North-Eastern Part of Moesia Inferior. In T. Bekker-Nielsen (Ed.), *Rome and the Black Sea Region: Domination, Romanisation, Resistance.* Aarhus, Denmark: Aarhus University Press.

Phang, S. E. (2001). *The marriage of Roman soldiers (13 B.C. - A.D. 235): law and family in the imperial army.* Leiden, Netherlands: Brill.

Pliny. *Natural History.*

Rossi, L. (1971). *Trajan's Column and the Dacian wars.* Ithica, NY: Cornell University Press.

Ruscu, D. (2004). The Supposed Extermination of the Dacians: the literary tradition. In W. S. Hanson & I. P. Haynes (Eds.), *Roman Dacia: the making of a provincial society.* Portsmouth: Journal for Roman Archaeology.

Schmitz, M. (2005). *The Dacian Threat: 101-106 AD.* Armidale, Australia: Caeros Publishing.

Sozan, M. (1997). *Ethnocide in Romania.* Safely Harbor, FL: Simon Publications.

Strabo. (1924). *The Geography* (J. R. S. Sterrett & H. L. Jones, Trans. Vol. VII).

Tóth, E. (2002). The Roman Province of Dacia. In B. Köpeczi, L. Makkai & A. Mocsy (Eds.), *History of Transylvania* (Vol. I). Boulder, CO; New York, NY: Social Science Monographs.

Varga, R. (2008). The Peregrine Names from Dacia. *Acta Musei Napocensis, 43-44*(I), 244-245.

Vegetius. *Epitome rei militaris.*

Vekony, G. (2000). *Dacians, Romans, Romanians.* Budapest, Hungary: Corvinus Library.

Wanner, R. (2010). *Forts, fields, and towns: communities in Northwest Transylvania from the first century BC to the fifth century AD.* Leicaster, UK: University of Leicaster.

4. LOSING DACIA: EVACUATION, PROPAGANDA, AND INCOMPETENCE

Roman Dacia is fundamentally important to Romanian origins as it created a Daco-Roman culture, solving the problem of Romanization. In effect: it explains how the Romanians got their language and their name. Romanian history however becomes more controversial from this point on. Nothing lasts forever and Dacia was no exception. Rome learned the hard way that its jutting province was an expensive investment. Dacia was not only the last province to be added to the Roman Empire, but also the first to be abandoned. The question remains: did the Romans leave anything behind?

Holding Dacia proved problematic from the start, as it came immediately under threat from the nomadic barbarian horsemen to the east and west.(Bennett, 1997, p. 167) An attack in 107 and again in 117 nearly convinced Hadrian to surrender the province, but he reconsidered when he realized the impossibility of evacuating the province and just how many Roman citizens would be left as a result;(Everitt, 2009, p. 173) Rome had gone in too deep to pull back now. The emperor instead swapped around Rome's forces, leaving Dacia with two rather than the originally-intended three legions but strangely with more troops. It is noteworthy that Hadrian saw evacuating the large number of civilians as physically impossible (hence: he could not let them fall into barbarian hands).(Bejan, 1998, p. 161) Dacia continued to experience raids and attacks for most of its history up until its fall. It had to be reorganized repeatedly in order to deal with its problematic borders.

We should not take this to mean that Dacia did not prosper. The Carpathians protected much of the province from attack and the cities were encircled by walls from the start, such that only exterior buildings were affected whenever barbarians paid an unannounced visit.(Goldsworthy, 2009, p. 121) The region's increasing prosperity is noted during the reign of Septimus Severus (193-211) which saw the promotion of several of Dacia's cities to *municipium* status, with one even becoming a top-tier *colonia*.(Goldsworthy, 2009, p. 165) Sarmizegetusa was also promoted to *metropolis* status in the early third century. In spite of harassment from barbarians, the Roman authorities actually saw its hold on the western provinces as being much more precarious;(Kulikowski, 2007, p. 40) Dacia was seen for its early history seen as a defensible and prosperous province.

Dacia's abandonment was spurred on by the "arrival" of the Goths. Romanticist ~~fantasy~~ history of the nineteenth century envisaged these barbarians as blond-haired Germans that migrated to the Balkans from Scandinavia, but recent evidence presents another picture. Little proof exists for any sort of migration out of Scandinavia,(Kulikowski, 2007, pp. 67-70) and chances are that such an idea was a German nationalist invention based on the sixth century writer Jordanes, who ironically identified the Dacians as the ancestors of the Goths, but believed that the Dacians came from Scandinavia themselves at a much earlier time!(Jordanes, 1960XI, 67) His famous work, "The Origins and the Deeds of the Getae" (or *Getica*) has the last word (mis)translated to "Goths" by modern authors who still support the migration theory. The *Getica* itself should not be taken too seriously. Written centuries after the events it describes, it is as historically valuable as Dan Brown's *The Da Vinci Code*. Yet, the historians who find Jordanes' claim of a

Dacian origin of the Goths laughable readily accept his account as evidence of a Scandinavian migration! (Jordanes, 1960, IV, 25)

Archeologically at least, the Goths appear as a cocktail of Dacian, Carpic, Germanic and Sarmatian culture, shaken and stirred up by the Roman frontier. Like the western Franks, the Goths were not the result of migration, but rather one of having the Romans as neighbours: "two or three generations after Roman provincial culture began to develop inside the frontier [in Dacia and elsewhere], new and more sophisticated barbarian polities appeared along the [Roman] periphery";(Kulikowski, 2007, p. 41) think gentrification's more violent cousin. The Goths, if anything, look like a fusion of local cultures rather than the invasion of a new one.

Of course, it might be hard to completely deny a migration given that the Goths spoke a Germanic language and not Dacian. The translation of the bible into Gothic in the fourth century clearly shows its Germanic character. Furthermore, a people called the *Gothones* were noted in the Baltic area in the first century, and it is possible that they had moved southward two centuries later, losing a few syllables of their name along the way. Yet, even if these new Germanic rulers had come from the north, the archaeological evidence suggests the newcomers were only a small ruling nucleus in a large confederation.

Dacia's abandonment was not considered just because of this change of barbarian hats: Dacia had failed in its purpose for the empire. It was designed to protect the Balkan provinces but things were not going according to plan. By the mid-third century the hotspots for barbarian invasions were Moesia and Pannonia; not Dacia.(Husar, 2002, p. 597) All roads lead to Rome, but the barbarians realized the fastest path was not through Dacia. The province therefore fared better than Pannonia during the Marcomannic Wars, and better than the southern provinces during the Gothic-Carpic invasion of 248-251.(Bejan, 1998, p. 170)

Dacia was also no longer profitable. The famous war that was supposed to "pay for itself" had in its occupation proven more expensive than could be imagined. The salaries of the garrisoned soldiers was greater than any taxes that could be extracted from the residents and the land had been so thoroughly Romanized that the best farmlands were legally exempt from taxation. As for all of that Dacian gold that was supposed to pour out of the province: it mostly enriched the colonists and their contractors.(A. Diaconescu, 2004, p. 120) The similarity to some modern wars is in many ways striking.

The Romans finally did the smart thing and pulled out, but when it happened and what mess was left behind is unclear. Six sources record Dacia's abandonment.[f] Five claim that Dacia was lost under Emperor Gallienus[g] and four claim it was lost under

---

[f] Aurelius Victor, Eutropius, Rufius Festus, the *Historia Augusta*, Orosius and Jordanes.
[g] All of them except for the *Historia Augusta*.

Aurelian,[h] meaning three sources end up with the absurd testimony that Dacia was lost twice![i] What the withdrawal meant is also questionable. No sources mention any evacuation under Gallienus, one source states Aurelian withdrew only the legions, while the remaining three argue that Aurelian evacuated the civilians as well.

The Roman sources, when contrasted, are clear as mud. We may think it safe to believe the general evacuation account told by the three authors… but all three appear to have copied more or less verbatim from a single (propaganda) source that repeated an "official" story. The source in question, Vopiscus, is both confused and confusing. Vopiscus claims that Dacia's colonists were moved to Moesia literally in the same sentence in which he informs the reader that Moesia was lost from the empire! Maybe it was only hyperbole, but there are other problems: the South Danubian provinces were by then bearing the brunt of barbarian raids. Moving the settlers from Dacia to Moesia would only have put them in harm's way.[(Bejan, 1998)] Even if we assumed Aurelian was so uncaring, it is doubtful Dacia's inhabitants, nestled in the Carpathians, would have been dying to move to a warzone. In short: a lie repeated a thousand times becomes the truth, but three times is rarely convincing, and other evidence must be used to solve this mystery.

On the surface Dacia during Gallienus' reign appears to have stopped working altogether. This is hardly surprising however, since its residents were no longer getting paid! The province's mint closed down in 256 and few coins were imported thereafter.[(A. Diaconescu, 2004, p. 130; Goldsworthy, 2009, p. 122)] The number of inscriptions commissioned for production declined rapidly as a result. Dacia's strategic value, or lack thereof, had forced Gallienus to relocate part of its two legions to Pannonia in 260.[(Watson, 1999, p. 155)] Hungarian historians argued that the entire legions were removed from the province and concluded, *ipso facto*, that nothing was left behind in Dacia to be defended; the province must therefore have been completely evacuated as well. According to this interpretation, Aurelian's later withdrawal was just a formality, tying up the loose ends of a province that was already abandoned;[(Mócsy, 1974, p. 209)] Aurelian just "removed everybody from Dacia still under Roman rule."[(Vékony, 2000, p. 141)]

The argument looks convincing but quickly loses strength once we note what was happening throughout the empire. Firstly, we should note that no source mentions any evacuation by Gallienus. Given that Gallienus was disliked by the Roman authors, it is surprising that he did not get blamed for evacuating Dacia; someone would have jumped to the occasion to point out that Gallienus had caused hundreds of thousands of Romans to lose their homes if it truly were the case. Secondly, the time in which Gallienus and Aurelian ruled was part of the "Crisis of the Third Century", an era that stretched from 235 to 284. The Roman Empire in this time suffered invasion after invasion and the average emperor was lucky to reign for two years. Only three out of twenty-two emperors (not including usurpers) died of natural causes (two of plague and

---

[h] All of them except Aurelius Victor and Orosius.
[i] While you could figure out who they were by the info provided, I will spare you the headache. They are Eutropius, Rufius Festus and Jordanes.

43

one in Persian captivity) averaging between themselves an above-par reign of three years. To say the least, there were a lot of widows and funerals. What was happening in Dacia was in many ways no different than events in the rest of the Roman Empire.

Dacia actually fared well relative to the rest of the empire. Rather than going into decline, the province appears to have prospered. Dacia received favourable attention and development in terms or roads, cities, and monuments. In 253 the city of Apulum earned the title of *Chrysopolis*, the "city of gold". Rather than going into terminal decline, Dacia's economy flourished. The maximum amount of coin circulation in Dacia took place during the reigns of Decius and Gallus (249-253), just prior to the joint reigns of Valerian and Gallienus. There was no sign at all in this time that the empire intended to abandon its salient province,(Husar, 2002, pp. 600-604) which would make the actions of Gallienus – if they occurred at all – rather sudden.

The joint emperorships of Valerian and Gallienus were disastrous for the empire, and events in Dacia must be understood in this light. Rome was attacked on all fronts: the Goths headed for Greece, the Marcomanni broke through Pannonia and Illyria, the Borani overran Asia Minor, and the Alans threatened Rome itself... yet Dacia was sidestepped completely. Gallienus did take the title of *Dacicus Maximus,*[j] implying that some fighting occurred in the province,(Husar, 2002, p. 609) but that is all the evidence we have for it. There are no signs of destruction, a far cry from the claim that Dacia "bore the brunt of this new attack."(Mócsy, 1974, p. 206) Gallienus' title itself is questionable. His coregent Valerian strangely did not receive it as well, and the title is only attested in some unreliable documents. To historians these are red flags indicating the title was just pulled out of Roman creativity (to put it politely). The people who wrote those documents knew of the fighting on the Danube and just assumed that a *Dacicus* was going to be thrown in among the emperor's other titles;(Peachin, 1989, p. 81) the emperor of course did not mind. Archaeologically Dacia was at peace until 259. Altars and temples were completed at Tibiscum and Potaissa, honorary inscriptions were made at Mehadia, and one inscription was dedicated to Valerian at Sarmizegetusa.(Bejan, 1998, p. 176)

In 260 the empire went from crisis to nosedive. Valerian had gone east to fight the Sassanids of Persia, leaving the mess in Europe to his coregent, but his defeat and capture in 260 almost ruined the empire. Valerian's blunder caused two large swathes of the empire to break off and form independent states: the Gallic Empire in the West, and Palmyra in the East. Both would last until Aurelian dealt with them over ten years down the road. The Danubian provinces had comparatively mild usurpers that were immediately crushed. The most interesting of these was Regalianus, a man who claimed to have been a kinsman of Decebal himself.(*Historia Augusta*, 1921-1932, 8) Whether this was true remains speculation, but it is clear the claim did not help him much as Dacia's legions

---

[j] Whenever Roman Emperors scored a victory abroad they often took an appropriate title to commemorate it. If a Roman emperor won against the Goths he was called *Gothicus*, if he defeated the Parthians he would be called *Parthicus*. Unfortunately these names can also be ambiguous. A name like *Germanicus* could mean "victor over the Germans"... or it could mean "victor in Germania." The latter seems to be the case for all of the *Dacicus* titles we see after the mid-third century.

remained faithful to the emperor, unlike other legions in Gaul and Palmyra. It is little wonder then that Dacia's legions were granted the title of "faithful and loyal" (*pia fidelis*).[(Husar, 2002, p. 614)]

The straw that broke the camel's back was a barbarian invasion through Pannonia headed for Italy itself, one that convinced the emperor to redraw the empire's defense. The changes we see in Dacia take part in this context, and Dacia was hardly the only province affected by the reorganization. More importantly, Dacia's reorganization was not a sign that it was being evacuated. Dacia's monetary decline in the 250's also occurred in neighboring provinces,[(Husar, 2002, p. 609)] none of which are ever claimed to have been evacuated. Some of Dacia's garrison was moved to Pannonia, but we know for certain that some also remained behind. An inscription dated after 260 indicated that the Legion XIII's commander was still at the Dacian Herculane baths,[(Husar, 2002, p. 608)] and it is doubtful that the legion would have left without him! Dacia was also not the only province to have its garrison downsized, as units from Britain and Germania were also moved into Pannonia.[(Husar, 2002, p. 614)] It was part of a rethinking of Roman strategy: previously the legions had been stationed at the empire's border, but the problem was barbarians kept finding holes in the armor-clad meat-fence. The Roman army's response was thus limited to intercepting booty-laden barbarians on the return-trip. Gallienus instead placed the troops at important crossroads behind the frontier, allowing an interception of barbarians as they moved in. The rearrangement strengthened the core regions at the expense of the frontier, and since Dacia was the furthest out it also lost the most.

This also solves the question of where all the money went. Dacia was left with a minimal garrison. Fewer soldiers equated into fewer people getting paid, which meant less money going into the province. It is for this reason that Dacia appeared strapped for cash after Gallienus' military withdrawal,[(Husar, 2002, p. 615)] and though the wealth of the province decreased, life continued unabated. Houses built after 260 (obviously implying someone was left behind to do the building) were smaller as people were poorer, but the cities themselves did not diminish in size. The central fortresses also display continuous life and refurbishment.[(Husar, 2002, pp. 617-619)] The diminishing number of inscriptions is partially caused by inscriptions falling out of fashion in the entire empire,[(A. Diaconescu, 2004, p. 132)] and partially caused by the poor economy; it is certainly not evidence of abandonment. More importantly, that inscriptions continued at all attest to the permanence of provincial culture even in trying times.[(Ardevan, 2007)] No archaeological evidence exists for Dacia's evacuation under Gallienus.[(Hügel, 2003, p. 287)]

The loss (*amissa*) of Dacia spoken of by Roman authors was not an evacuation nor even a territorial loss, but rather a loss of military[(Husar, 2002, p. 616)] and financial[(Gãzdac, 1998)] control. Later on this event was exaggerated by authors who were quite spiteful to Gallienus and quite friendly with Aurelian. Though it is clear Aurelian was the true evacuator of Dacia, it would have been too much to suggest Aurelian, the "global restorer" (*restituto orbo*), lost Roman land without precedent.[(Southern, 2001, p. 120)] Gallienus was made the scapegoat, even if the propaganda ended up contradicting itself by claiming Aurelian later *also* evacuated Dacia. As with modern politicians, the Romans were quite good at blaming the previous administration.

Dacia's actual loss under Aurelian did not come about in a major barbarian victory, nor in some major invasion, but ironically due to a Roman victory! Aurelian's ascension to the throne in 270 was interpreted by the Goths as an opening in which to plunder the empire, but Aurelian had other things in mind for his uninvited guests. When he arrived in Moesia in 271 he not only forced the Goths over the Danube but even chased them beyond it and killed their king in the resulting battle. It was the most decisive victory the Roman army witnessed in the entire third century and utterly crushed the barbarian threat in the area for some time.(Watson, 1999, pp. 54-55) Aurelian could finally reorganize the empire's defences without any pestering invaders getting in the way.(Watson, 1999, p. 155)

Aurelian's first step was to finally abandon the dysfunctional Dacia, all but useless in Roman strategy by now, but the exact year when this occurred is difficult to pin down. Most believe it happened shortly after his victory over the Goths. Aurelian was about to embark on a hard campaign against Palmyra and would later return to fight in Gaul. He needed troops and a stable frontier and evacuating Dacia gave him both. The year 271 is therefore the most commonly given date for the withdrawal.(Husar, 2002, p. 626) In spite of the sound logic, all the evidence on the ground suggests an abandonment around 274/275.(Bejan, 1998, p. 179) A later date is not so unbelievable either, as it would not have been the first poorly-timed decision made by a Roman emperor. Whatever the case, we can say that another four years of occupation would not have mattered much for the already-Romanized province.

Aurelian abandoned *Dacia Traiana* and carved a chunk of land from Moesia to form a new province, unimaginatively named *Dacia Aureliana*. It was a strange move for someone sought to restore the empire, but Aurelian was a military man who valued practical solutions.(Watson, 1999, p. 156) Politically, the move was long overdue: it freed up military units to go fight in the East and drastically shortened Rome's borders. The power vacuum left north of the Danube also would have, at least temporarily, divided the barbarians squabbling over it.(Mócsy, 1974, p. 211)

Some argue that it was not only the province's name that moved south, but also its residents. By far the strongest evidence comes from the written sources but there are other hints. That a new *Dacia* was made at all gives reason for concern. Dacia's two legions, after being sent east to crush Palmyra, were also garrisoned in the new Dacia south of the Danube, and some extrapolated from this that the colonists had followed suit (obviously not all the way out to Palmyra!) and gone south as well. Relocating the civilians made good sense as it would have repopulated a region ravaged by wars and plagues and kept the empire's valued tax-payers.(Tóth, 2002, p. 340) More importantly, crushing the barbarians granted Aurelian the respite needed for such an operation. At the very least he could have evacuated the cities, had he intended it.

There are so many arguments against "total evacuation" however that even recounting them is arduous. While the legions were indeed moved south, Dacia's more numerous auxiliaries just vanished after its abandonment.(Goldsworthy, 2009, p. 122) If this were taken as any indication, it would appear Aurelian left not only civilians behind but much of the army as well. No evidence exists for new settlers in Aurelian's province as no new cities appear south of the Danube, implying that any population transfer must have been insignificant.(Husar, 2002, p. 632) It is noteworthy that Jordanes' account of Aurelian's withdrawal – Jordanes being the only author actually born near Dacia(Jordanes, 1960, 217) – mentions only relocated legions and no civilians. Barbarian settlement in the former province was also suspiciously slow, maybe because Aurelian set terms forbidding them from moving into former imperial lands, or even hired them as the old Dacia's protectors.[50] Dacia was not just handed over to barbarians, and Aurelian's protective policies strongly suggest he was forced to leave the colonists behind.(Husar, 2002, p. 632) Indirect evidence for this is that Aurelian settled the *Carpi* south of the Danube in 272, and many other barbarian settlements followed,(Watson, 1999, p. 157) making it clear that the southern provinces had not been repopulated by Roman colonists from the north.

It is doubtful Aurelian intended to lose Dacia at all, let alone evacuate it. Coins were struck across the empire featuring "Happy Dacia" (*Dacia Felix*) in the first year of Aurelian's reign,(Husar, 2002, p. 624) and Aurelian could hardly have meant it as a sarcastic joke. It is clear that Dacia's abandonment was brought on by a moment of duress: Palmyra had occupied Egypt and thus threatened Rome's grain supply directly, and Aurelian needed troops fast. Dacia's abandonment in this case would not have been intended as a permanent arrangement.(Southern, 2001, p. 121) Returning to Dacia once Palmyra had been crushed was seemed reasonable, but Aurelian's assassination in 275 changed the plan.(Southern, 2001, p. 225) Even if he did not intend to return to Dacia, it is known that Aurelian was a military man to whom a complete evacuation would have looked like a logistical nightmare.(Watson, 1999, p. 157) A total evacuation of any land that large is completely unheard of. The creation of a new Dacia represents Aurelian's need for cheap propaganda:(J. Lewis, 2010, p. 119) he was not about to go down in history as the first emperor to lose Roman land, so he just created another province to make it appear on paper as if nothing had changed.

The only way to bury the debate over Aurelian's evacuation is – ironically – by digging it up. Archaeological evidence can confirm whether Aurelian left behind anything more than a *terra deserta*.(Ellis, 1998) One hundred and fifty years ago it would have been difficult to make any conclusive arguments on the issue, as archaeology in Romania consisted of little more than random discoveries by peasants ploughing their fields.[k] Many of the previous debates were thus reduced to useless speculation: questions like "what would Aurelian have wanted to do?" or "would the Roman inhabitants really have abandoned their homes?" could never resolve what actually happened. Today

---

[k] See the Treasure of *Nagyszentmiklós* (Sânnicolau Mare), a beautiful golden hoard dating from Late Antiquity, as an example.

47

however, there is ample evidence to determine if life and civilization continued in post-Roman Dacia.

The fate of the province's settlers is best solved by looking at that of its city-dwellers, not the least because they are the best studied group in Dacia. Much of Dacia's countryside was not well-known until the fall of communism. As one can imagine, archaeology in Romania was (and still is) not exactly opulently funded, and projects to discover rural sites received little attention. Getting funded to study something that *might* exist is a tricky proposition. The "big money" (if one can talk of such things) went to central projects like Dacian fortresses, resulting unfortunately in a rural *terra incognita*.(Haynes & Hanson, 2004, p. 29) Those arguing for complete evacuation find this "absence of evidence" convenient, but assuming evidence of absence is logically fallacious.[1] Findings on the countryside are rare because nobody has gone to town (well, out of town) looking for them, rather than because it is not there. Recent archaeological surveys in Romania have indeed revealed numerous findings.(Oltean, 2007)

There is another reason why looking at the urban population is critical: the urbanites would have been the most prone to leaving the province with the army. Cities housed imperial officials and administrative personnel, people whose jobs depended on continued Roman government. Their residents were undoubtedly the wealthiest segment of the population, and therefore the most able to start anew south of the Danube. Unlike veterans of the army garrisons, who had served for 20 years for their own small plot of Dacian land, the city dwellers had far fewer attachments to the province. Cities were also centers for Romanization: whatever "feeling Roman" meant, it is certain that it was felt more in the city than outside of it. The urban population would therefore have been the most concerned with finding itself outside of the empire's borders.

Lastly, we should note that cities would have been the simplest to evacuate, if it was truly intended. Many of Dacia's cities had substantial garrisons, so rounding up the citizens when it was time evacuate would have been easy enough. It certainly was easier than combing 200,000 square kilometres of rugged countryside for every Roman villager. What's more, we know all the cities were abandoned eventually as their names have not continued into modern times. This at least removes one uncertainty when investigating: the cities were *eventually* abandoned. However, *when* and *how* the cities' former residents moved out is an entirely different matter. Did they leave abruptly with the Roman administration, or did they (and their descendants) live on nearby?

The fate of urban population is thus decisive as it is a "worst case" scenario for Daco-Roman Continuity. If Aurelian intended the province's evacuation then the cities would have been the first to go. The Romans would not have evacuated the countryside and left the cities as they were. In what regards survival, the cities were magnets for

---

[1] The fallacy is known as "argument from silence" (*argumentum ex silentio*). In essence it means "absence of evidence is not evidence of absence." This is particularly true in the case of Dacia's inhabitants, where accepting the fallacy would result in everyone disappearing, since there is also no evidence that they went anywhere else.

barbarians and therefore their inhabitants would also have been annihilated long before the barbarians found each and every farmer. An end to city life with Aurelian's withdrawal would weaken the odds of Daco-Roman continuity, but it would not entirely rule out its survival in the countryside. However, if urban life continued, then the entire provincial population must have continued as well. Understanding Dacia's fate therefore, rests on the fate of her cities.

Porolissum, situated on the northern fringe of Dacia (and "civilization") was as bad a spot as any during this tumultuous period, yet it survived well into the post-Roman period. The army predictably abandoned its post as the nearby fort was deserted after the third century, but the citizens decided to dig in. Excavations reveal a plethora of changes: the forum and colonnades were fortified, and multiple new structures were built, including water basins.(Wanner, 2010, p. 117) A few stragglers would have been hard-pressed to build all of this, Roman industriousness aside. A substantial Daco-Roman community was clearly left behind. The city bristled with life for at least a century after the army's withdrawal. Its defense may have been organized by the recently discharged ("abandoned" is such a strong word) auxiliary garrison, given that they were never mentioned again within the empire. Trade continued in the region, though the Romans seemed to have at least evacuated the city of its pocket change; very few coins are found hereafter.(Wanner, 2010, p. 115)

Napoca, the next city south, is a bit harder to analyze. Very little activity is noted past the 280's. There are no coins, no Christian relics... almost nothing at all. There are a few constructions, even one with a Latin inscription, but nothing even close to Porolissum's activity. Aside from some graveyards, there is little of note in the fourth century. Life was noticeable... in the same way a New Yorker would notice life in Kansas, but clearly few of the inhabitants remained inside the city.(Wanner, 2010, pp. 118-119) Yet, if we look just a little ways outside the city limits, we see something rather amazing (or not). Villages were founded all around the former urban center. Roman graves containing coins and pottery leaves little doubt as to who the inhabitants of these new rural settlements were.(A. Diaconescu, 2004, p. 133) It is clear that even though the city was abandoned, its former residents did not go very far. Napoca's abandonment might be explained by the fact that it had no garrison; it was an entirely civilian city.(A. Diaconescu, 2004, p. 121) In the post-Roman world this was about the equivalent of having a "loot me" sign posted on the city walls. Its residents realized how exposed they were and dispersed into the countryside for safety. In general they were right in doing so, as pots and fabrics all attest a strong Daco-Roman presence in the nearby villages up until the seventh century. A nearby grave of a Gothic prince, dated to the fifth century, even took up the title *patricius Romanorum* in honour of his new-found subjects.(A. Diaconescu, 2004, p. 134)

Potaissa's, Northwestern Transylvania's largest city, is interesting as it also housed the legion *V Macedonica*.(Wanner, 2010, p. 107) The strongest evidence for post-Roman life comes (ironically) from nearby cemeteries. One discovered a dozen miles to the northeast proved conclusively that civilians lived on in the surrounding area.(MacKendrick, 1975, p. 126) More recent surveys(Wanner, 2010) confirmed that burial sites continued to be used in the south and west well into the fourth century, when they curiously stop. This is not because (as some might believe) everyone had died off, but rather due to another phenomenon: Christianity. Finds from the city confirm the religion's spread after the withdrawal, and the new faithful were hesitant to give their dead a pagan burial. The new spot chosen for the cemetery, inside the old Roman fort, was still not terribly appropriate either, but at least it was not sacrilege.

Apulum, according to recent studies,(A. Diaconescu, 2004, pp. 135-136) fared similarly to Potaissa, which is unsurprising since it housed Dacia's other legion (*XIII Gemina*). Continued habitation is proven by fourth century cemeteries though, as in Potaissa, they stopped being used due to the spread of Christianity. Apulum's most interesting change is the militarization of the locals, similar to that which occurred in Britain after its own abandonment. Garments, belt buckles, and brooches indicate a continuity of Roman military tradition and ranks. It is doubtful that they mattered much anymore, but posterity sometimes has its own value. Similar items were found at other military sites like Potaissa but rarely in civilian settlements like Napoca. Not only had the settlers of Apulum lived on in the region, but their traditions continued long after the province had been forsaken.

Sarmizegetusa, Dacia's first city, evidences a slow decline rather than a sudden abandonment.(A. Diaconescu, 2004, pp. 131-133) The city center was looted and destroyed… but it was not barbarians doing the looting, but rather the Roman Christians! This much is proven by the Christian symbols found on the looted goods scattered about. One well-known change in the city was the fortification of its amphitheatre in 375,(Goldsworthy, 2009, p. 122) on the eve of the Hun Invasion, a structure which could easily have defended thousands of inhabitants. And yet, no evidence exists for a barbarian raid or any violent destruction in this time. Rather than barbarians, the structure's purpose was to defend the city's inhabitants from Roman brigands and outlaws who saw the retreat of authority as a chance to steal from the rich and keep for themselves. Clearly an organized Roman community survived in the city after Aurelian's withdrawal, and the Roman pots, lamps, and other goods have been found that date up to the sixth century.

Sarmizegetusa's population slowly radiated to the city outskirts. The center was abandoned (and looted) early on, with the Romans moving to new suburban communities. One house even had a swimming pool, because being ostentatious was too Roman a trait to lose. By the sixth century however the houses had moved even further out and became multi-generational complexes. The reason for the move is easy to understand: the diminished economy of the province (never mind the near-complete absence of coins) made it hard for cities to import grains from the countryside. In a battle between fountains and food, food took precedence, and the citizens slowly moved outward and became self-sufficient. The name of the city likewise lost to its inhabitants as they drifted into the rural unknown.

The former city-dwellers may have abandoned their homes, but their vocabulary seems to have survived, though in a terribly misused state. The Latin word for pavement (*pavimentum*) came to be used for "earth", something which may bring a chuckle to someone familiar with Romania's rural roads. The word has survived in modern

Romanian as *pământ*. The same is true of the word *monumentum* which replaced the word *tumba* (tomb) when being used for graves; it has survived in Romanian as *mormânt*. The bizarre adoption of urban terms to rural life could only have happened if the urban settlers moved out to the country at an early date[Madgearu, 2001, p. 37] and this phenomenon did not occur anywhere else in the Roman Empire. Similarly, the loss of the word *civitas* for city (the current word in Romanian, *oraș*, is derived from Hungarian) could only be explained if the Romanians' ancestors lived in an area where city life had essentially disappeared. Indeed, in modern Romanian *civitas* became *cetate*, meaning fortress, which reflects the trend of Dacia's former cities became *ad-hoc* fortresses.[Madgearu, 2008a, p. 90] Similarly, when the proto-Romanians abandoned the cities and moved into smaller villages, these were often fortified as well. It is little wonder then that the Romanian word for village, *sat*, is derived from the Latin *fossatum* meaning a fortification ditch. In other words: the linguistic evidence lines up perfectly with Dacia's post-Roman history.

The southern part of Trajan's Dacia remained largely unchanged by Aurelian's withdrawal. The region remained densely populated, with hundreds of settlements dotting the landscape.[Bejan, 1995; Micle, 2008] Roman forts (Sucidava and Drobeta) on the northern bank of the Danube continued to be used well into late antiquity.[Ellis, 1998] Perhaps this was because the army believed it was to return shortly, as happened in 332 when Constantine the Great subdued the Goths and reclaimed part of the former province. Constantine's campaigns may have something to do with the revival of coinage in the region shortly after.[Găzdac, 1998] A monument erected in Romula in 376 attested a sense of Roman permanence felt by its inhabitants.[Madgearu, 2001, p. 34] Unfortunately the Huns overran the entire territory later that year.

In civilian life Aurelian's withdrawal was a non-event. Dacia's cities remained inhabited until the seventh century, though an even later date is not out of the question.[A. Diaconescu, 2004, p. 129] Aurelian was only able to withdraw the army and administration, and even that met with partial success. The resulting power vacuum was not filled by barbarian kings, but rather by the local strongmen, who liked to emphasize their Roman origin with conspicuous swag. The discoveries of *fibulae* with Latin inscriptions as well as Roman military gear and rank insignias indicate an aristocracy with Roman traditions.[Madgearu, 2001, p. 35; 2008a, p. 88] These leaders were usually former aristocrats who now competed with each other, but whose power came from the idea that Roman administration would one day return.[Wanner, 2010, pp. 311-317] Roman culture survived, even if the finer aspects of Roman life were lost. All things considered, Aurelian's withdrawal must only have been an administrative in character: everyone else stayed on and made use of what they could remember of Roman traditions.[MacKendrick, 1975, p. 143]

It should be noted that those arguing for a complete withdrawal often have a political stake in the matter. In some cases, the factual errors caused by such ulterior motives are easy to spot: one author for instance claimed that there was a strong Greek influence in Dacia,[Vékony, 2000, p. 154] something hard to believe given that Greek inscriptions in Dacia amount to only 1% of all inscriptions discovered, while Latin inscriptions dominate the landscape. If we consider the evidence in an unbiased manner, we can only conclude that Dacia was Romanized and that the colonists of the province stayed on after Aurelian's withdrawal.

Of course, the story does not end there. Roman Dacia's history solved the questions of Romanization and abandonment. Now we have one last hurdle: survival. For the next thousand years Dacia served as the generous (if unwilling) host of many barbarian tribes. The list looks like something Roman mothers would use to scare their children: Goths, Vandals, Huns, Slavs, and many others all settled in Dacia for shorter or longer periods of time. What happened to the proto-Romanians in this time? Did they die off or get evicted from Dacia? Did they become the lower class of this new barbarian order? Or, is it possible that they still played a role in this era?

Works Cited

Ardevan, R. (2007). *On the Latest Inscriptions of Roman Dacia*. Paper presented at the 13th International Congress of Greek and Latin Epigraphy, Oxford, UK.

Bejan, A. (1995). *Banatul in secolele IV-XII [Banat in the 4th to 12th centuries]*. Timisoara: Editura de Vest.

Bejan, A. (1998). *Dacia Felix: Istoria Daciei Romane*. Timisoara, Romania: Editura Eurobit.

Bennett, J. (1997). *Trajan Optimus Princeps: A Life and Times*. London, UK New York, NY: Routledge.

Diaconescu, A. (2004). The towns of Roman Dacia: an overview of recent research. In W. S. Hanson & I. P. Haynes (Eds.), *Roman Dacia: the Making of a Provincial Society*. Portsmouth, RI: Journal of Roman Archaeology.

Ellis, L. (1998). Dacia Terra Deserta: Populations, Politics, and the [de]colonization of Dacia. *World Archaeology, 30*(2).

Everitt, A. (2009). *Hadrian and the Triumph of Rome*. New York, NY: Random House.

Gazdac, C. (1998). Coins and the abandonment of Dacia. *Acta Musei Napocensis, 35*(I).

Goldsworthy, A. (2009). *How Rome Fell: Death of a Superpower*. New Haven, CT: Yale University Press.

Haynes, I. P., & Hanson, W. S. (2004). An Introduction to Roman Dacia *Roman Dacia: the making of a provincial society*. Portsmouth, RI: Journal of Roman Archaeology.

Historia Augusta.

Hügel, P. (2003). *Ulitemele decenii ale stăpânirii romane in Dacia (Traianus Decius - Aurelian)*. Cluj-Napoca: Nereamia Napocae.

Husar, A. (2002). *Din Istoria Daciei Romane*. Cluj-Napoca, Romania: Presa Universitară Clujeană.

Jordanes. *Getica* (Vol. XI).

Kulikowski, M. (2007). *Rome's Gothic Wars*. Cambridge, UK: Cambridge University Press.

Lewis, J. (2010). *Nothing LEss than Victory: decisive wars and the lessons of history*. Princeton: Princeton University Press.

MacKendrick, P. (1975). *The Dacian Stones Speak*. Chapel Hill, NC: University of North Carolina Press.

Madgearu, A. (2001). *Rolul Crestinismului in Formarea Poporului român*. Bucharest, Romania: BIC ALL.

Madgearu, A. (2008). *Istoria Militara a Daciei Post-Romane, 275-376*. Targoviste, Romania: Cetatea de Scaun.

Micle, D. (2008). *Digital Cartography and Spatial Analysis of Elements of the Dacian-Roman Rural Habitat in South-Western Dacia between the 2nd and the 5th century A.D.* Sibiu: Lucian Blaga University.

Mócsy, A. (1974). *Pannonia and Upper Moesia: a history of the middle Danube provinces of the Roman Empire*. London, UK Boston, MA: Routledge & K. Paul.

Oltean, I. (2007). *Dacia: Landscape, Colonisation and Romanisation*. New York, NY: Routledge.

Peachin, M. (1989). *Roman imperial titulature and chronology, 235-284*. Leiden, Netherlands: Brill.

Southern, P. (2001). *The Roman Empire from Severus to Constantine*. London, UK; New York, NY: Routledge.

Tóth, E. (2002). The Roman Province of Dacia. In B. Köpeczi, L. Makkai & A. Mocsy (Eds.), *History of Transylvania* (Vol. I). Boulder, CO; New York, NY: Social Science Monographs.

Vekony, G. (2000). *Dacians, Romans, Romanians*. Budapest, Hungary: Corvinus Library.

Wanner, R. (2010). *Forts, fields, and towns: communities in Northwest Transylvania from the first century BC to the fifth century AD*. Leicaster, UK: University of Leicaster.

Watson, A. (1999). *Aurelian and the Third Century*. London, UK: Routledge.

5. I SURVIVED 1,000 YEARS AND ALL I GOT WAS THIS HÂT

The withdrawal of Roman administration from Dacia signifies the start of a new (and worse) era in Romanian history. An old Romanian proverb explains this time period in a nutshell: "the water passes, but the stones remain." A barbarian torrent poured over Romania: Goths, Huns, Gepids, Slavs, Avars, Bulgars, Magyars, Pechenegs, Cumans and Mongols all paid a visit. A thousand years would pass from the abandonment of Dacia to the creation of the first Romanian states. In one sense, this could be viewed as a tragic time in Romanian history and yet, in another sense, it would be hard to see the development of a separate Romanian identity without it. There would be no Romanians today if the barbarians did not cut the imperial umbilical cord. So what happened to the Daco-Romans in this time? How is it that *Romanus* became *Român*?

What strikes the archaeologist first is that there was no sudden breakdown in communication between the empire and its former Dacian province. Dacia's situation was nothing like in post-Roman Britain; the Danube may be big but it is not the English Channel. There was never anything like a Roman "Iron Curtain" on the Danube either. Roman forts remained on its northern bank, and with them came Roman influence and good. Trade continued throughout late antiquity. Though some (mostly Hungarian) historians argue that Roman goods do not prove "the survival there of a 'Daco-Roman' population, because such objects have been unearthed over almost the whole of Europe,"[Kazar & Makai, 2001, p. 22] the case of Dacia is unrivaled in the whole non-Roman world.[Ellis, 1998] We are not talking a few coins here and there, but many hundreds of objects at any given time!

The second aspect an archaeologist must remember is that a change in material culture does not imply a change in population, even if they appear quite sudden. One glaring example is in the changing burial practices in Dacia.[Ellis, 1998] By around the fourth century the burial practices began to change from cremation to inhumation. This presents an interesting problem since it is known that the Romans cremated their dead while the Germanic Goths (who were arriving on scene at the time) buried their own; you say potato, I say… inhumation. Taken in isolation, the evidence suggests that the Goths had completely replaced the Romans, and that Roman culture came to an end. The argument sounds logical, until one realizes that the same change from cremation to inhumation occurred in Gaul and Italy and in many other Roman provinces where no barbarians had settled. In other words, far from inhumation being a "non-Roman" practice, this change of customs is just an evolution of Roman culture, and could even be seen as evidence of cultural exchange between post-Roman Dacia and the empire.

With this backdrop, we are finally ready to be introduced to Dacia's first wave of barbarian settler who, incidentally, was more Dacians! Known as the *Carpi*, they are perhaps the most fearsome tribe to have a name with evokes a type of fish. They "invaded" Dacia immediately after the Roman abandonment, but this was not some glorious Dacian Reconquista. Rather, the Dacians were fleeing from the Goths, other barbarians that had taken over their former Moldovan homeland. Gothic expansion came directly at the expense of the Carpi, and the Carpi moved into Dacia as a result.

The saga of the Carps seems to be a case of out of the frying pan and into the fire. Having escaped their barbarian pursuers, they entered the crosshairs of the Roman army by trespassing into the former province. In 272, possibly in retaliation for entering Dacia, Aurelian attacked them and claimed to have moved them south of the Danube. It is telling that even here Rome's "resettling" policy was half-baked at best, as the Carpi remained a constant factor north of the Danube for nearly 50 years. Diocletian found plenty of Carpi in Dacia, which he claimed to have settled in Pannonia in 296. Even then, Galerius had ample supply for his own resettlement in 307, consisting of a "great number of captives."(Eutropius, IX, 25) Roman exaggerations aside, the Carpi were more than willing to be moved due to their pressing Gothic neighbors,(Kulikowski, 2007, p. 78) a willingness noted by many Roman historians such as Aurelius Victor.(Victor, 1970, 43)

Constantine the Great hammered the final nail in the coffin of the Carpi during his campaigns in 317, a year after which the Carpi disappear as a major tribe. The last we hear of them is in the fifth century(Zosimus, IV, 114) when they are mentioned by an author[m] that is infamously referred to as the most incompetent historian the empire had ever seen (an "honor" for which he had stiff competition!).(Thompson, 1982) His reference is completely unreliable, and it is certain that a major Carpic presence had ended in Dacia by the early fourth century, after only 40 years.

The Carpi were replaced by the Goths: vicious, bloodthirsty primitives who sacked Rome and nearly ended civilization… or perhaps they were something else? It is hard to describe the Goths around Dacia as genocidal barbarians, mostly because it is not true. If anything, the Goths were quite cosmopolitan: Roman provincials, Dacians, Germans, and other tribes all visibly influenced Gothic culture.(Halsall, 2007, p. 134) Though there was undoubtedly a "Gothic" elite, and Gothic political dominance, the settlements north of the Danube were predominantly non-Gothic.(Burns, 1991, p. 32) There was no "barbarization"; rather, the Goths imitated the Romans in practically every aspect! It was not uncommon to see Roman goods and (if linguistic evidence is anything) even Roman manners at a Gothic dinner table.(Green, 2000, p. 208) Some aspects were undoubtedly lost in translation but it seems Roman culture continued to spread in Dacia even after Rome formally abandoned it.

The Gothic takeover of Dacia was hardly a *blitzkrieg* either. The first traces of them appear in Dacia around 300 AD, but a major expansion beyond the Carpathians

---

[m] The author, Zosimos, and his mention of the Dacians, was a favorite of Romanian communist historians. It was common during the communist era for Romanian historians to emphasize the "Dacian" aspect of Romanian ethnicity, and Zosimos allowed for Dacian influence to be spread over several more centuries than was truly warranted. This had to do with Ceaușescu's desire to portray himself as both independent of Moscow ("the Slavs") and the West ("the Romans"). The idea was simple: the Romanians were "mostly Dacian", Romania was a "2050 year old [Dacian] state", and Ceaușescu was the Burebista's heir as absolute ruler of the Dacians/Romanians. This fifth century mention by the author Zosimos was used to strengthen the Dacian presence in Romanian history at the expense of the "barbarians." It was one of the worst bastardizations of Romanian history, and unfortunately it stained the reputation of Romanian historiography for some time.

occurred only fifty years later.(Burns, 1991, p. 111; Wanner, 2010, pp. 27-28) Why did the Goths take so long to take over what was, some claim, abandoned territory? Aurelian's (still hypothetical) peace terms that shielded Dacia may have been a factor early on. Even if Aurelian's treaty never set any formal stipulations, the Romans civilians left behind in Dacia may also have played a role, as the Goths were not looking to give the Romans *casus belli* to "rescue" their citizens.(Burns, 1991, p. 31) Another explanation may come from barbarian organization (or lack-there-of): intertribal warfare left little time for exploration.

The Goths' slow advance after they became more unified in the 330's is more difficult to explain. Transylvania remained out of Gothic control even when they had the strength to take it. A Gothic army raided into Central Transylvania in 334, but "after defeating and plundering the Vandals, [they] returned home again," a home which evidently was still East of the Carpathians.(Wolfram & Dunlap, 1988, p. 63) Even in 370, at the peak of Gothic power north of the Danube, their central region was still Moldova.(Wolfram & Dunlap, 1988, p. 71) Needless imperialism seems to not have been on the Gothic agenda.

Transylvania remained out of Gothic hands for one reason: it was seemingly pointless to conquer. There had been some barbarian squabbling over Dacia,(Wolfram & Dunlap, 1988, p. 56) but by the fourth century everyone knew the real action was in the Roman Empire. A Roman general would pay good money for a chance at becoming emperor, and a little barbarian help could go a long way in that regard. The Goths knew this: they were a part of both Constantine's army, and that of his rival Licinius during their struggle for emperorship.(Wolfram & Dunlap, 1988, p. 59) If work failed to pay, raids were always an acceptable alternative. Barbarians were thus drawn towards the Danube and away from Dacia. The Roman Empire still had plenty of coin, while Dacia had hardly any.

What is most interesting in this time is that the Romans never gave up on Dacia. Aurelian's abandonment was considered a "strategic withdrawal" by later Romans, one that was hoped to be reversed. Constantine's stone bridge across the Danube, built in 328, was an ominous portent for the barbarians. Ending the subsidies paid to barbarians made things even more obvious: Constantine was clearly preparing to retake Dacia.(Burns, 1991, p. 35) In 332 he launched a thorough campaign in the region to show the barbarians who was in charge. To some extent he succeeded: Roman forts on the northern bank of the Danube were repaired, and a new milestone situated far north of the Danube suggests the advance at least reached central Oltenia.(MacKendrick, 1975, p. 163) Coin circulation increased tremendously south of the Carpathians, both in towns and fortresses.(Găzdac, 1998, pp. 273-274) Roman confidence was reflected in their propaganda: Constantine took the title *Dacicus Maximus* and issued coins claiming "Gothia" was subdued and that Dacia was restored(Wolfram & Dunlap, 1988, p. 22) a fair bit before either had occurred. It was a Roman "Mission Accomplished" *sans* aircraft carrier. Constantine's death and a barbarian backlash in 337 brought things to a grinding halt. The Romans did retake Oltenia, but Transylvania never saw another Roman governor. Similarly, coin circulation north of the Carpathians never increased enough to indicate a return to pre-Aurelian days. Still, the Danubian toehold was enough for Rome to influence developments in the region for over a century.

By far the biggest cultural change in Dacia in this time was the spread of Christianity. Even at the northern tip of the province in Porolissum one sees pagan temples converted into churches in the early fourth century.[Wanner, 2010, p. 116] Similarly, a *donarium*[n] discovered at Biertan (southern Transylvania) with a Latin inscription[o] confirms a Latin speaking Christian community in the region.[Pop, 1997, pp. 26-27] Hungarian historians that argue against Romanian continuity tried to minimize the discovery's significance by suggesting the artefact was Greek since its donor bore a Greek name,[Vékony, 2000, p. 160] but this ignores the very language the donation is written in! The Roman Empire was multiethnic, and Greek names should not surprise us, but whoever received the gift must have known Latin.[Varga, 2008] The *donarium* serves as evidence for Latin as the major language of correspondence in Dacia, and that Christianity was spread in this language in post-Roman Dacia is confirmed by the Latin-based fundamental Christian terms in modern Romanian.[p]

This does not mean, of course, that Dacia became some Christian haven as some have proposed.[Stefanescu-Draganesti, 1986] The Christians north of the Danube received their fair share of persecution. They were undoubtedly not very numerous during Roman rule, and this did not change much immediately following Aurelian's withdrawal. The spread of Christianity in Dacia occurred very similar that in the rest of the empire: with slow but sure steps.

We can say the Goths actually helped bring Christianity to Dacia. Prisoners taken by the Goths during their raids south of the Danube were being settled north of the river since the mid-third century.[Vasiliev, 1958, p. 85] By the fourth century many of these prisoners were Christians and they acted as a proselytizing force on the Goths (and anyone else in the region).[Cusack, 1998, pp. 39-40] The Christianization of the Goths of course makes it difficult to identify the owner of discovered religious artifacts, though most scholars agree that Arian Christian[q] artifacts are predominantly Gothic while those of the Trinitarian variety belong to Roman settlers and prisoners.[Vasiliev, 1958, p. 86] The battle between the different type of Christianity is however a minor detail to the fact that Christianity was spreading in the region, in one form or another. It may come as a surprise, but were it not for the Goths (and their prisoners) the Romanians would likely have been Christianized centuries later, and not have gained the Latin Christian vocabulary they possess today. Ironically, barbarians were essentially further Romanising the Daco-Romans!

---

[n] A fancy term for "gift."

[o] The inscription reads "*EGO ZENOVIUS VOTUM POSVI*", or "I, Zenovius, offer this gift."

[p] This might seem like an odd argument, since it relies on the Romanians being Christianized in Dacia. However, as Greek was the predominant language in the Balkans, the Romanians would certainly have had a few Greek words in their Christian vocabulary had they been Christianized there. The dominance of Latin in Romanian Christian terminology is an indication that the Romanians converted to Christianity in the region as well.

[q] One of the theological schools of thought popular at the time but which was declared heretical in the fourth century.

One well-recorded individual sheds much light on the ethnic situation north of the Danube. His name was Ulfila, and he would become the "bishop of the Goths" and translate the bible into Gothic a half-century before it was even translated into Latin! Not only is his Bible important, as it reveals Latin loanwords in Gothic, but Ulfila's life reveals many facts about life in Dacia in its own right. His ancestors were prisoners taken by the Goths out of Asia minor, but he was a third generation Goth, born north of the Danube and outside of the empire.(Wolfram & Dunlap, 1988, p. 76) Nevertheless, Ulfila knew both Latin and Greek, languages that must evidently still have been in wide use in post-Roman Dacia.(P. Heather, 1996, p. 91) Furthermore, his title of "bishop of the Goths" is a misnomer: he was actually "bishop of the Christians in the Getic [Gothic] Lands." This is not an arbitrary distinction: it evidences that Ulfila was presiding over a multiethnic Christian community north of the Danube, composed of Romans, Goths, and other barbarians.(Wolfram & Dunlap, 1988, p. 77)

Gothic power north of the Danube ended in 376 when the Huns thundered in from the east. Ambrose covered the event with ludicrous brevity: "the Huns threw themselves upon the Alans, the Alans upon the Goths, and the Goths upon the Taifali and Sarmatae"(Ambrose, X, 10) and so another round of barbarian billiards ended. Some Goths fled to Transylvania but most went to the Danube to ask Emperor Valens to be let into the empire. Pure chaos ensued once the Romans had let them inside: "Thrace, Pannonia, and the whole country as far as Macedon and Thessaly were filled with Barbarians, who pillaged all in their way."(Zosimus, IV) It was another not-so-brilliant decision in Roman history, as only two years later the Goths would crush the Romans at Adrianople and eventually sack Rome itself. This is however, where we will leave the Goths: they ironically completely fall off the radar of Romanian history just as they become hugely important for the Romans. Gothic rule had come to an end in Dacia. Their domination of 75 years was not even half as long as the Roman one, and it was certainly far less thorough.

With all this talk of expulsions, migrations, and conquest, it is important we consider who was moving where and how much is truth or exaggeration. Most of the historians from the colonial times of the nineteenth century promoted an idea that tribes completely displaced one another and never mixed.(Kulikowski, 2007, pp. 64-65) This was a result of their take of Roman authors at face-value. Ancient authors made a clear divide between Romans and barbarians.(Procopius, 1940, IV, 5) Historians thus considered the ancient world as having well-defined boundaries between regions where one could place labels as "Huns" or "Goths" or "Romans," essentially trying to draw up nation-states at a time before nationalism. Thus, when the Huns took over Dacia politically, historians assumed that they had wiped the slate clean of people as well. Nothing could be further from the truth: Europe, Dacia included, was polyglot and multiethnic for much of its ancient history.

No migration into Dacia ever wiped out the previous inhabitants. The Goths that fled to Transylvania to escape the Huns called their new home *Caucaland* after the Dacian tribe of the *Caucones*, and undoubtedly their new home harbored Dacians,

Sarmatians, and Romans.(Wolfram & Dunlap, 1988, p. 93) The Huns were likewise not genocidal. Priscus, a Greek diplomat from the fifth century, noted that Gothic, Hunnic and Latin were all spoken in Hunnic lands.(Murgescu, 2001, pp. 65-66) Even the Gothic settlements – now supposedly abandoned – did not change in culture for forty years after their supposed abandonment!(Kulikowski, 2007, p. 155; Wanner, 2010, p. 47) Wars of extermination were both difficult and a waste of valuable manpower, and the barbarians were never foolish enough to attempt them.

Roman influence north of the Danube did not end with the arrival of the barbarians. Coins found in post-Roman Dacia attest to almost constant trade with the empire,(Curta, 2005b) especially in the purchase of luxury goods;(Brezeanu, 2003) vanity was not something exclusively Roman. Peaceful trade between the barbarians and Romans was more common than war.(Goldsworthy, 2009, p. 273) Ulfila himself is a testament of this cultural exchange: he may have been born a Goth but he died a Roman.(Goldsworthy, 2009, p. 181)

With the survival of Roman influence one notes also the survival of the Latin language. Latin's development and use in Dacia was much more profound than in other provinces such as Britain.(Wollman, 1993, pp. 8-11) Britain had witnessed superficial Romanization and Latin eventually disappeared after the Romans withdrew from the island. Even so, Latin might also have disappeared in Dacia, had it fallen out of use among the new rulers as occurred in Britain. Latin however survived as Dacia's *lingua franca* as the new barbarian rulers needed to negotiate with the powerful Roman Empire immediately across the Danube. Priscus evidenced its vigorous use during the Hunnic era, claiming jesters at Attila's court even made jokes using "a confused jumble of Latin, Hunnic, and Gothic"! Latin remained the international language in Dacia.(Brezeanu, 2003)

The whole gamut of evidence makes it clear that the Danube was only a political frontier and not an ethnic or cultural one. The region was ruled by barbarians *de facto*, but this does not mean that no Romans lived there among them. The unfortunate aspect is that primary authors cared more for politics than ethnography and most of their writings deal only with ruling (barbarian) elites.(Spinei, 2009, p. 188) Conquered people like the Goths, or the Daco-Romans before them, simply fell off of the radar screen. The dethroned Goths were "in a sense passed over by history... one would doubt their existence were it not for the well-documented archaeological sites"(Wolfram & Dunlap, 1988, p. 73) and it is doubtless that the Daco-Romans were in a similar position. Modern historians (those who do not believe in magically disappearing tribes) have to piece together the truth from archaeology, which attests to an ethnically mixed landscape.

The new Hunnic masters were a mysterious group. Almost nothing is known about their language, though it is believed they originated from within Asia. The Romans first encountered them in the late fourth century in the eastern province of Armenia,(Goldsworthy, 2009, p. 295) and the first mention of Huns on the Danube is only in the year 400.(Kulikowski, 2007, p. 154) A powerful Hun state emerged in the area in the 420's when, largely bolstered by Roman tribute paid to Hunnic chiefs.(Goldsworthy, 2009, p. 320) Even then it is unclear who the Huns really were: from what we can tell most of their army was

Germanic,[Goldsworthy, 2009, p. 315] and even the name Attila is believed to be Germanic in character.

Whoever the Huns were, they made their presence felt, causing unprecedented destruction south of the Danube.[Kulikowski, 2007, p. 138] Being unable to stop the barbarian threat with force, the Romans switched to their other tested method of dealing with barbarians: tribute. Ironically, this only encouraged further attacks by empowering local chieftains, resulting in even higher tribute and the Huns were able to consolidate their dominance north of the Danube with Rome's generous – if unwilling – financial backing. Attila used his wealth to redecorate the Roman frontier by smashing every Roman settlement on it. The archaeology of most settlements south of the Danube reveals a generous twenty-inch thick ash layer in the archaeological record due to his actions.[MacKendrick, 1975, p. 165]

For all the harm they caused to their enemies, the Huns were not particularly cruel to their subjects. This is not to say they became docile creatures laden with Roman loot in their own lands, but in general the Huns, not being overly numerous,[Goldsworthy, 2009, p. 319] needed subjects on their farms and in their armies. The Huns of Priscus' days in the mid-fifth century were not the nomads that lived two generations prior. Influences from Roman and barbarian subjects made Hunnic society a bit more sedentary and "civilized."[Brezeanu, 2003] Priscus described villages ruled by Hunnic chiefs, with Romans living happily under the Huns. Priscus notes his surprise at finding a fellow Greek happily living among the barbarians, who described the barbarian way of life as consisting of "enjoying what they have got, and [being] not at all, or very little, harassed." Whether this "noble savage" idea was entirely valid is another issue, but Priscus' surprise at finding another Greek north of the river is a subtle hint that the majority of the Romans in the area were Latin-speakers.[Brezeanu, 2003]

Transylvania appears to have been mostly ignored by the Huns. The center of Hunnic power in the late fourth century was in Moldova or Muntenia and in the fifth century it moved to the Pannonian plain.[Madgearu, 2001, p. 34] Transylvania – situated between these two centers – shows no trace of Hunnic settlement.[Wanner, 2010, pp. 46-47] It is easy to understand why the Huns never spread to Transylvania however. Though rich in natural resources such as salt and gold, the Huns could easily enjoy the spoils of the province just as tribute from Gothic or Daco-Roman settlers in the region. Even if the Huns wanted to invade Transylvania, chances are they would not have been able to do so; the terrain was simply not suitable to the Hunnic way of warfare. Mounted archery was impractical if not outright hazardous to use in Transylvania's forested and mountainous land, and the Huns may have decided to leave well enough alone.

The Huns vanished almost without a trace after Attila's reign. Attila's death was arguably ancient history's greatest anticlimax: a combination of drunkenness and a nosebleed was an unexpected way to go for a man who had cowed both the Western and Eastern Roman Emperors. With no direct successor, it was Hun against Hun, with everyone else taking the chance to reassert their independence.[Williams, 1999, p. 88] Some tribes tried to pick up the pieces while others decided to find a new home south of the Danube.(Williams, 1999, p. 89)

The regions north of the Danube became a political mess for the next 100 years, with the Gepids enjoying a short-lived dominance, though never outright hegemony in the region.(Curta, 2006b, p. 54) The Eastern Roman Emperor tried to cushion the empire from the turmoil in the north by establishing client kings in the region. One barbarian royal burial discovered in Transylvania is littered with symbols of Roman power and the owner bore a ring inscribed with the Roman title of *vir glorisissimus*,(Madgearu, 2010, p. 69) essentially the barbarian chief's way of letting everyone know they were friends of the emperor. Transylvania in this time experienced a sort of *pax Gepidica* (Gepid Peace) where – at least archaeologically – the local Romanic culture appears to have bounced back from the shock of the Huns.(Dumitrașcu & Sfrengeu, 2006)

The fragmented kingdoms north of the Danube were unified by force in 567 by a new barbarian group: the Avars. Like the Huns, they too were nomads hailing from the unknown plains of Central Asia. Centered on the Hungarian plain, they remained the most powerful barbarian force for nearly two hundred years. Both Germanic and Roman life continued in the region, with some settlements continuing since the days of Roman administration in the region.(Vida, 2008b, pp. 31-39) Much like the Huns, the Avars rapidly assimilated into the cultures of their clients: even within 30 years the Avars looked completely different from those that had burst into Hungary through the Ukrainian Carpathians.(Curta, 2006b, p. 62)

A familiar people also make an entrance on history's stage in this time: the Slavs. Their origin is a mystery to this day. According to the (lack of) information in Roman sources, the Slavs just appeared on the Danube in 545. There is no record of how they got there, but this might be typical Roman myopia ignoring anything happening beyond the frontier. Some argued that they came from northeastern Europe, but the evidence is tenuous. Others have found another explanation: the Slavs were simply made up by Byzantine/Roman[r] historians!(Curta, 2006b, pp. 59-61) That is not to say that the Slavs are a myth (given that there are hundreds of millions of Slavic people today), but rather it indicates that "Slav" was, much like "Goth", an umbrella term for many different people that gathered around an aristocracy which had risen to power by waging wars against the Romans. They only emerged from the shadows when the Romans recognized them as a unique threat.

The Byzantine response to their changing neighbours was to lock the door and throw away the key, attempting to make the Danubian border impregnable. The idea was not exactly new –Julius Caesar had thought of fortifying the Danube five centuries

---

[r] The term "Byzantine Empire" came to designate the Eastern Roman Empire during the Middle Ages. It is entirely a fabrication of modern historians, as no work written until the empire's fall in 1453 ever called it "Byzantine." In spite of its completely fabricated nature and its derogatory connotation (or perhaps because of it) the name has stuck in modern historiography. To prevent confusion, the term "Byzantine Empire" will be applied throughout the rest of this book.

earlier – but the new emperor Justinian was the first to seriously attempt it. The project ended up wildly over budget (not atypical for government projects), resulted in the construction (and reconstruction) of over 600 fortresses, and left the empire economically exhausted. The attempted exclusion of the barbarians, coupled with the empire's strained finances, caused Byzantine coin circulation to stop north of the Danube for two decades. The defences were somewhat of a mixed success: immediately they created a definite divide between the empire and the barbarians, but by stifling trade the new defences actually made the barbarians more aggressive. When the barbarians could not buy the Roman goods they wanted, they attempted to take them by force,(Madgearu, 2010, p. 81) and hardly a year went by when the Balkans were not attacked as a result.(Curta, 2006b, p. 53)

A unique Romanian culture began to take shape north of the Danube by this time. The culture emerged across the entire territory of modern Romania, in spite of the fact that archaeologists gave it three names.[s] The cause of this spread was likely a gradual diffusion of settlers from Transylvania to the eastern and southern plains, where they were reinforced by newly-settled captives from the empire.(Madgearu, 2001, pp. 76-77) Romanian culture maintained strong ties with the empire; the cemeteries at Bratei in Transylvania showed remarkable similarity to Roman traditions south of the Danube.(MacKenzie, 1986, p. 116) Justinian's walls however, had created a very real divide between the northern and southern Romans, and this was reflected by the cultural drift in the region.

The terms Roman and Christian were considered largely synonymous in this time, both in the Balkans and in Romania. The number of artefacts, including moulds of cross-shaped jewelry, indicates the religion's spread among the Daco-Romans, who thankfully did not mind being ostentatious about it.(Madgearu, 2001, pp. 81-83) Though we should not assume that it was exclusively Roman, nevertheless the vast majority of such artefacts are discovered in Daco-Roman settlements, and it may even be that bronze pectoral crosses acted as both religious and ethnic identifiers in the north, differentiating Christian Romans from pagan barbarians.(Madgearu, 2001, pp. 85-87; 2010, p. 94)

The conversion of the Romanians occurred in a slow and rather anticlimactic fashion. Most history books portray conversion as a distinct event: in some year some leader decided that everyone he ruled should become a Christian. Constantine and Theodosius II's conversion of the Roman Empire, or Clovis' conversion of the Franks in 496, are two examples that come to mind. By contrast, there is no concrete date, no Year X, in which we can say the Romanians converted to Christianity, nor can the work be credited to any one man. They are not alone in this regard: the Lombards, Ostrogoths, and Gepids also do not have a precise date of conversion but they nevertheless converted. It is in some sense unrealistic to portray conversion as an official order at all, but rather as a cultural movement.(Curta, 2005a, pp. 181-182) When Theodosius II declared

---

[s] In Muntenia it is called Ipoteşti-Cândeşti-Ciurel, in Transylvania it is called Bratei, and in Moldova it is called Costişa-Botoşana.

Christianity the official religion of the Empire he was mostly acknowledging a *fait accompli*; much of its inhabitants had converted long before that date. Therefore, there is nothing surprising or unique about the fact that the conversion of the Romanians just happened without official decree. It was expected, if not downright predictable, given the close ties between the Romanians and Eastern Roman/Byzantine Empire.

The Byzantine defenses ruptured like a water balloon in the seventh century, with the Slavs spilling all over the Balkans. The Avars breached the border in 602, and the Slavs followed in their wake. The Byzantine emperor have been caught off-guard by the whole event[(Curta, 2006b, p. 3)] though it soon became clear the Slavs were not going to go home, as whole tribes were settling in the Balkans.[(Curta, 2001a, p. 107)] It was a move that would redefine this corner of Europe: the Slavs would dominate and assimilate the lands south of the Danube, while the Romanians would dominate the north (at least in Romania).[(Georgescu, 1991, p. 12)] The Slavic invasion also effectively separated the Latins of Southeastern Europe. The Aromanians of the Balkans and the modern Romanians would from this point on develop as separate people.[(Georgescu, 1991, p. 13)]

The role of the Slavs in Romanian history is complicated, often being minimized or exaggerated depending on which political wind was blowing through Bucharest.[(Curta, 2001b)] Archaeologists in Communist Romania fluctuated between making the Slavs docile creatures and warlike brutes; the only constant was that they were considered primitives, lacking the potter's wheel, migrating everywhere, and still cremating their dead as pagans (in contrast to the Christian Daco-Romans). After the Prague Spring of 1968, Romanian scholars tried to turn the early Slavs into an analogy for the Soviets, painting them as aggressors who destroyed a budding Romanian civilization. They argued that all effects of their invasion were detrimental: material culture declined, church organization collapsed, and pagan rituals were revived.[(Madgearu, 2001, pp. 92-106)] Romanian archaeologists also sought to minimize the Slavic presence, reducing it to a simple layover on their journey from Ukraine to the Balkans.

To some extent the Romanian scholars were right: it is hard to deny that the Slavs cremated their dead or that they lacked the potter's wheel. Minimizing a Slavic presence in Romania was wrong however – they had been present since the mid-sixth century at least – but the Slavic influence upon the Romanians was small at the time. Whether this is because their culture was too primitive or because they lived in separate villages is up for debate. Romanian is peppered with Slavic loanwords for state organization (*voievod* – "warlord", *boier* – "noble", *războinic* – "warrior", *etc.*) and religious structure (*preot* – "priest", *botez* – "baptism", *călugăr* – "monk"), but the Slavs at this time hardly had any organization themselves, let alone enough to inspire those around them. Instead, linguists believe most of these words were only injected in early Romanian in the ninth century, and they have a particular Bulgarian tint. The Bulgars, at this time hundreds of miles away near the Caucasus, still needed to come in and shake things up.

Bulgar raids on the Danube were first noted in 480, but they only established a permanent presence in the region in the region after 650. Hardly the conquering invaders some sought to paint them as, the Bulgars were actually refugees forced out of the steppes. They settled in Dobrogea,(Fiedler, 2008, p. 152) though hardly any archaeological evidence exists to show for it until the eighth century.(Curta, 2006b, p. 82) The Bulgars quickly realized the Balkans were not a tranquil land and used the nearby Slavs as a buffer against Byzantium and the Avars, creating the first Bulgarian state between the Balkan Mountains and the Danube.

Unfortunately, piecing together the relations between the Romanians and their neighbours during this time is difficult. The eighth century is one of the worst-recorded in Eastern European history, and Romania is no exception. Even great powers of the time, such as the Avars, disappear completely from history for nearly a century.(Curta, 2006b, pp. 90-92) Relying on written sources to prove a Romanian presence is therefore illogical. Trying to attribute graves to ethnic groups proves difficult as the whole of Eastern Europe was an ethnic mess. One common assumption is that cremation graves are said to be Slavic, inhumation graves with the axis going North-South are Bulgar, and inhumation graves aligned East-West are Romanian.(Fiedler, 2008, p. 157) The ethnic mixture is reflected in the multilingual landscape: in one recorded case, a Slavic man from north of the Danube was able to pass himself off as a Roman general by fluently speaking Latin,(Procopius, VII, 14) signifying that there were Latin speakers in the north able to teach him this language. Perhaps the linguistic diversity of the region is best shown by the word "Vlach", a word of Germanic origin that came to be used by the Slavs to denote the Romanians.(Curta, 2004) This polyglot nature did not deter the Byzantines from pejoratively calling all northern people barbarians however.

Whatever one can say of Bulgar-Byzantine relations, the Bulgars did not turn a blind eye to the north. The Avars were wiped out in at the start of the ninth century by a combined Frankish-Bulgarian effort, with Bulgaria occupying much of its eastern holdings, called afterward as "Bulgaria beyond the Danube" in Byzantine texts. Although modern Bulgarian historians often expand this area to all of modern Romania and then some, in reality this may only have stretched a slightly into southern Transylvania. In some instances this land acted as a repository for Byzantine prisoners of war, as happened to the inhabitants of Adrianople in 813. Bulgar rule was weak however, and the locals were left to their own devices so long as the Bulgars could control the salt trade from Transylvania.(Madgearu, 2005c, pp. 106-107) This trade in turn enriched the Romanian and Slavic nobility and allowed them to take over lands of their rivals and thereby form larger states.(Madgearu, 2005c, p. 109)

Though the Romanians and Slavs coexisted since the sixth century,(Nandriş, 1939) the majority of the Slavic influence upon the Romanians came during the ninth century under Bulgar rule.(Nandriş, 1946) This came about, in particular, with the introduction of Slavonic language and the Cyrillic alphabet in Romania. Bulgaria's conversion to Christianity in the ninth century produced profound reverberations north of the Danube, where Bulgar culture permeated the local nobility. This exchange was not entirely one-directional: changes in Bulgarian grammar dated from the 800's indicates a Romanian influence.(Curta, 2004, p. 136)

The pertinent question, given the rapid succession of barbarian tribes in Romania, is if a "Roman" identity could have survived this tumultuous time. Did the Daco-Romans not mingle with the newer settlers, and thus been assimilated and disappeared? Perhaps the best answer is given in the *Deeds of St. Demetrius*, an ancient text discussing the fate of Roman prisoners under the Avars that were taken in the late seventh century and settled in Pannonia. It seems the prisoners made themselves at home, "mixed with the Bulgars, Avars, and other nations" and, in other words, were fruitful and multiplied. The chronicle goes on to state, however, that these Romans retained their identity and traditions.(Curta, 2006b, p. 106; *Miracles of Saint Demetrius*, II, 5, 292) This well-recorded group, a rarity for this time, serves as an enlightening case-study for the rest of the region's Romanized population.

It seems that a Roman-like identity could have survived north of the Danube, but its mutation into something distinct of Byzantine culture was inevitable. The proto-Romanians adopted the customs of their neighbours and thus produced their own identity. This cosmopolitanism did not go unnoticed by sources of the time. The *Strategikon* of Emperor Maurice, written in the late sixth century, that any "refugees" from north of the Danube were to be treated with suspicion, for though they were Romans, they "forget their own people, and prefer to gain the good will of the enemy."(Brezeanu, 2003; Maurice, XI, 30-31) If such tendencies were noted even in the sixth century, by the ninth century the link between Romanians and the Eastern Roman Empire was, at least in a political sense, broken. The Transdanubian Latins however remained a source of manpower and supplies for the Byzantine Empire, especially during incursions north of the Danube.(Gândilă, 2009, pp. 457-458) The barbarian influence thus, while never erasing the Roman heritage of the Romanians, was strong enough to produce a distinct local identity that we can finally call "Romanian."

Though *de facto* untrue since Hunnic domination, the Byzantines continued to think the lands of former Dacia as "Roman," even when they had no way to enforce such a claim. One telling episode is the incursion of a Byzantine general named Priscus north of the Danube in the late sixth century.(Simocatta, VII, 7) Byzantine armies frequently transgressed north of the Danube as a show of force to the barbarian rulers in the area, and Byzantine generals are even recorded as telling barbarian chiefs flatly that Dacia was "Roman land." The Qagan's diplomats told the general he was "walking on a foreign land" and warned that the general "threatens the peace [between the qagan and the Emperor]", the most diplomatic way of telling Priscus to get lost. Priscus indignant reply is all we need to know about Byzantine attitudes on the former Dacia: "the land is Roman," with the obvious implication that a Roman general may trample about it as he wished. It serves as evidence that the Byzantines continued to see the old territory of Dacia as Roman soil. Priscus knew this was wishful thinking, since even he admitted that "the Barbarian [pretends] that the Romans lost it [the land] through the agency of the armies and of the law of war," but it shows that Dacia was not lost and forgotten to the Romans.

The eighth and ninth centuries were period of recovery for the Romanians, and also the time at which the Romanians became a distinct people. The entire region witnessed substantial demographic growth. The plains of Muntenia began to be repopulated, likely an expansion from the foothills into the plains.[Madgearu, 1997, p. 194] A similar expansion of Roman-style goods is found in eighth century northwestern Transylvania, suggesting a migration from the mountainous Transylvanian heartland,[Băcueț-Crișan, 2005] and also expanded into mixed Slavic-Romanian communities in these regions.[Pinter & Țiplic, 2006]

The relative peace was due to a particular nomadic group living hundreds of kilometres away: the Khazars. A peculiar group that both Byzantium and the Arabs attempted to convert to Christianity and Islam respectively, the Khazars eventually snubbed both and chose Judaism. Allying with the Byzantines against the Arabs and Persians, the Khazars established a large empire north of the Caucasus and over Ukraine, acting as a roadblock for other nomads hoping to reach Europe, and thus shielding the Romanians.[Spinei, 2009, pp. 49-50] The ensuing peace – a *Pax Chazarica* – played a central role in the emergence of the Romanians from the Dark Ages.

The ethnic landscape however ensured that the cultural resurgence would be Slavic and not Latin in nature. The Bulgarians had cut the Roman umbilical cord, and the society that emerged was inspired by Bulgarian (and indirectly, Byzantine) models, as shown in the region's archaeology.[Curta, 2006b, p. 161] The strongest Bulgarian influence was felt in the territories the Bulgarians controlled directly. Slavic terms like *boier* (noble), *cneaz* (prince), *jupan/zhupan* (administrator), and *războinic* (warrior) entered the Romanian vocabulary, and the Slavonic form of Orthodox Christianity pervaded the land.[Păcurariu, 2007, p. 190] Religious terms of Slavonic origin were incorporated in Romanian, including *blagoslovire* (blessing), *utrenie* (morning service), and *liturghie* (liturgy).[Firică, 2008]

Archaeologists refer to the culture forming in this time as the Dridu Culture,[†] which stretched from the southern Carpathians to the Balkan Mountains. In spite of efforts by Romanians to make the culture exclusively Romanian on the one hand, and Bulgarian efforts to make it exclusively "Bulgarian" on the other, in reality it was both. Undoubtedly the goods, pots, or even burials that someone used cannot correlate exactly with the language they spoke. Given that much of Romania were enveloped by the Bulgarian Empire, it is not surprising that the Romanians took up aspects of Bulgarian culture. There was no longer a religious barrier between the Romanians and Slavs, and this accelerated the cultural mixing between the two groups.[Nandriș, 1946] The culture was not exclusively Bulgarian as it persisted in the Romanian lands even after the Bulgarian Empire lost control of the region,[Fiedler, 2008, p. 216] but the Bulgarian-inspired Dridu culture served as the bedrock on which Romanian medieval culture developed.

Thus, by the start of the tenth century, things were looking up for the Romanians. The Slavo-Bulgarian influences upon Romanian had finalized the process of

---

[†] Like all other cultures with names that seem impossible to pronounce, the Dridu culture was named after the settlement in which it was first discovered by archaeologists.

ethnogenesis. We can finally do away with weird hyphenated names and "proto" prefixes and finally call the inhabitants of this region "Romanians." The autonomous nature of "Bulgaria beyond the Danube" allowed for the formation of small Slavo-Romanian states around the salt trade routes, with capital strongholds that acted as centers of power in Transylvania.[Madgearu, 2004] The Romanians (along with their Slavic cohabitants), if left alone, were well on their way towards entering the Middle Ages.

Being left alone is too much to ask for in Eastern Europe. The invasion of the Hungarians in the late ninth century, followed by those of the Pechenegs, Cumans, and Mongols in the following centuries, effectively delayed the entry of the Romanians on the world stage for another three centuries. Nevertheless, these new groups could no longer play a fundamental role in the formation of the Romanian people.

Works Cited

Ambrose. Expositio evangelii secundum Lucam.

Băcueţ-Crişan, D. (2005). Depresiunea Silvaniei în secolele VII-XI. *Bibliotheca Septemcastrensis, XII.*

Brezeanu, S. (2003). The Lower Danube Frontier during the 4th-7th Centuries. An ambiguous Notion. *Annuario, Instituto Romeno di cultura e ricerca umanistica, 5.*

Burns, T. S. (1991). *A History of the Ostrogoths.* Bloomington, IN: Indiana University Press.

Curta, F. (2001a). *The Making of the Slavs.* New York, NY: Cambridge University Press.

Curta, F. (2001b). Pots, Slavs, and Imagined Communities. *European Journal of Archaeology, 4*(3), 367-384.

Curta, F. (2004). The Slavic Lingua Franca: (linguistic notes of an archaeologist turned historian). *East Centra Eurpe, 31*(1), 125-148.

Curta, F. (2005a). Before Cyril and Methodius: Christianity and the Seventh-Century Danube Frontier. In F. Curta (Ed.), *East Central & Eastern Europe in the Early Middle Ages.* Ann Arbor, MI: University of Michigan Press.

Curta, F. (2005b). Frontier Ethnogenesis in Late Antiquity: The Danube, the Tervingi, and the Slavs. In F. Curta (Ed.), *Borders, barriers, and ethnogenesis: frontiers in late Antiquity and the Middle Ages* (pp. 449-471). Turnhout: Brepols.

Curta, F. (2006). *Southeastern Europe in the Middle Ages: 500-1250.* Cambridge, UK: Cambridge University Press.

Cusack, C. M. (1998). *Conversion among the Germanic Peoples.* London, UK: Cassell.

Dumitraşcu, S., & Sfrengeu, F. (2006). Relaţiile interetnice în Dacia Occidentală in secolele IV-VI. In I. M. Ţiplic (Ed.), *Bibliotheca Septamcastrensis: Relaţii interetnice în Spatiul Românesc (secolele VI-XIII)* (Vol. XXI). Bucharest: Departamentul pentru Relaţii Interetnice; Altip.

Ellis, L. (1998). Dacia Terra Deserta: Populations, Politics, and the [de]colonization of Dacia. *World Archaeology, 30*(2).

Eutropius. *Breviary.*

Fiedler, U. (2008). Bulgars in the Lower Danube Region: a survey of the archaeological evidence and of the state of current research. In F. Curta & R. Kovalev (Eds.), *The Other Europe in the Middle Ages: Avars, Bulgars, Khazars, and Cumans.* Leiden, Netherlands; Boston, MA: Brill.

Firică, C. (2008). Slav influence upon the Romanian language - direct references to Croatian. *Rustvena Istrazivanja, 19*(3), 511-523.

Gândilă, A. (2009). Face value or Bullion value? Early Byzantine coins beyond the lower Danube border. In M. Woloszyn (Ed.), *Polish Academy of Arts and Sciences* (Vol. III). Krakow, Poland.

Găzdac, C. (1998). Coins and the abandonment of Dacia. *Acta Musei Napocensis, 35*(I).

Georgescu, V. (1991). *The Romanians: a history* (A. Bley-Vroman, Trans.). Columbus, OH: Ohio State University Press.

Goldsworthy, A. (2009). *How Rome Fell: Death of a Superpower.* New Haven, CT: Yale University Press.

Green, D. H. (2000). *Language and History in the Early Germanic World*. Cambridge, UK: Cambridge University Press.

Halsall, G. (2007). *Barbarian Migrations and the Roman West, 376-568*. Cambridge, UK: Cambridge University Press.

Heather, P. (1996). *The Goths*. Cambridge, MA: Blackwell.

Kazar, L., & Makai, J. (2001). *Transylvania, in search of facts*. Linfield, Australia: Trianon Forum.

Kulikowski, M. (2007). *Rome's Gothic Wars*. Cambridge, UK: Cambridge University Press.

MacKendrick, P. (1975). *The Dacian Stones Speak*. Chapel Hill, NC: University of North Carolina Press.

MacKenzie, A. (1986). *Archaeology in Romania: the mystery of the Roman occupation*. London, UK: Hale.

Madgearu, A. (1997). *Continuitate si discontinuitate la Dunarea de Jos in secolele VII-VIII*. Bucharest, Romania: University of Bucharest.

Madgearu, A. (2001). *Rolul Crestinismului in Formarea Poporului român*. Bucharest, Romania: BIC ALL.

Madgearu, A. (2004). Voievodatul lui Menumorout în lumina cercetărilor recente" (The Duchy of Menumorout in the light of the recent researches). *Analele Universităţii din Oradea. Istorie-arheologie, 11*.

Madgearu, A. (2005). Salt Trade and Warfare: the rise of the Romanian-Slavic military organization in Early Medieval Transylvania. In F. Curta (Ed.), *East Central & Eastern Europe in the Early Middle Ages*. Ann Arbor, MI: University of Michigan Press.

Madgearu, A. (2010). *Istoria Militară a Daciei Post-Romane*. Târgoviste, Romania: Cetatea de Scaun.

Maurice. *Strategicon*.

Miracles of Saint Demetrius.

Murgescu, B. (2001). *Istoria României în Texte*. Bucharest, Romania: Corint.

Nandriş, G. (1939). The Earliest Contacts between Slavs and Roumanians. *The Slavonic and East European Review, 18*(52), 142-154.

Nandriş, G. (1946). The Beginnings of Slavonic Culture in the Roumanian Countries. *The Slavonic and East European Review, 24*(63), 160-171.

Pacurariu, M. (2007). Romanian Christianity. In K. Parry (Ed.), *The Blackwell Companion to Eastern Christianity*. Maiden, MA: Blackwell.

Pinter, Z. K., & Tiplic, I. M. (2006). Scurta istorie a Transilvaniei - perspective arheologice. In A. Dragota & I. M. Tiplic (Eds.), *Piese de Podoaba si Vestimentatie la Grupurile Ethnice din Transilvania (sec. 7-12)*. Alba Iulia: Departamentul pentru Relatii Interetnice.

Pop, I.-A. (1997). *Istoria Transilvaniei medievale: De la etnogeneza românilor pînă la Mihai Viteazul [The History of Medieval Transylvania: from the ethnogenesis of the Romanians to Michael the Brave]*. Cluj-Napoca, Romania: Cluj University Press.

Procopius. Buildings.

Procopius. History of Wars.

Simocatta, T. History.

Spinei, V. (2009). *The Romanians and the Turkic Nomads North of teh Danube Delta from the Tenth to the Mid-Thirteenth Century*. Leiden, Netherlands: Brill.

Stefanescu-Draganesti, V. (1986). *Romanian Continuity in Roman Dacia: linguistic evidence*. Miami Beach, FL: Romanian History Studies.

Thompson, E. A. (1982). Zosimus 6. 10. 2 and the Letters of Honorius. *The Classical Quarterly, 32*, 445-462.

Varga, R. (2008). The Peregrine Names from Dacia. *Acta Musei Napocensis, 43-44*(I), 244-245.

Vasiliev, A. (1958). *History of the Byzantine Empire, 324-1453* (Vol. 2). Wisconsin: University of Wisconsin Press.

Vekony, G. (2000). *Dacians, Romans, Romanians*. Budapest, Hungary: Corvinus Library.

Victor, A. *De Caesaribus*.

Vida, T. (2008). Conflict and Coexistence: the local population of the Carpathian Basin under Avar rule (sixth to seventh century). In F. Curta & R. Kovalev (Eds.), *The Other Europe in the Middle Ages: Avars, Bulgars, Khazars, and Cumans*. Leiden, Netherlands; Boston, MA: Brill.

Wanner, R. (2010). *Forts, fields, and towns: communities in Northwest Transylvania from the first century BC to the fifth century AD*. Leicaster, UK: University of Leicaster.

Williams, S. (1999). *Rome that did not Fall: the Survival of the East in the Fifth Century*. Florence, KY: Routledge.

Wolfram, H., & Dunlap, T. J. (1988). *History of the Goths*. Berkeley, CA: University of California Press.

Wollman, A. (1993). Early Latin loan-words in Old English. In M. Lapidge (Ed.), *Anglo-Saxon England*. Cambridge, UK: Cambridge University Press.

Zosimus. *New History*.

6. LIGHT AT THE END OF THE DARK AGE TUNNEL

By the ninth century the Romanians had gained a distinct identity but still lacked a country of their own. Emerging from the Dark Ages was, for many people in Europe, the result of creating a state. One could hardly imagine the English in the Middle Ages without England nor its (contested) founder William the ~~Bastard~~ Conqueror, nor can one imagine the French without Clovis setting the foundations of the Frankish kingdom. The creation of a state in essence meant entering the Middle Ages as it represented a return of proper administration, law, and literature in the form of court and religious records. Romania, unfortunately, was sorely deficient in all three aspects in the ninth century.

In one part of Romania, the Basarabi-Murfatlar cave churches, the beginning of medieval life is literally written in stone. The ancient graffiti on the churches' walls – written in three alphabets – indicates the rising literacy in the region. Many of the "artists" gave themselves ruling titles that indicate some political organization as well. However, this center was undoubtedly dependent on Bulgarian patronage. Without a proper state present in Romania, literacy and order could deteriorate as soon as the old power left the region. Indeed, that seems to have been the case: the Cyrillic alphabet used Romania in the Middle Ages has a strong similarity to thirteenth and fourteenth century Bulgarian rather than to that of the ninth century. Literacy must have ceased of the Danube in the ninth century and been reintroduced later.(Deletant, 1980)

The Bulgarians abandoned their outposts north of the Danube in the late ninth century due to the arrival of a new invader: the Magyars, known today as the Hungarians. Like almost everything else in Romania's post-Roman period, the Magyars came from the East. Linguistically different from anyone else in the region, they formed part of the Finno-Ugric family of languages, with the Finns as their closest European relatives. Unlike the Finns however, the Magyars spent their early history surrounded by the nomadic Turkic tribes of the Caucasus and adopted nomadism as a result. Even the name "Hungarian" derives from the Turkic word "Onogour."(Engel, 2001, p. 9) By the time the Magyars became known to Arab and European authors in the ninth century, they were practically indistinguishable from their neighbours: many referred to them as "Turks" and their lands as "Turkey."(Porphyrgenitus, 1967, pp. 168-169; Róna-Tas, 1999, p. 277)

The Magyars took control of the Steppe lands north of the Black Sea. The first we hear of them in Europe is in 837, when a revolt by Roman prisoners broke out north of the Danube. The rebels were largely unopposed as the Bulgarian army was stationed south of the Danube, causing the Bulgars to request help from the Magyars. Thankfully, the Byzantine fleet on the Danube was able to evacuate the prisoners before they could become Magyar target practice.(Curta, 2006b, p. 166) For the Magyars' first mention, it was a bit of a non-event. They are next encountered by the Cyril and Methodius, famous missionaries noted for their role in converting the Slavs to Christianity, on their way to the Khazar Khaganate in 860. Their mission's intent was to make the Khazars "cast off heathen abominations and lawless marriages";(Life of Constantine, 1983-10) hardly a diplomatic description of Judaism. On this trip, Cyril encountered the Magyars in the Crimean Peninsula, where they came "howling like wolves" and wishing to kill him, but managed to leave peacefully. Whatever one could say of Magyar hospitality, the account indicates that these nomadic warriors had gained possession of the Black Sea steppe. Methodius encountered the Magyars again in 880, when he met with their king near the Danube, showing that the Magyars were already drifting further and further west.

The Hungarian homeland at the time was called Etelkuzu, but its exact location is a matter of dispute. Some specialists believe the name comes from a Hungarian expression for "between rivers" – a nomadic Mesopotamia, sans ziggurats – while others believe it simply means "the Don [River] Country." Indeed, the Magyar word for the Don was *Etul*. Some argue that their lands stretched from the Romanian Danube to the Don, excluding Transylvania.(Engel, 2001, p. 10) Unfortunately, there is that no archaeological evidence for this claim. No Magyar grave in Moldova or Wallachia is dated from this time.(Curta, 2006b, p. 124) Local settlements also show no sign of suffering from nomadic raids or Magyar rule.(Spinei, 2009, pp. 67-69) Whether this is caused by the Magyars' nomadism (permanent remains are hard to come by for a people whose way of life had little permanence at all) or by their absence from the region remains an open question.

The Magyars did not stay in their homeland (wherever it was) for long. Their westward migration was forced by the invading Turkic Pechenegs to their east, who were themselves pushed west by another Turkic tribe, the Uzes. Their movement into the region signalled the end of *Pax Khazarica* and the collapse of the Khazar empire. Chaos ensued shortly after: devastating Magyar raids are recorded in Frankish holdings and in Moravia (Czech Republic) in 862, 881, 892, and 894. One Frankish monk recounted how the Magyars "carried off the young women alone with them like cattle to satisfy their lusts, and reduced the whole of Pannonia to a desert."(The Annals of Fulda, p. 129) The Magyars were, however, not the remorseless demons they were made them out to be. Their raids were a result of their need to attract allies, which in steppe diplomacy could only be achieved by flexing one's muscle and accumulating wealth.(Todorov, 2010) This was little consolation to the farming settlements affected by this nomadic popularity contest.

The Byzantines, who were in a Bulgarian-caused world of hurt, were more than happy for the Magyars' arrival. The Magyars were on sour terms with the Bulgarians since 892, and Emperor Leo VI jumped at the opportunity to gain an ally conveniently placed behind enemy lines. At the behest of the emperor, the Magyars inflicted a devastating attack on Bulgaria in 894, forcing the Bulgarian tsar Symeon to sue for peace with the Byzantines. Leo, forgetful that he had just forced a Magyar-Bulgarian war, quickly accepted Symeon's offer. The Magyars were left practically surrounded by enemies as a result. Deciding to give the Magyars a taste of their own medicine, Symeon convinced the eastward Pechenegs to attack the Magyars from the east while Symeon pressed from the south.(Spinei, 2009, p. 66) The devastation inflicted upon the Magyars in 895 was so great that it reverberated in Hungarian folklore.(Engel, 2001, p. 12) The results however, are not entirely due to Symeon's strategic brilliance, as the Pechenegs were already being prodded into Magyar territory by the aggressive Uzes and Khazars in the east. The invasion was largely inevitable; its satisfaction of Bulgarian strategic aims was mere coincidence.(Porphyrgenitus, 1967, pp. 166-167)

The bonus of being nomadic is that one can move when the going gets tough, and the Magyars started moving as fast as they could. Under a new chief named Árpád, they opted to flee to the Pannonian plains, distancing themselves from Pechenegs as possible. Where they settled and what path they took is controversial. Hungarian historians claim that the Magyars occupied both the Danube Plain and Transylvania simultaneously, some claiming even that this occurred even before they were forced to leave Etelkuzu.[Engel, 2001, p. 11] Romanian historians, on the other hand, claim that the Magyars did not enter Transylvania until much later. The oldest preserved Hungarian account of the event, the *Gesta Hungarorum*, claims the Magyars travelled through Galicia (Halych, Ukraine; not the Spanish Galicia) and entered the Pannonian plain through the Verecke Pass in Ukraine.[Anonymous, 2008, XII] On the other hand, later Hungarian chronicles like the *Chronicon Pictum* ("Illuminated Chronicle", since "Picture Book" is too dismissive) claim that the Hungarians travelled to Pannonia through a region called *Erdelw*, which Hungarian historians identified with Transylvania (called *Erdely* in Hungarian). For now, the evidence points to a migration through the Verecke Pass into Pannonia and side-stepping Transylvania: all the Magyar graves belonging to people born outside of Pannonia are only found around this pass; all other graves date from the tenth century or later.[Madgearu, 2005b, p. 91]

While the *Chronicon Pictum* hints that *Erdelw* is Transylvania, this seems to be a mistake made by later copyists of the text. Up until the invention of the printing press, the only way to preserve texts was to copy them by hand. As one can imagine, a mix of poor lighting, bad eyesight, and somewhat illegible handwriting (including frequent use of shorthand) made this an error-prone operation. *Erdelw* might originally have been "forest" (*erdö*), meaning the Ung Forest near Verecke, and it was likely distorted by later copyists into Transylvania. This interpretation would make the *Chronicon Pictum* consistent with the older *Gesta Hungarorum* and other chronicles that retell the Hungarians migration through the Ung forest near the Verecke Pass.[Spinei, 2009, p. 72] Transylvania, buttressed by the Carpathian Mountains, was side-stepped completely.

A deciding factor in how and from where the Magyars entered Transylvania comes from the way the Magyars marked the boundaries of their realm: the *indagines*. Strips of deserted land, more than just a nomadic version of a white picket fence, they were a powerful defensive measure that acted as an early-warning system for invasions. When we consider the *indagines* in Transylvania, there is a clear west-to-east expansion of these lines from the Someş river in *c.* 900 all the way to 1200 when they finally reach the eastern Carpathians.[Pop et al., 2005, p. 211] These convenient lines of demarcation indicate that the Magyars advanced into Transylvania from the west, where they encountered the Romanians.

Romanian nationalism considered the arrival of the Magyars and the conquest of Transylvania to have been a disaster for the Romanians: the Romanian states were erased before they could fully develop, and the Romanians became the servant-slaves of these barbarian overlords. This is however, not how it happened at all. The *Gesta Hungarorum* describes the events as a conquest, but one solidified only by the locals choosing Magyar chiefs as rulers.(Anonymous, 2008, XXVII) Events likely did not happen exactly as specified in the *Gesta* which, it must be admitted, was written two centuries after the fact. One reason to doubt a literal interpretation is that the *Gesta*, by its very nature, is propaganda designed to attribute everything important in the foundation of the kingdom to Árpád, the founder of the first Magyar dynasty, including the conquest of Transylvania.(Madgearu, 2005b, p. 26) But this author also places the defeat of the Magyars at Lechfeld, having taken place in 955, in "the fifth year of King Conrad [915]" just after Árpád died.(Anonymous, 2008LV) The author of the *Gesta* had a tendency of pushing events slightly back in time. As such, the conquest of Transylvania did not happen, as the author claims, during Árpád's reign, but likely later.

The *Gesta* however, had to be consistent with contemporary political realities: its author needed to historically justify the special, autonomous rights the Romanians possessed, and needed to justify Hungarian sovereignty over Transylvania.(Madgearu, 2005b, p. 92) Portraying the Romanians as willingly submitting to the new Hungarian rulers thus solved both issues. An agreement between the Romanian locals and the Magyars was not without precedent. A similar "agreement" had occurred between the Croatians and Hungarians in 1102 (the *Pacta Conventa*), whereby the Croatians retained an autonomous status within the kingdom. In all likelihood it is more than coincidence that both Croatia and Transylvania were the only autonomous regions in the Hungarian Kingdom.

Archaeologically, different parts of Transylvania seem to have entered the Hungarian dominion in different ways. Western sections of the region resemble a typical conquest; Magyar settlements saturated the landscape and displaced whatever natives happened to be there. Still, other areas had only a minority of Hungarian settlements.(Sălăgean, 2005) The persistence of the title of *voievod* (*vajda* in Hungarian), the same title as the rulers of the two future Romanian states of Moldova and Wallachia, indicates that some of the old Romanian-Slavic political system was kept in place. Furthermore, noble families from the Romanian regions described in the *Gesta* also bore such a title as a personal name.(Sălăgean, 2005) The Romanians were not under ruthless subjugation during the early days of Magyar rule in Transylvania. Only later, with the "Westernization" of the Hungarian kingdom, would the Romanians face a significant loss of rights.

East of the Carpathians the Pechenegs helped themselves to the former lands of the Magyars. As nomads that scared even other nomads, one might expect a level of brutality from the Pechenegs, but once again the facts on the ground contradict our expectations. It is true that the Pechenegs were troublesome in Ukraine, where most sedentary sites were abandoned in the early 900's as a result of Pecheneg attacks, but in Romania settlements continued with little change.(Curta, 2006b, p. 185) The Romanians were of course not entirely spared. The *Gesta Hungarorum* attests that the Romanians in Transylvania could not resist the Magyar invaders from the west as they were already significantly weakened by Pecheneg raids from the east,(Anonymous, 2008XXV) raids that must have occurred in the early tenth century.

Though the Pechenegs may have weakened the Romanian states in Transylvania, they might also have been responsible for keeping Transylvania out of Magyar control for some time. Abu Ubayd al-Bakri, an eleventh-century Arab geographer using sources that dated from the mid-tenth century, mentioned that the Magyars and the Pechenegs kept a "deserted land", a Medieval version of a demilitarized zone, between themselves.(el-Maqdisî, 1907; Madgearu, 2005a) As for where this region was situated: some Hungarian authors have tried to place it in Moldova,(Kristó, 2003, p. 59) conveniently insinuating that the Magyars controlled Transylvania. Written sources never mention the area exactly, but the Byzantine *De Administrando Impero* ("On the Governance of the Empire") offers some hints. Its claim that the Pechenegs were separated from the Magyars by four days of travel(Porphyrgenitus, 1967, pp. 34-49) rules Moldova out of the question (barring some very slow horses). The time however, is much more reasonable for crossing the rugged mountain passes of Transylvania. Eastern Transylvania must have formed the buffer region between the two tribes.

Even though the Pechenegs did not control Transylvania, some of them did settle there. In general, the Pechenegs of Transylvania are remembered by two types of place names: those derived from "Pecheneg" (obviously) and those derived from "besenyö," the Hungarian word for Pecheneg. The latter term was only introduced when the Hungarians used the Pechenegs as border guards, as these border guards came to be known by the word *bisseni* in medieval documents. (Anonymous, 2008, XXV; LVII; Madgearu, 2005a)

The use of the *bisseni* border guards by the Hungarians was delayed for some time in Transylvania, and for good reason: their main adversaries on the other side of the Carpathians were still the Pechenegs. Needless to say, the Hungarian kings grasped the illogical nature of inviting the Pechenegs into the kingdom in order to keep the Pechenegs out. Any terms in Transylvania relating to *bisseni* must date from the early twelfth century onward, when Pecheneg power in Wallachia and Moldova collapsed.(Madgearu, 2005b, pp. 116-117)

Thus, the two forms of the place names (those derived from *Pecheneg* and those derived from *Bisseni*) relate to two different periods of Pecheneg settlements: one where the Pechenegs moved in out of their own interest and the other where they were settled by the Hungarian kings. In Wallachia and Moldova, most of the place names remembering the Pechenegs are of the form *Pecheneg* (*Pecineaga*, *Peceneagul* etc.), while in Transylvania and Banat the majority are of the form *Bisseni* (e.g. *Beşeneu*, *Beşinou* etc.). However, there are still a few names in Transylvania that carry the form *Pecheneg*, such as the mountain *Peceneaga* (in southern Transylvania). These names could only have been preserved if the Romanians lived among the Pechenegs in Transylvania before the settlement of the *Bisseni* in this region, and therefore before the arrival of Hungarian rule.(Madgearu, 2005b) The Romanians must have taken this name at a time before the collapse of Pecheneg power in Wallachia and before the Hungarian takeover of Transylvania.

The Romanians finally appear in the torrents of history in the tenth century, when they are mentioned explicitly by their ethnic name in written sources. Ironically, the first people to write of the Romanians were not any people near them, but a distant Arab author: Mutahhar al-Maqdisi. His account briefly lists off the neighbors of the Pechenegs as "Khazars, Russians, Slavs, *Waladj*, Alans, Greeks and many other peoples..." While some have tried – largely without any logical basis – to argue that the Waladj are some mystery people from the Caucasus, the similarity between *Waladj* and *Wallach* (Romanians) cannot be overlooked: the author could only have been referring to the Romanians.(Spinei, 2009, p. 82)

Incidentally, the tenth century is also the time of the first mention of the Balkan Vlachs in chronicles. John Skylitzes, a Byzantine chronicler from the eleventh century, recounted how David, the brother of the future Bulgarian tsar Samuel, was "killed between Kastoria and Prespa [modern Macedonia] by some vagabond Vlachs."(Skylitzes, 2010XVI) Arguably, not the most flattering portrayal of the Vlachs, but sometimes you take what you can get. From this moment on, the Balkan Vlachs would be progressively mentioned more frequently in the coming centuries.

The near-simultaneous mention of the *Wallachs* and the *Vlachs* brings up a critical question: could the Byzantine author and the Arab author have been referring to the same Vlachs south of the Danube and therefore not to the Romanians? Though some Hungarian historians trying to erase the Romanians from north of the Danube before the thirteenth century desire such a conclusion, it can be shown that the two authors are referred to different people. The Arab historian would hardly have chosen a small population within of the Byzantine Empire as neighbors of the Pechenegs, never mind that the Pechenegs were separated from Macedonia by several hundred kilometers. When al-Maqdisi was referring to neighbors, he could only have been referring to politically independent people, and therefore his *Wallachs* must have been living outside of Bulgaria, the Byzantine Empire, and Russia. This leaves only Romania as their geographical location. He may even have been referring to the same Transylvanian Romanians mentioned in the *Gesta Hungarorum*, something that would be more than coincidence. Whatever the exact location, it is clear that the tenth century written sources confirmed the presence of both Romanians north of the Danube and Vlachs in the southern Balkans.

A second Arab writer from the tenth century, Ibn al-Nadim, similarly listed off the people of Eastern Europe, and again mentioned a people known as the *Blaghā*, which may be yet another reference to the Romanians.(Al-Nadim, 1970, pp. 36-37) The similarity to the word "Vlachs" is easy to see when we realize that the letters B and V were often interchanged in Medieval documents on Southeastern Europe due to Greek authors often acting as intermediaries on the region for other sources. The Greek word for Vlach was βλαχοι and even Bulgaria was sometimes referred to by the less-flattering name of "Vulgaria." When later crusader chronicles mentioned the Vlachs, they often called them *blaci* or *blachi*,(R. L. Wolff, 1949) again due to the Greek influence. *Blaghā* thus could very easily be a distortion of *Vlach*, given that the author was playing 'telephone' with his Greek sources on another continent.(Spinei, 2009, p. 83) The *Blaghā* were politically independent and must have been situated north of the Danube in Romania and probably in Transylvania, the last place in the region that remained a political no man's land.

The Arabs are however, not the only unusual source we have for news on the Romanians: we also find them in several interesting Viking accounts. The Vikings of Eastern Europe, known as the Rus or Varangians, played a fundamental role in founding the first Russian states. While the inaccurate stereotype of Vikings as horn-helmed raiders might make one doubt the Vikings ever founded anything, these much-maligned people were actually among the more industrious state-makers in Europe. Normandy, England, Russia and Sicily all have the Vikings (be they Normans or Varangians) to thank them into the Early Middle Ages. According to the Russian "Chronicle of Bygone Times" (*Povest Vremennykh Let*), sometimes also called the Russian Primary Chronicle, written by a monk named Nestor in the early twelfth century, the Slavs supposedly invited the Vikings into Russia, saying "our land is great and rich, but there is no order in it. Come to rule and reign over us."(Nestor, 1953, p. 7) Whether things really played out as such or if Nestor was just trying to cover the embarrassment of being conquered is anyone's guess, as even more modern Russian historians found the idea of a foreign foundation as "dishonourable."(Honig, 2001, p. 5) What is clear is that by the late ninth century the Varangians had established several states within Russia, stretching from the Baltic to the Black Sea.

Many Vikings however, did not stop in Russia but rather continued further south, where they found lucrative trade with Byzantium and even more distant Arab lands, and stumbled upon the Romanians along the way. When the Vikings saw the wealth to be had in Constantinople – both through trade and through employment as mercenaries – they quickly spread the news back home and this resulted in one of the most active trade routes in all of Europe, known as the "Route of the Varangians to the Greeks." The exact path taken by the Viking traders is not entirely clear once it reaches the Black Sea. Most left by boat from the Crimean Peninsula and sailed to Constantinople. Some evidence suggests there were stopping points north of the Danube along the way. The discovery of Arab coins in southern Moldova and Wallachia, as well as the carvings of Viking longboats and heraldry at the Basarabi-Murfatlar church complex, indicates that Viking travellers frequented the Romanian lands as well.(Spinei, 2009, pp. 53-54)

The tales of one Viking merchant's encounter with the Romanians is recorded on a rune stones at the Sjonhem cemetery, on the isle of Gotland in Sweden, dated to the early eleventh century. The rune stone speaks of a man called Rodfos, stating "Rodvisl and Rodälv had these stones erected in memory of their three sons. This stone in memory of Rodfos. He was betrayed by *Blakumen* ["Vlach men"/Wallachians(Jesch, 2001, p. 257)] on an expedition abroad. God help Rodfos' soul. God betray those who betrayed him."(Jansson & Foote, 1987, p. 63) Arguably not the most flattering publicity the Romanians received, but a valuable source nonetheless. As the Vlachs betrayed Rodfos, we can conclude Rodfos must have been a Norse merchant who had entered into some agreement with the Romanians before being done in. Rodfos must have encountered the Romanian Vlachs somewhere around the Varangian path, possibly on the Dniester if not further east.(Curta, 2006b, p. 303)

There are however, some who believe that *Blakumen* were not Vlachs (*Blaku-Men*) but rather "Black Cumans" (*Bla-Kumen*). Thankfully, there are two other Norse sources that also mention *Blakumen* which we can use to clarify who these people were: they are the *Eymund Saga* and the *Ring of the World*. The *Eymund Saga* records the dynastic disputes between Yaroslav the Wise and Sviatopolk over the throne of the Kievan Rus. In it, Sviatopolk is mentioned as hiring "Turks" and Wallachians (*Tyrkir ok Blokumenn*) as mercenaries from the land of the Turks (*Tyrkland*) in 1019. This passage is more than a little problematic for those arguing that the *Blokumenn* are Cumans. Firstly, the Cumans would not arrive in the region until several decades. Secondly, "Turks" acted as a generic term for the variety of nomadic horsemen north of the Danube. A statement like "Turks and Cumans" is therefore redundant. Thirdly, the substitution of *o* for *a* in the world *Blokumenn* is reminiscent of the Russian word for "Vlach" (*Volohi*), a language that undoubtedly influenced the Varangian writers. Lastly, and possibly most importantly, the Germanic word for "Cuman" was not *Kumen* but rather *Valwen*! As such, *Blokumenn* – a word that would be a strange mix of German and Latin – makes no sense at all; it would have to be *Blavalwen* if it were written in Norse. All of this leaves no doubt that the *Blakumen*/*Blokumenn* were Romanians.[Hazzard-Cross, 1929; Spinei, 2009] Sviatopolk was able to recruit these mercenaries together, we can only conclude that the Wallachians in question came from Moldova or Wallachia

The third Norse source that mentions Romanians is the *Ring of the World*, written by Snorri Sturluson in the early thirteenth century. The text recounts how the emperor Alexios I Komnenos (*Kirjalax*) of Byzantium waged a war in the land of the Vlachs (*Blokumannaland*[u]), reaching the "Pecheneg (*Pezina*) Plains."[Sturluson, 1964, XXI] It is interesting that the author uses the term *Blokumannaland* a century before Wallachia's foundation as a country, thereby signifying the importance or preponderance of the Vlachs in the region. The three Norse sources mentioned thus provide compelling evidence that the Romanians north of the Danube were becoming increasingly important in trade, warfare, and politics.

The Pechenegs were pushed out of the region by the arrival of the Uzes, a Turkic people, in the mid-eleventh century.[Psellus, VII, 67] Many Pechenegs thus moved into northern Bulgaria, where they first were a headache for the Byzantines, but later became a buffer against other potentially troublesome nomads. The Uzes thus achieved domination of the plains north of the Danube. As for the sedentary Romanians: living under one nomadic overlord or another did not matter much. There is evidence for the continuation of settlements in the region, and an account of the Uzes using wooden boats (undoubtedly "borrowed" from the locals) hints to the survival of the Slavic and Romanian people.[Spinei, 2009, pp. 115-116] In any case, the relationship between the Uzes and the Romanians was short-lived, as in little more than a decade they were pushed out by the invading Cumans.

---

[u] Some have interpreted "Blakumen" as "Black Men" and thus moved the event recounted to Ethiopia. This interpretation however, is morphologically not sound and geographically out of the question given that Emperor Alexios never set foot in Africa.

The Cumans came crashing into the Danube area in around the 1060's and 1070's, bowling over the Uzes, Romanians and anyone else in the region. By their own account preserved in the eleventh century *Oghuz-name* chronicle the Cumans defeated a variety of people in the area, including the Vlachs (*Ulâq*).[Curta, 2006b, p. 306] These were undoubtedly the same Romanians that had allied with the Pechenegs in their raids on the Rus lands a few decades earlier. Though the account is told in a mythical style, its events nevertheless line up with archaeological evidence: many settlements on the plains north of the Danube either disappeared or moved further north into densely forested areas,[Curta, 2006b, p. 307] a phenomenon that continued into the 1100's.[Curta, 2006b, p. 318] The Byzantines and Hungarians likewise had a fair share of Cuman-related headaches, as raids persisted in both realms throughout this time. The Cumans were keen on establishing their territory, and the lands south and east of the Carpathians came to be known as *Cumania* until the mid-fourteenth century.

The unrest along the Danube frontier caused the Balkan Vlachs to play an increasingly important role in the Byzantine Empire, usually to its detriment. Known largely as a resilient people inhabiting the mountains – the Slavs had helped themselves to the fertile valleys – the Vlachs were a relatively autonomous people of the empire, enjoying tax privileges while being entrusted to defend the Balkan mountain passes.[Tanaşoca, 2001] Known for their transhumance pastoralism,[v] they proved difficult to rule. In 1066 they took part in a serious revolt alongside the Bulgarians and Greeks against harsh taxation. The Vlachs were led by the provincial governor Niculitsa – a strongman with a private army at his disposal – who opposed the revolt but later found himself as both hostage and leader of the rebels;[Fine, 2000, p. 216] a difficult situation to explain to the emperor. Similar events unfolded along the Danube delta in 1078. A local governor was appointed to the region in hopes of preventing rebellion, but the governor – likely a Vlach[Angold, 1997, p. 121] – became one of the rebellion's leaders. The Vlachs increasingly resented the empire. During a Cuman invasion in 1091, the Vlach sentries guarding the mountain passes willingly acted as guides to the nomadic invaders.[Komnena, II] Some Vlachs however remained loyal to the emperor: a Vlach nobleman warned the emperor of Cuman invasion in 1091 and in 1164 some Vlach trackers had captured a pretender to the Byzantine throne on the border of Galicia,[Choniates, 1984, V, 368] undoubtedly in northern Moldova.[Curta, 2006b, p. 316]

Vlach-Byzantine relations continued to deteriorate in the next century. When the Jewish traveller Benjamin of Tudela passed through the Balkans in the mid-eleventh century, he wrote of the Vlachs living in Macedonia as being fond of descending from the mountains and raiding the hapless Greeks in the plains. He described them as impossible to rule, and even claimed they were not Christians[w]! Benjamin curiously argued that the Vlachs and Jews were brothers because "whenever they meet an

---

[v] Transhumance pastoralism implies a seasonal movement of herders with their herds, while still maintaining a permanent settlement to which they return to in the off-season. In this sense the Vlachs were not really "nomadic."

[w] The allegation might have been made because a "proper Christian" within the empire had to be loyal to the emperor, which the Vlachs were not.

Israelite, they rob, but never kill him, as they do the Greeks."(Tudela, 1888, p. 72) When it came to the treatment the Jews received in Europe, the bar obviously was not set high.

All of these events foreshadowed a massive Vlach-Bulgarian rebellion in 1185 that permanently changed the Balkan political landscape. It was the most important event of twelfth-century Balkan history, and the Vlachs took center stage. Bulgaria had been destroyed in 1018 by Emperor Basil II, who gained the title "the Bulgar-slayer" for quite obvious reasons. His actions put an end to the three hundred year-old Bulgarian threat and re-established Byzantine authority on the Danube. The revolt of 1185 however, would result in the permanent loss of the area for Byzantium.

According to Nicetas Choniates, a Byzantine historian contemporary to the events, the revolt was started in the Haemus [Balkan] Mountains by the Vlachs who were dissatisfied that their taxes had gone to fund the lavish wedding of the emperor's daughter.(Choniates, 1984, pp. 203-204) Their leaders were two brothers, Peter and Asen, also Vlachs. The uprising took the Byzantines by surprise,(Spinei, 2009, p. 138) which is in itself surprising given the warning signs mounting throughout the past century. According to Choniates, the two brothers built a church and brought into it "demon-possessed" people "with crossed and bloodshot eyes" who proclaimed that God had "consented to their freedom."(Choniates, 1984, p. 205) Thus roused, the Vlachs began their attacks... and were completely routed by the emperor's forces. The two brothers fled across the Danube, from where they returned with Cuman assistance, and ultimately succeeded in their revolt and founded the Second Bulgarian Empire. Vlachs from north of the Danube also likely participated in the revolt, as they did in 1198 when they crossed the Danube with the Cumans to assist the incipient Bulgarian state.(Choniates, 1984, p. 74)

The Vlach-Bulgarian rebellion essentially recreated Bulgaria, a state that lasted until the Ottoman conquest in the fourteenth century and that was not revived until the nineteenth century. It is an extremely important event in Bulgarian history and unsurprisingly there have been controversies, namely as to who the Vlachs were. Romanian historians tend to believe the Vlachs were, obviously enough, Vlachs. Bulgarian historians have tried, on the other hand, to prove by a variety of means that the Vlachs were actually other Bulgarians.(Tanaşoca, 2001; R. L. Wolff, 1949) Similar to Russian insecurities about Varangian founders, Bulgarian historians likewise do not wish to believe they were ruled by a Vlach dynasty. Some believe (in all seriousness) that there was a conspiracy among Byzantine historians to avoid writing "Bulgarian", and therefore they used "Vlach" instead... even though "Byzantine writers use the word 'Bulgar' quite freely when they are talking about Bulgars, and use 'Vlach' only to refer to Vlachs."(R. L. Wolff, 1949)

Bulgarians often buttress their argument on a passage from the Byzantine historian Nicetas Choniates, who stated that "the barbarians who lived in the vicinity of Mount Haimos [the Balkan Mountains], [had] formerly been called Mysians and [are] now named Vlachs."(Choniates, 1984, p. 204) As Mysian was term often used for Bulgarian, they argue that the "Vlachs" were therefore Bulgarians. This explanation however, suffers from a major flaw: "Mysian" is not an ethnic term, and it does not mean

"Bulgarian." It is only a geographical term that means "inhabitants of Moesia", pointing to the name of the ancient Roman province. As Bulgaria roughly overlapped with Moesia, it is not surprising that the name was often used by the Byzantines when writing of the Bulgarians, but it was not exclusively used for Bulgarian. When the Pechenegs moved south of the Danube due to the attacking Uzes, they too gained the name "Mysians." Thus the fact that the Vlachs were "formerly called Mysians" does not have any relevance on their ethnicity: it just means that they lived in the lands of the former province.

The Vlachs in question must have been a separate ethnic group. Nicetas Choniates' account includes the story of a Greek priest captured by the rebels, in which the priest pleaded with Asen in the "language of the Vlachs."[(Choniates, 1984, p. 257)] Unless one was to believe that Bulgarian shepherds spoke their own secret language, one must conclude that they spoke in a Vlach dialect, likely Aromanian. Byzantine accounts are corroborated by crusader sources. The chronicler Ansbert, who passed through Bulgaria in 1189, also wrote of "the Vlach Kalopetrus and his brother Assanius."[(Ansbert, 2010, 33)] Geoffrey de Villehardouin 1204 further drives the point: "John [i.e. Kaloyan], who was King of Wallachia and Bulgaria. This John was a Wallachian."[(Villehardouin, 1908, p. 51)] Pope Innocent III addressed the successors of Kaloyan as "king of Bulgarians and Vlachs" and references Kaloyan's "Roman ancestry" and that his people "assert that they are descended of Roman blood."(Migne, 1862) Meanwhile, Kaloyan gave himself the title "emperor of all Bulgarians and Vlachs" and mentions the Roman ancestry of his people, something corroborated in a letter from the archbishop of Tarnovo. This proves both that the Vlachs were a real ethnicity and that they were aware of their distinct ancestry.[(Hurmuzaki, 1887, II; III; V; XXIII; ; Murgescu, 2001, p. 77)] No stretch of the imagination could justify Kaloyan claiming that he intended to give himself a title as ridiculous as "emperor of Bulgarians and Bulgarian shepherds." Clearly, the Second Bulgarian Tsardom was a multi-ethnic endeavor.

This should not be taken to the other extreme of distorting the event into a Romanian national awakening. The Vlachs were not Romanians, and the tsardom never extended into modern Romania, as some earlier Romanian historians argued.[(Tanaşoca, 2001)] The motive for the revolt was also economic in nature, not ethnic. Ideas about nationalism were not as important in the Middle Ages. Ultimately, creating a legitimate kingdom was seen as more important than to ensure that it remained Vlach in character. The rulers of the new kingdom thus drew on parallels between the new Bulgaria and the old one.[(Tanaşoca, 2001)] Kaloyan himself claimed he was a descendant of the old Bulgarian emperors, which remains an unproven fantasy but one that doubtlessly helped him solidify his rule. That is why within a few decades the state became Bulgarian in nature. It does not prove however that the Vlachs were "stealth Bulgarians" all along, but rather that ethnicity was not important.[(Vásáry, 2005, p. 25)] Obviously, the Romanians basing their political history on a country that became Bulgarian would be impossible, and we must look to events more than a century later for the beginnings of Romanian statehood.

North of the Danube things were heating up. The Kingdom of Hungary reached the Carpathian frontier and contacts with the Romanians became increasingly noted and troublesome. Hungary was at the time attempting to prove itself to be a fine Western kingdom, and the best way to do this in the thirteenth century was with unbridled religious intolerance. King Andrew II had joined the Fifth Crusade in 1217, but his success (or lack thereof) in the Holy Land meant he had yet to prove himself. Thankfully by virtue of the Fourth Crusade in 1204 – in which Christian "holy warriors" sacked Constantinople and looted churches – Orthodox Christians were now on the menu, and Andrew II seized at the opportunity. Indeed, while the Muslims proved to be prohibitively far away, the Orthodox Romanians were conveniently nearby. Andrew could practically crusade from the comfort of his own kingdom; no perilous voyage, no hot weather, no problem. It was going to be a rough period for the Romanians.

Andrew's decision to do some religious landscaping in Transylvania was a change in the way Hungary handled its minorities. It was a far cry from the days of Saint Stephen, Hungary's first king, who stated that "a kingdom of one language and one custom is weak and fragile."[(N. Berend, 2006, p. 40)] Indeed, up until the thirteenth century Hungary was a remarkable example of ethnic and religious tolerance, allowing for Romanians to coexist in their own Orthodox *cneazates* and *voievodates*.[(Papacostea, 1993, pp. 70-71)] Now, with the aegis of the Roman Catholic Church, Hungary's new rulers made some changes to Saint Stephen's lesson: Catholic immigrants were welcome, but Orthodox people need not apply.

The wake of the Fourth Crusade soon reached the Romanian lands. In 1205 the Pope sent a letter to the Archepiscope of Calocea in Transylvania, wherein he mentions "the lands of the sons of cneaz Béla [possibly Bâlea]" (*Bele knese*) where there was an church that was under the jurisdiction of the Orthodox Church in Constantinople, and argued to rectify this "oversight."[(Migne, 1862, pp. 610-611)] As this church must have been Orthodox Christian in nature, and Béla's title of cneaz indicates that he was ethnically Romanian. Elsewhere, Hungarian nobles conquered the fortress of Mediaş in northwestern Transylvania with royal assistance, taking it "from the hands of the Vlach [Romanian] schismatics" sometime between 1204 and 1215.[(Papacostea, 1993, pp. 59-60)] Protests by the Romanians to the royal court, as was attempted in 1291, proved futile.[(Papacostea, 1993, p. 73)] The new spirit of the times was clearly evoked by King Béla IV in a letter sent to the Pope in 1234 where he declared he would "drive out the heretics… and false Christians from our land."[(Fejér, 1830, p. 118)]

Vlach lands were redistributed to new Catholic colonists from Western Europe. One document from 1223 mentions that Andrew II donated lands taken from the Vlachs (*exempta de Blaccis*) in southern Transylvania to the nearby Cistercian monastery of Cârţa, the donation taking place around 1206.[(Tuetsch & Fimhaber, 1857, pp. 28-30)] Along with knights and monks came Transylvania's German settlers: the Saxons. Hungarian kings granted these German settlers a wide array of privileges in order to attract them to develop the Transylvanian countryside. The Hungarian crown gave the Saxons free reign in former Romanian lands, as a document from 1222 entitled the Saxons to use the "forest of Vlach and Pechenegs" (*silvam Blacorum et Bissenorum*) in southern Transylvania.[(Spinei, 2008)] Their privileged status naturally cause a level of hubris and isolationism in the Saxons, and the discrimination the Romanians faced at their hands was far in excess of what they received from the Hungarians. In the Saxon city of Braşov (*Kronnstadt*) for instance, the Romanians were only permitted entry one day a year, a day that is today curiously considered a holiday.

Many Romanians fled across the Carpathians in response, but Andrew II was one step ahead of them. He invited the Teutonic Knights into his kingdom, expert crusaders from the Holy Land, where they gained much knowledge on religious tolerance and how to get rid of it. Their settlement in Burzenland (modern Ţara Bârsei) was designed to protect against the Cumans, but the almost stereotypically industrious Teutons chose to take the fight to the enemy instead, claiming to have successfully converted some of the Cumans. The conversions however, had less to do with the actions of the Knights as it did with those of the Mongols to the east.[Hurmuzaki, 1887, lxxxviii] In 1223 a Mongol raiding party inflicted a crushing defeat on the combined forces of the Rus states and the Cumans at the battle of Kalka River. Fearing an invasion, the Cumans figured they would fare better to gain Catholic Hungary as an ally. Andrew II could tell the Knights were getting too big for their boots, and expelled them in 1225. Zealous as Andrew II was, he knew that having harbouring an elite army loyal only to the Holy See was not particularly wise.

Further east, between the Olt and Siret rivers in Wallachia and southern Moldova, the Hungarians established the Bishopric of Cumania, hoping more Cumans would join the faith. It was not the first mission outside of the Carpathians, as earlier one had been sent to the lands of Severin (modern Oltenia), targeted at the "schismatics and heretics." While the Schismatics proved largely unreceptive, the Cuman diocese actually met with some success, once again mostly due to the Mongols. In 1227 the Mongols conquered the lands of the Kievan Rus and later that year the Cuman chief Bortz converted to Catholicism along with the rest of his followers, and were thus allowed to seek refuge in the kingdom. It was not the first politically-motivated conversion to Catholicism. Indeed, though in Rome it was believed that the Cumans would settle, make towns and villages, and become good (taxable) farmers, the Cumans had no intention of abandoning their nomadic ways,[Hurmuzaki, 1887, lxxxviii] nor even many of their pagan rituals! More Cumans converted in 1239, as the Mongols came practically within spitting distance of the Bishopric of Cumania. The Hungarian kings were keen to accept them, viewing such missionary activity as part of their efforts to expand outside of the Carpathians. Hungarian kings had already adopted the title of "King of Cumania" in anticipation, though it should be noted that Hungarian kings often exaggerated their own reach. When Béla IV listed his titles as "King of Hungary, Dalmatia, Croatia, Ramae, Serbia, Halych, Lodomeria, Bulgaria, and Cumania"[Spinei, 2008] only around half were true even by the most optimistic accounts.

For a place named the Bishopric of Cumania, there was a peculiar absence of Cumans within its domains. For the most part the priests presided over Romanians,[Curta, 2006b; Hurmuzaki, 1887, cv] which may have been as much as surprise for them as it is for us. Pope Gregory IX's more-than-slight-annoyance at this "oversight" is evident from a letter he sent to King Béla IV in 1234:

"As I was informed, there are certain people within the Cuman bishopric named Wallachians, who although calling themselves Christians, gather various rites and customs in one religion and do things that are alien to this name. For disregarding the Roman Church, they receive all the sacraments not from our venerable brother, the Cuman bishop... but from some pseudo-bishops of the Greek rite."(Spinei, 2008)

"Pseudo-bishops" was more than just a jab at the "schismatics": it meant that the Orthodox priests in the area were not ordained, and therefore must have been local priests belonging to some now-defunct Romanian episcopacy rather than being Bulgarian missionaries.(Rogerius, 1938, p. 564) The letter also mentions that "Hungarians, Teutons [Saxons], and others Schismatics" were leaving the Hungarian kingdom to join the Wallachians and become Orthodox Christians. This must have looked like one step forward and two steps back: while Christianity was spreading in the region, its Orthodox flavour was hardly what the Pope had in mind. He recommended giving the Romanians "a Catholic bishop, as is fit for that people" to goad them towards the Apostolic See, but undoubtedly Romanian Catholic bishops were in short supply. The Romanians had somehow scored a small Orthodox victory against Catholic proselytism, but it was not enough to turn the tide. Fortunately, the Romanians were about to receive their salvation from the most unlikely of people.

In 1241 the Mongols burst into Europe from the Ukrainian steppe, trampling all in their path as far as the Adriatic Sea. Though they thrashed the Poles at the Battle of Legnica, their main target was Hungary. The major force of the Mongol army broke through the Carpathians at the Verecke Pass, pretty much every other nomad had crossed earlier. King Béla decided wage a winner-take-all battle at Mohi in 1241. Unfortunately, the Hungarians had lost much of their former nomadic prowess and their army was mostly composed of armor-clad knights, the equivalent of arrow-fodder for the Mongols. It was a catastrophic defeat that left the Mongols free to pillage the land.

Other branches of the Mongol invasion had simultaneously proceeded through the Romanian lands. According to Roger of Maggiore, who visited the region after the Mongols were gone, the Mongol chief Bochetor proceeded through Moldova and into the episcopacy of Cumania, where local resistance was easily crushed.(Epure, 2011) Unfortunately, the name "Bochetor" does not match that of any known Mongol general, but certainly the Cuman bishopric did not destroy itself, and the handiwork of the Mongols can be seen archaeologically.(d'Ohsson, 1852, p. 628) The Persian writer Rashed-od-Din gave a more detailed account of the Mongol invasion, but his spelling also left much to be desired, and most names and places are left to mere speculation. According to him one branch of the Mongols "traversed the country of Ilaut [probably Oltenia]" and "vanquished Bezerenbam [likely the Ban (ruler) of Severin]." Meanwhile, a second branch "moved against the Sassans [Saxon Germans] and defeated them in three battles." Lastly, a third army "entered Kara-Ulag, being Transylvania or Wallachia], vanquished the people of the Ulag [Vlachs], crossed the mountains and invaded the country of Miscelav, where he defeated the enemy, who was awaiting him."(Spinei, 2009, pp. 142-143) "Kara-Ulag" has been translated as "Black Wallachia" and "Ulag" as Romanians.

The identity of Miscelav remains unclear, though some believe he was a Romanian voievod in Wallachia. The Romanians and Szeklers (Hungarian border guards) also tried together to seal the mountain passes, actions that resulted in yet another glorious defeat for the overmatched defenders, something not unlikely given the Orthodox Christian garrisons in mountain pass fortresses such as that of Bâtca Doamnei.[Curta, 2006b, p. 408] While not a shining moment in Romanian military history, the records show that the Romanians were actively involved in the defense of their lands as well as Hungary. In retrospect however, sitting this one out might have been a better idea.

The Mongols left just as quickly as they had come. They had never been intent on annexing Hungary, which may explain why they sacked the kingdom. News that the Mongol Great Khan had died forced the leading Khan of the expedition, a potential successor, to return and squabble for the throne. Some Mongol presence was maintained in Wallachia and Moldova in the Romanian lands.[Hurmuzaki, 1887, cxciii] For the Romanians things could not have been better (well, except getting annihilated). The resultant power vacuum in the region caused by a Hungary too weak to act and a Mongol Empire to distant to care was the environment necessary for the Romanians to assert their independence. They had finally received their lucky break, even if it came at a heavy price.

The first records of Romanian statehood are found in a Hungarian document from 1247: the Diploma of the Knights of Saint John. King Béla IV of Hungary invited the Knights of Saint John (Knights Hospitallers), another famous crusader order, into the kingdom and gave them lands in Severin. Thankfully, due to the Hungarian King's predisposition to parcelling out lands that belonged to others, the diploma mentions that the knights were given lands belonging to the cneazes (princes) John and Farkas. However, some of the lands belonging to the voievod Litovoi was parcelled out as well, but most was "left to the Romanians."[Rădvan, 2010, p. 123] The knights were given permission to expand to the east in Cumania (by now an outdated name), "except for the lands of Seneslav, voievod of the Romanians."[Vásáry, 2005, p. 147]

Even though there is no evidence that the Knights of Saint John ever accepted the invitation, the document elucidates the political realities outside of the Carpathians. An important detail is the use of the term "voievod" in lands south of the Carpathians. It was not just another strange Orthodox title: rather, the *voievods* had larger holdings and more power than a mere *cneaz*.[Curta, 2006b, p. 408] Romanian power was consolidating as smaller holdings were being unified into larger states. The document also called upon the knights to not accept any peasants from the kingdom as colonists, suggesting that there was still a migration of peasants out of the kingdom and into Wallachia. The new spirit of the document was also telling: the Hungarian king was no longer able or willing to extend his rule beyond the Carpathians.[Spinei, 2009, p. 163] He tried to keep the people in the region as vassals, tasking them with protecting the kingdom, but most Romanian rulers opted for Mongol suzerainty, as in the example of a duke *Olaha* at the Mongol court in 1247.[Hurmuzaki, 1887, ccclxvi] Many Romanian rulers doubtlessly knew the Hungarian king had lost his long arm in the Mongol invasion.

Around the year 1272 Litovoi, the same voievod mentioned in 1247, struck out to make an independent Romanian state in Wallachia. He was undoubtedly still bearing a grudge against the Hungarians who had taken away his lands. He threw off the Hungarian yoke and occupied the land of Severin as an act of defiance. It was a case of David versus Goliath, except this time David lost in spectacular fashion as Litovoi was killed in battle against the Hungarian army. His brother, Bărbat (literally meaning "man"), in spite of his name, chose to surrender and paid his own massive ransom while swearing fealty to the king.[1](Rădvan, 2010, p. 129) It was the first test-flight of an independent Romanian state, and it came crashing down rather quickly. Though it had failed, it still had some successes: Litovoi's successors likely kept the lands he had occupied during his revolt.(Papacostea, 1993, p. 169) Nevertheless, it was just the tip of a growing Romanian political iceberg. Sooner or later something was going to give.

By the fourteenth century the Romanians were ready to try again, and this time they succeeded. From the late thirteenth to the early fourteenth centuries the states south of the Danube continued to unify into one larger state. One ruler, Basarab, bore the title of "great voievod", implying that he (or his predecessor) had united all of the smaller voievodships.(Hurmuzaki, 1887, cccclxvii) Hungarian documents clearly made him out to be a vassal, as in 1324 he was charmingly referred to as "our transalpine voievod."(Berza & Pascu, 1977, p. 37) However, less than a year later Basarab became "unfaithful to the holy crown"(Rădvan, 2010, p. 130) likely due to a territorial dispute.(Brezeanu, 2001)

The Hungarian king Charles-Robert of Anjou decided to nip his Wallachian problem in the bud, and invaded Wallachia in 1330. Anjou considered that the former kings erred by not annexing Litovoi's state. He planned to both get rid of Basarab and erase Wallachia from the map. Charles-Robert's large army of knights and nobles set off in September 1330, and his invasion was carefully recorded in the Hungarian *Chronicon Pictum*.(Vásáry, 2005, p. 154) After forcing Basarab out of Severin, Basarab sued for peace with an offer of 7,000 pieces of silver and his oath of fealty. Charles was feeling confident however: he told Basarab's emissary that Basarab "is the shepherd of my sheep and I will take him from the mountains by his beard." Charles proceeded to Basarab's capital of Curtea de Argeş, which he found completely deserted. Much like Napoleon when he was confronted with an abandoned Moscow during his Russian campaign, Charles was unable to decisively end his campaign and set fire to the city out of frustration. And, much like Napoleon again, with winter approaching and food becoming scarce, the Hungarian king realized his strategic blunder. The Wallachian voievod on the other hand, though in a tight spot, had managed to fortify his position in the mountains. Faced with a stalemate, the Hungarian chronicle claimed Charles-Robert achieved an armistice with Basarab in which Wallachian guides were to lead Charles army through the Carpathians back to Hungary. Basarab however, was not about to let Charles-Robert's army return to try again in the coming summer. The army was lead straight into an ambush and was subsequently annihilated.(Florescu, 1999, p. 65) It is questionable whether the armistice had actually been agreed upon or if it was historical reediting by Hungarian chroniclers to make up for the humiliating defeat suffered at the hands of the Wallachians during the retreat.(Ludescu, 1998, p. 104, 2-4)

The annihilation of the Hungarian army at the Battle of Posada could not have been more lopsided. The Romanian voievod had placed his army on the sides of the ravine overlooking the path that the Hungarians took, from which they shot down arrows and threw stones upon the now-impotent knights. What followed was like shooting fish in a barrel; even the chronicle likened the Hungarians to "fish trapped in nets." Hungarian "young and old warriors, princes and noblemen fell without distinction of rank." Charles-Robert barely escaped with his life by exchanging clothes with one of his soldiers, among the most awkward scenes to have graced any battlefield. With the utterly crushing victory Basarab ensured the independence of his principality and became the first independent ruler the Romanians had seen in four centuries.

For Basarab's great importance in Romanian history, his identity is still unclear. Medieval Romanian chronicles paint the picture of an entirely different man, making no mention of Basarab but rather of a certain Radu Negru ("Radu the Black"), sometimes called Negru Vodă ("The Black Warlord"). In the seventeenth century chronicle, *Istoria Țării Românești* (History of Wallachia), Radu is said to have been a prince from southern Transylvania who came to Wallachia in 1290 with numerous followers.(Rădvan, 2010, pp. 130-131) The chronicle then claims that the boyars of the Basarab family in Oltenia pledged fealty to Radu Negru, and thus unified the country.

For the longest time modern historians considered this only a myth, but certain events and facts of Romanian history continue to line up with the so-called legend. It must be more than coincidence that Radu Negru left southern Transylvania in 1290, the same year that Hungarian nobles gained ownership of some Romanian lands in Southern Transylvania, and the Romanians were then denied their appeal at the Hungarian court;(Popescu, 1963, p. 5) Romanian chronicles even make reference to this event!(Gusztáv, 1862, p. 197) Hungarian documents from the late thirteenth century also mention "driving out the schismatics"(Rădvan, 2010, p. 266) and undoubtedly some Orthodox Romanians fled to Wallachia. Similarly, later Romanian medieval documents refer to land grants given to boyars by Radu Negru in 1292, the date being so close to that of the legend that it must be more than coincidence.(Florescu, 1999, p. 64) The fact that Wallachia's initial capital of Câmpulung was right beside the Carpathians and later capitals continued to move further south is understandable if Wallachia's first founder was originally a Transylvanian. The very name *Muntenia* implies the state was created by people who had crossed the mountains, and also the term in popular folklore for the Romanian foundation – *descălecare* ("dismounting") – implies Radu came from somewhere else.(Florescu, 1999, pp. 57-67) Câmpulung's first ruler was a Transylvanian Saxon named Laurencius, perhaps a man who had come with Radu Negru to the south.

All of this has prompted historians to seriously reconsider this supposed "myth." Some consider that Basarab was Negru Vodă, and that one ruler unified the entire country.(Djuvara, 2007) An alternative theory is that Negru Vodă was Basarab's father Thocomerius, and therefore Basarab inherited Negru Vodă's unification.(Rădvan, 2010, pp. 131-132) Still more believe the two people were unrelated, with Radu Negru unifying the country and Basarab being a usurper who took over someone else's work.(Papacostea, 1993, pp. 171-173) Whatever the case may be, it is evident that the foundation of Wallachia was not a self-contained event: Wallachia was created as an independent state in response to the collapse of Romanian political autonomy in southern Transylvania.(Vásáry, 2005, pp. 171-173)

That is not the only question that has been raised about the Romanian voievod Basarab: many wonder how "Romanian" he was at all. Basarab's name is of Turkic origin, being a conjugate of *basar-aba* ("father-king"). Similarly, Basarab's father's name, recorded as *Thocomerius* in Latin documents, is close to the Turkic *Togomer* rather than the Romanian-Slavic alternative *Tihomir* proposed by many Romanian historians (who are themselves reluctant to accept a Turkic origin).(Madgearu, 2005a) While Radu Negru's capital had a Romanian name of Câmpulung (meaning "long field") Basarab's capital at Argeş had a (debatably[x]) Turkic name,(Berza & Pascu, 1977, p. 37) perhaps more proof that the initiative of a Romanian ruler had been usurped by a Turkic dynast. Furthermore, a document in 1325 also mentions that a Cuman lord from Hungary boasted that the Hungarian king could barely reach up to Basarab's ankles.(Hurmuzaki, 1887, ccccxcviii) Taken together, some consider this compelling evidence that Basarab was of Cumanic origin.

All those arguments considered, Basarab was unanimously referred to as a Romanian (*Olacus*) in contemporary documents and there are several reasons why we should take this at face-value.(Vásáry, 2005, p. 138) The Mongol invasion of 1241 resulted in the expulsion of many Cumans from Wallachia,(Spinei, 2009, p. 353) and only a number of Romanian nobles were of Cuman extraction, suggesting that Cumans played a small part in the foundation of Wallachia. Turkic names were likely adopted by some Romanian elite like the Basarabs because it was seen as fashionable to associate oneself with the nomadic rulers. The case of the early Magyars reflects such tendencies, as even Árpád bore a Turkic name, yet no credible argument has been made for Árpád being Turkic.(Spinei, 2009, pp. 356-359) Archaeological evidence for peaceful Romanian-nomad interaction remains very small, and a Cuman-Romanian symbiosis is unsubstantiated. The nomadic Cumans and the sedentary Romanian simply lived in two different worlds. Any Cumans that settled among the Romanians were isolated families and were rapidly assimilated.(Rădvan, 2010, p. 315) When we look at Basarab, even if his family was originally Cumanic, by the time of his rule he was considered just as Romanian as his subjects.

Further east a second Romanian state was about to emerge: Moldova. Thankfully, the origin of Moldova is less controversial. Romanian states had been noted in the region for some time. In 1300 Otto of Bavaria, a competitor for the Hungarian throne, was imprisoned and sent by the Hungarian king to a Romanian ruler in Moldova.(Vásáry, 2005, p. 158) That is unfortunately the most informative account of Moldovan statehood until 1345 when the Hungarian king Louis the Great began an offensive against the eastward Mongols. Louis had no trouble pushing the Mongols out of Moldova, but he was unsure of what to do with the land he had just conquered. Thankfully, many Romanians from Maramureş participated in the offensive and Louis

---

[x] The precise etymology is unclear. Some Romanians do not accept the Turkic etymology, but believe the name is from the Dacian word *Ordessos*, or possibly the fortress *Argedava*. This is itself doubted by Romanian medievalists.

was happy to leave the mess made to one of them, a cneaz name Dragoş. The small Romanian principality – at the time barely covering northwestern Moldova in Romania – was designed to be little more than a tool used by the Hungarian king to protect his actual kingdom.(Vásáry, 2005, p. 159) Hungarian documents also readily acknowledged that Dragoş ruled "our land Moldova." Moldova had changed ownership from the Mongols to the Hungarians, even if it was ruled by a Romanian.

It was not long until Moldova saw a new leader, Bogdan of Cuhea, who established her independence. Some have tried to identify this Bogdan with another mentioned in 1335, "Bogdan voievod, son of Mikula" who immigrated into the Hungarian kingdom with his followers in that year.(Spinci, 1986, p. 204) This is identification is unlikely given Bogdan's vast holdings in Maramureş that he would have had trouble building up in only twenty years.(Spinci, 1986, p. 205) The document makes no reference as to where the son of Mikula had moved to, and there is no reason to believe that one "Bogdan" is as good as another. In all likelihood, Bogdan of Cuhea had always lived in Maramureş.

A dispute between King Louis I and Bogdan resulted Bogdan's lands and titles being granted to another noble, as Bogdan is referred to in 1343 as the "former voievod of Maramureş."(Deletant, 1986; Vásáry, 2005, pp. 159-160) Bogdan would, in turn, extract his revenge by conquering the larger Moldova! He crossed the Carpathians to conquer the new principality in 1363 or 1364.(Thuroczy, 1766, 49) Hungarian chronicles described how "Bogdan, the voievod of the Vlachs of Maramureş lead his Vlachs of his districts into the land of Moldova."(Berza & Pascu, 1977, pp. 80-81) The demographic growth of the Vlachs in Moldova was thus coupled with their decline in Transylvania. The foundation of an independent Moldova was yet another failure of the Hungarian policy towards the Romanians: dismantling Romanian districts within Transylvania resulted in a bigger state for the Romanians (and a bigger headache for the Hungarian kings) outside of the Carpathians. Bogdan drove Dragoş's son from Moldova, and Dragoş's grandson left his followers behind and reportedly fled to Transylvania, where the king rewarded him with Bogdan's former possessions.(Makkai, 2002, p. 488) Hungarian historians cite the flight of Dragoş's descendant into the kingdom as an example of Vlach immigration into Transylvania,(Christich, 1923) but such an interpretation forgets that these immigrants were originally Transylvanians. In any case, Bogdan was the clear winner of this game of Moldovan musical chairs, and came to be viewed as the rightful founder of an independent Moldova. Later documents even referred to the country as *Bogdania* as a result.

Contentions between the Hungarian kingdom and the Romanian states strengthened the pull of the Orthodox Byzantine world on the Romanians. Though writers on Romania from the early twentieth century noted that "a Latin country which is not Catholic is an anomaly,"(Hurmuzaki, 1887, x) Romania's religious nature was a consequence of medieval politics. A state in the Middle Ages required its own religious hierarchy to be considered legitimate. Hungary, for example, only became a proper kingdom after the conversion of Saint Stephen to Catholicism in the year 1000. Beforehand, Hungary was seen as being no more than some land temporarily seized by

Magyar warriors. Practically speaking, conversion did not change this, but in a legal sense it made Hungary an actual state. The Vlachs were aware of this truism: Kaloyan's letters to Innocent III bore the maxim "an empire without a patriarchy cannot stand"[Tanaşoca, 2001] and pleaded for Innocent III to establish a mission in Bulgaria as to legitimize the new state. Kaloyan's appeals indicate that the Vlachs may have had an ethnic affinity for Catholicism;[Hurmuzaki, 1887, ccclxxvi] if left alone or if favorable terms had been offered, they might have realized they could understand Latin a lot better than they could understand Slavonic. Indeed, there are several documents in which the Pope in Rome sings praises both to Basarab[Hurmuzaki, 1887, dli] and his successor Nicolae-Alexandru for being faithful to Catholicism and referred to the Romanians as *Olachi Romani* ("Vlach Romans").[Deletant, 1986] Likewise, in 1370 the Moldovan prince Laţcu addressed the Pope in a letter, asking for the Pope to establish a diocese in his lands; the fact that he sent it directly to the Pope and not through a Hungarian proxy suggests Laţcu was trying to pre-empt a Hungarian invasion.[Hurmuzaki, 1887, ccccxcviii]

The biggest roadblock to a Romanian acceptance of Catholicism was the Hungarians. To Basarab and his Wallachians, accepting Catholicism would have meant accepting Hungarian domination. Indeed, Basarab only possessed *de facto* independence after his victory at Posada. As far as Catholic Europe was concerned, he was still a vassal of the Hungarian king and his rule rested only on the force of arms. It was this political threat that prompted the Romanian princes to seek Constantinople's patronage.[Brezeanu, 2001, pp. 85-86; Seton-Watson, 1934, p. 29] When the Orthodox metropolitanate of Wallachia was established in 1359, it legitimized Wallachia as a real country and not just some warlord's temporary holdings. Similar events played out in Moldova, where the establishment of the Byzantine Metropolitan in 1402 ended Hungarian aspirations on the region. Wallachia and Moldova chose Constantinople as a guarantor for independence.

The establishment of Romanian independence was the final step in their ethnic development. Though it had taken over a millennium to form, the Romanians as a nation finally became a reality. The road was bumpy, but at its end emerged a Latin people that had adopted the Eastern Orthodox rite of Christianity. Their established states created a sense of demographic and cultural permanence on the European landscape. As such, this is where the discussion of Romanian origins ends. Though many people would add to the Romanians over the coming centuries, be they Turks, Russians, the French, or even the English, these influences would be minor touches on an already completed work. The Romanians had firmly established their place in Europe.

Works Cited

Al-Nadim. (1970). *The Fihrist. A Tenth-Century Survey of Muslim Culture*. New York, NY: Columbia University Press.

Angold, M. (1997). *The Byzantine Empire, 1025-1204: a political history*. London, UK ; New York , NY: Longman.

The Annals of Fulda. (T. Reuter, Trans.). Manchester, UK: Manchester University Press.pres

Anonymous. (2008). *Gesta Hungarorum* (M. Rady, Trans.).

Ansbert. (2010). *Historia de expeditio Frederici Imperatoris.* Farnham, UK Burlington, VT: Ashgate.

Berend, N. (2006). *At the Gate of Christandom: Jews, Muslims, and "pagans" in medieval Hungary.* Cambridge, UK; New York, NY: Cambridge University Press.

Berza, M., & Pascu, Ş. (1977). *Documenta Romaniae Historica.* Bucharest, Romania: Academia de Ştiinţe Sociale şi Politice a Republicii Socialiste România.

Brezeanu, S. (2001). A Byzantine Model for Political and State Structure in Southeastern Europe between the Thirteenth and Fifteenth Centuries. In R. Theodorescu & L. C. Barrows (Eds.), *Politics and Culture in Southeastern Europe.* Bucharest, Romania: UNESCO.

Choniates, N. (1984). *O City of Byzantium: annals of Nicetas Choniates* (H. J. Magoulias, Trans.). Detroit: Wayne State University Press.

Christich, E. (1923). Dacians of To-Day. *New Blackfriars, 4*(42), 1070-1076.

Chronicon Pictum Vindobonense. Lipsiae: 1883.

Curta, F. (2006). *Southeastern Europe in the Middle Ages: 500-1250.* Cambridge, UK: Cambridge University Press.

d'Ohsson, C. (1852). *Histoire des Mongols, depuis Tchinguiz-Khan jusqu'a Timour Beyou Tamerlan.* Amsterdam: Frederik Muller.

Deletant, D. (1980). Slavonic Letters in Moldova, Wallachia and Transylvania from the Tenth to the Seventeenth Centuries. *The Slavonic and East European Review, 58*(1-21).

Deletant, D. (1986). Moldova Between Hungary and Poland 1347-1412. *The Slavonic and East European Review, 64*(2), 189-211.

Djuvara, N. (2007). *Thocomerius-Negru Vodă. Un voivod de origine cumană la începuturile Ţării Româneşti.* Bucharest, Romania: Humanitas.

el-Maqdisî, M. b. T. (1907). *Le Livre de la Création et de l'Histoire.* Paris: Cl. Huart.

Engel, P. (2001). *The Realm of Saint Stephen: A History of Medieval Hungary, 895-1526.* London, UK: Tauris.

Epure, V.-A. (2011). Invazia Mongolă în Ungaria şi in spaţiul românesc [The Mongol Invasion in Hungary and the Romanian space]. *ROCSIR Revista RomâROCSIR Revista Romána de Studii Culturale (pe Internet).*

Fejer, G. (1830). *Codex Diplomaticus.* Budae: Regiae Universistatis Ungaricae.

Fine, J. v. A. (2000). *The Early Medieval Balkans: a critical survey from the sixth to the late twelfth century.* Ann Arbor, MI: University of Michigan Press.

Florescu, R. R. (1999). *Essays on Romanian History.* Iasi, Romania; Oxford, UK; Portland, OR: Center for Romanian Studies.

Gusztav, W. (1862). *Monumenta Hungariae Historica.* Pest, Hungary: Magyar Tudomanyos Akademia.

Hazzard-Cross, S. (1929). Yaroslav the Wize in Norse Tradition. *Speculum, 4*(2), 177-197.

Honig, B. (2001). *Democracy and the Foreigner.* Princeton, NJ: Princeton University Press.

Hurmuzaki, E. (1887). *Documente Privitoare la istoria românilor [Documents relevant to the history of the Romanians]*. Bucharest, Romania: Academia Româna.

Jansson, S. B. F., & Foote, P. (1987). *Runes in Sweden*. Stockholm, Sweden: Royal Academy of Letters, History, and Antiques.

Jesch, J. (2001). *Ships and Men in the Lakte Viking Age: the Vocabulary of Runic Inscriptions*. Woodridge: Boydell & Brewer.

Komnena, A. Alexiad.

Kristo, G. (2003). *Early Transylvania (895-1324)*. Budapest, Hungary: Lucidus.

Life of Constantine. (1983). Ann Arbor, MI: University of Michigan.

Ludescu, S. (1998). *Letopiseţul Cantacuzinesc*. Chişinău, Moldova: Litera.

Madgearu, A. (2005a). Români şi pecenegi în sudul Transilvaniei [Romanians and Pechenegs in Southern Transylvania. In Z. K. Pinter, I. M. Ţiplic & M. E. Ţiplic (Eds.), *Relatii interetnice in Transilvania (secolele VI-XIII)*. Bucharest: Departmentul pentru Relaţii Interetnice.

Madgearu, A. (2005b). *The Romanians in the Anonymous Gesta Hungarorum*. Cluj-Napoca: Center for Transylvania Studies.

Makkai, L. (2002). Transylvania in the medieval Hungarian kingdom (896-1526). In B. Köpeczi, L. Makkai & A. Mocsy (Eds.), *History of Transylvania, vol I: from the beginnings to 1606*. Boulder, CO; New York, NY: Social Science Monographs.

Migne, J. P. (1862). Patrologiae Latina. *CCXV*.

Murgescu, B. (2001). *Istoria României în Texte*. Bucharest, Romania: Corint.

Nestor. (1953). *Russian Primary Chronicle, Laurentian Text* (S. Hazzard-Cross & O. Sherbowitz-Wetzor, Trans.). Cambridge, MA: The Medieval Academy of America.

Papacostea, Ş. (1993). *Românii in Secolul al XIII-lea: între Cruciată şi Imperiul Mongol [The Romanians in the 13th Century: between the Crusade and the Mongol Empire]*. Bucharest, Romania: Editura Enciclopedică.

Pop, I.-A., Barbulescu, M., & Nagler, T. (2005). *The History of Transylvania, I (up to 1541)*. Cluj-Napoca: CTS, Romanian Cultural Institute.

Popescu, R. (1963). *Istoriile domnilor Ţării Româneşti*. Bucharest, Romania: Editura Academiei Republicii Populare Romîne.

Porphyrgenitus, C. (1967). *De Administrando Imperio* (G. Moravcsik, Trans.). Washington: Dumbarton Oaks Center for Byzantine Studies.

Psellus, M. *chronographia*.

Rădvan, L. (2010). *At Europe's Borders: Medieval Towns in the Romanian Principalities*. Leiden, Netherlands; Boston, MA: Brill.

Rogerius. (1938). Carmen Miserabile. In E. Szentpetery (Ed.), *Scriptores Rerum Hungarorum* (Vol. II). Budapest: Academia Litter. Hungarica atque Societate Histor. Hungarica.

Róna-Tas, A. (1999). *Hungarians and Europe in the Early Middle Ages: an introduction to early Hungarian history*. Budapest: Central European University Press.

Sălăgean, T. (2005). Dextram Dantes, Notes on the Specificity of the Relations Between the Hungarian Conquerors and the Local Population in Northern Transylvania in the 10th-14th Centuries. In Z. K. Pinter, I. M. Ţiplic & M. E. Ţiplic (Eds.), *Relatii interetnice in Transilvania (secolele VI-XIII)*. Bucharest: Departamentul pentru Relaţii Interetnice.

Seton-Watson, R. (1934). *A History of the Roumanians*. Cambridge, UK: Cambridge University Press.

Skylitzes, J. (2010). *Synopsis of Histories* (J. Wortley, Trans.). Cambridge, UK: Cambridge University Press.

Spinei, V. (1986). *Modlova in the 11th-14th Centuries*. Bucharest, Romania: Editura Academiei Republicii Socialiste România.

Spinei, V. (2008). The Cuman Bishopric: genesis and evolution. In F. Curta & R. Kovalev (Eds.), *The Other Europe in the Middle Ages: Avars, Bulgars, Khazars, and Cumans*. Leiden, Netherlands; Boston, MA: Brill.

Spinei, V. (2009). *The Romanians and the Turkic Nomads North of teh Danube Delta from the Tenth to the Mid-Thirteenth Century*. Leiden, Netherlands: Brill.

Sturluson, S. (1964). *Heimskringla*. Austin, TX: University of Texas Press.

Tanaşoca, N.-Ş. (2001). Aperçus of the History of Balkan Romanity. In R. Theodorescu & L. C. Barrows (Eds.), *Politics and Culture in Southeastern Europe*. Bucharest, Romania: UNESCO.

Thuroczy. (1766). *Chronica Hungarorum*. Vienna.

Todorov, B. (2010). The value of empire: tenth-century Bulgaria between the Magyars, Pechenegs and Byzantium. *Journal of Medieval History, 36*(4), 312-326.

Tudela, B. o. (1888). *Itinerary of Benjamin of Tudela*. London, UK: Henry G. Bohn.

Tuetsch, G. D., & Fimhaber, F. (1857). *Urkundenbuch zur Geschichte Siebenbürgens*. Vienna.

Vásáry, I. (2005). *Cumans and Tatars: Oriental military in the pre-Ottoman Balkans, 1185-1365*. Cambridge, UK: Cambridge University Press.

Villehardouin, G. d. (1908). *Memoirs of the Fourth Crusade and the Conquest of Constantinople* (F. Marzials, Trans.). London, UK: J. M. Dent.

Wolff, R. L. (1949). The Second Bulgarian Empire: its origin and history to 1204. *Speculum, 24*(2), 167-206.

Part 1 Figures

a) Romania before and after the First World War. The large territorial expansion of the country, due to the large number of Romanians living outside of its former borders, caused significant political and historical controversy with its neighbors, especially Hungary and Russia.

b) The "Romanian Space" according to the historian Xenopol. A small inner triangle formed by the Transylvanian Carpathians is the center of Romanian people, from which their spread is bounded by the Tisza to the west, the Dniestr to the east, and the Danube to the south.

c) A depiction of the feared *falx* in action. The Roman soldier engaging the Dacian warriors has clearly upgraded his armor, as his a thick neck-guard segmented arm-guard try to keep all of his extremities safe.

d) A nation of road-builders, city-planners, metal-workers, and fanatical warriors, the Dacians of Burebista's time were hardly civilizational slouches.

e) Though the Dacians are depicted on Trajan's Column as fighting in nothing but shirts, the numerous suits of armor heaped up in a "victory pile" at the base of the column suggests the reality was far from what the artists wished to convey. It is doubtul the Dacians had left all of their armors at home when engaging the Romans, and most likely the Dacians were depicted without armor to clearly distinguish them from the Romans.

f) The frontiers of the Roman Empire in 150 AD, with Roman Dacia highlighted in yellow. Surrounded on three sides by barbarians, the province seems like a dumb idea in hindsight, but at the time it proved to be a great asset to the empire.

g) The Biertan Donarium, a gift donning a Latin inscription, represents solid evidence (both literally and figuratively) for a Daco-Roman Christian population in Dacia.

h) Eastern Europe at the start of the ninth century. Barbarian rule in Romania during this period was both a bane and a boon. On the one hand, the domination by the great powers of the Avars, Bulgars, and Magyars prevented the emergence of Romanian states. On the other hand, the Romanian space remained a marginal region for all three powers, and therefore was largely autonomous.

i) The battle of Posada as depicted in medieval chronicles. The Romanian peasant army, positioned on top of the cliffs, shot arrows and hurled boulders on helpless armor-clad knights and nobles below.

j) The Romanian states, namely Wallachia to the south and Moldova to the east, were largely unchanged after their establishment in the fourteenth century, as shown in this map of seventeenth century Southeastern Europe. Their foundation buffered the effect foreign powers would have on Romanian culture. Transylvania, though largely autonomous, was to remain a part of the Kingdom of Hungary for much of the Middle Ages.

a)

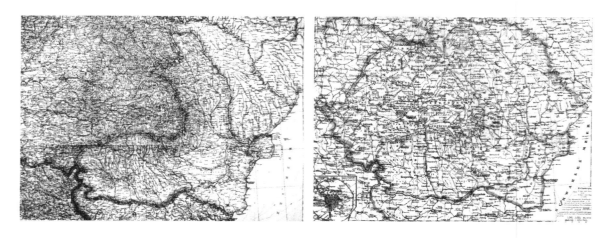

b)

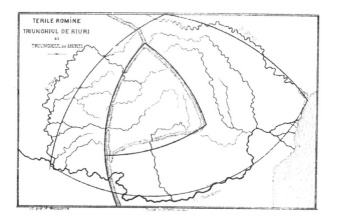

c)

d)

e)

f)

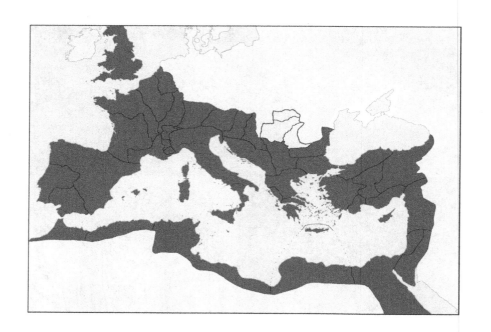

g)

h)

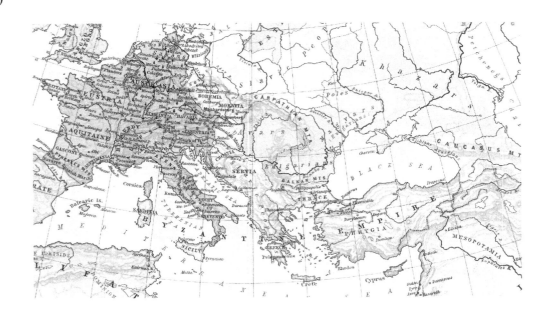

i)

j)

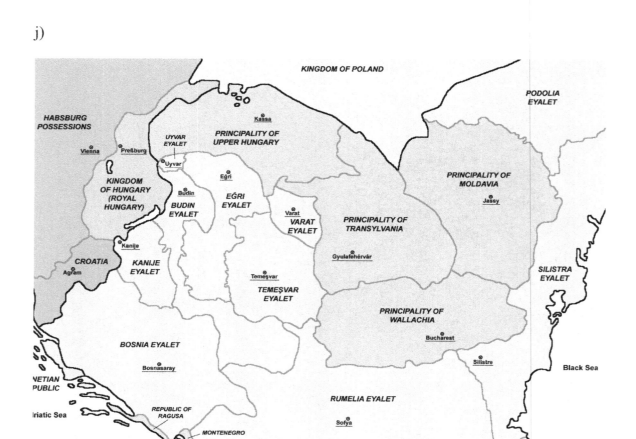

PART 2: THE CONTROVERSY

1. HISTORY AND POLITICS: A TOXIC ROMANCE

Even this brief glance at Romanian history reveals that there are still many unresolved questions. The relative obscurity of the Romanians throughout the Dark Ages and their unique position in Eastern Europe might have, in another world, created an environment of high-quality scholarship and academic cooperation. Unfortunately interpretations of history are often corrupted by politics. The origin of the Romanians has become in the best of cases a heated argument and in the worst of cases, a polemic of diatribes and propaganda. The argument has been primarily between Romanians and Hungarians over the rather childish game of "I was here first", the stakes supposedly being ownership of Transylvania.

This type of argument is not exclusive to the Romanians. Other examples include the Albanian-Serbian dispute over Kosovo, where Albanian use their "ancient origins" to buttress their claims to the region[H. Clark, 2000, p. xx] while Serbians largely deny the Albanian presence in the Early Middle Ages and point instead to Serbian cultural heritage in the region by way of the old Serbian churches.[Kostovicova, 2005, pp. 156-161] In the early twentieth century Greece sought the creation of a "Greater Greece" with many territories of the former Byzantine Empire, including Istanbul, and the Former Yugoslav Republic of Macedonia has border and history disputes with almost all of its neighbors (though the Macedonian government has formally denied any territorial irredenta). The argument boils down to "we were here since the year X and you only arrived here in the year Y. Therefore the land of Z belongs to us."

The mix of history and politics forms a rather deadly cocktail, but is the question of "first ownership" even relevant in the modern world? Modern borders are not determined by first settlement or kingly and imperial inheritances. It is laughable to imagine the United Kingdom today demanding the return of Normandy from France, or Germany asking Russia to surrender Kaliningrad on the grounds of prior ownership. The borders of today's states are legally justified by internationally-recognized treaties, and morally justified by ethic self-determination. When Kosovo was recently granted independence from Serbia, it was not on the grounds that Albanians were there first. It was not even entirely due to the numerical superiority of the Albanians in Kosovo and the threat they faced were they to remain a part of Serbia.[S. Wolff, 2004, p. 23] Therefore, the debate of "who was first in Transylvania?" has long-since become useless in modern politics. The Romanian historian A.D. Xenopol concluded in 1913 that ethnic self-determination was the only justification for a nation's borders as "the borders of state will lie together with those of its respective nation."[Xenopol, 1913, p. 23] Even if it were proven tomorrow that the Romanians all came from Greenland, it would not have the slightest effect on their ownership of Transylvania.

Unfortunately, some Hungarian historians refused Xenopol's argument. It was only natural for them to do so, as accepting Xenopol's logic would justify the fragmentation of their former kingdom. Instead, every shred of evidence has been put forward to argue in favor of a preconceived conclusion, namely that the Romanians are newcomers with no rights to their current country. Unfortunately the methodology employed of "here is our conclusion, now where can we find evidence to support it?" is prone to falsification. Listed below are but a few of the countless examples of historical manipulation that have occurred during a debate that is more than a century old.

One example is an argument made that in 1097 "Emperor Alexios Komnenos of Byzantium ordered the relocation of the Vlachs from the Chalkidike peninsula [in Northern Greece] to Peloponnesus [Southern Greece]. With this, the northward migration of the Vlachs [to Transylvania], ancestors of the Rumanians, began."(Wass, 1977, p. 14) The fact that Vlachs migrating were actually moving southward (away from Transylvania) was not considered. Other Hungarian historians claimed that the Vlachs came to Transylvania "fleeing from [the] Turkish advance on the Balkans"(Bodolai, 1980, p. 28) but the first Turkish incursions into the peninsula occurred over a century after the appearance of Vlachs in Hungarian official documents. The chronology therefore makes no sense. Even if we were to suppose a later migration of the Vlachs into Transylvania later due to the Ottoman occupation of the Balkans, this ignores the privileges and immunities Vlachs held within the Ottoman Empire(Malcolm, 1996, p. 78) that placed them in a privileged position from which they would hardly flee.

Sometimes the controversy does not arise from historical events but rather the interpretations of historical texts. The *Cantacuzino Chronicle*, written in the late 17th century, provides one example. Some historians considered the introductory passage as evidence for the "Vlach migration" into Transylvania:

"But first writing of the Romanians which separated from the Romans and ventured to the North. So crossing the Danube, they settled at Turnu Severin; others, in Transylvania ["the Hungarian country"] along the waters of the Olt, the Mureş, and the Tisa and reaching as far as Maramureş"(Ludescu, 1998, 1, 1)

Unfortunately, the choice of ending for this quote appears to be deliberate, as reading further provides an entirely different image.[13] The reader is shown a very small fragment of an otherwise substantial chronicle. The year of the events discussed is left as a mystery, as is what happened to the Romanians afterwards. However, the next passage of the chronicle helps clarify when, where, and what exactly happened.

"And those that settled at Turnu Severin extended themselves South of the mountains up until the Olt, others towards the Danube in the South. And thus, the whole land was filled with them up until the edge of Nicopolis.

Then they chose from among the boyars [Wallachian nobles] who were of great descendance. And they put as Bans [rulers] a family called Basarab and they set the capital first at Turnu Severin, the second capital at Strehaia, and the third at Craiova. And as such much time passed as they ruled that land.

And in the Year of Adam 6798 [A.D. 1290], a great voievod from Transylvania called Radu the Black, great Herzog of Almaş and Făgăraş, left those lands with his entire house and a great multitude of people, Romanians, Papists, Saxons, and all sorts of people and went down the Dâmboviţa to make a new country."(Ludescu, 1998, 1, 2-4)

While the original chronicler was sparse with important dates, there is still a lot that can be done with comparing to other texts that also cover that timeframe. The chronicle defines the area of Romanian settlement as only consisting of Transylvania, Oltenia, and Banat. This however runs contrary to written sources of the time, such the letter from Pope Gregory IX dated to 1234, that claimed Wallachians also lived in eastern Wallachia.(Spinei, 2008, p. 433) If there was a northward migration, it could not have taken place in the early thirteenth century.

But when did this migration occur if not in the thirteenth century? We first need to consider Ludescu meant in his opening statement when he said the Romanians had "separated from the Romans." Hungarian historians who place the date in the thirteenth century attempt to argue that the "Romans" were Greek Byzantines as medieval texts refer to the Byzantine Empire as the Roman Empire. To generalize this rule to the late Renaissance *Cantacuzino Chronicle* however, is a gross manipulation. Ludescu himself specifically refers to Greeks as Greeks, not Romans. Constantinople is referred to as "Tsarigrad" and never as "Rome", so the Romans of the chronicle could not have been the medieval Byzantine Empire. Instead, consistent with other Romanian chroniclers of the time, the text refers specifically to the Latin ancient Romans when discussing the origins of his people.

There is some cryptic evidence in the location of the settlement that many historians have not considered. The Romanians in the chronicle settled at Turnu Severin, then went northward into Transylvania, their homeland being bounded by the Mureş, Tisza, and Olt rivers, all the way to Maramureş. The eastern boundary was set at the Olt river from the Carpathians to Nicopolis (present-day Nikopol, Bulgaria), on the Danube. In other words, the region settled by the Romanians included Banat, Oltenia, and Transylvania. While it is possible that these boundaries were set arbitrarily by the author, they happen to perfectly coincide with the borders of Roman province of Dacia!(Oltean, 2007, p. 55)

The only conclusion possible is that the chronicle refers to the Roman colonization of Dacia, and thus linked the existence of the Romanians in the area to Emperor Trajan's conquest of the region. While the document does prove that the Romanians migrated from the Balkans to Transylvania, the one caveat is that it the migration occurred approximately 2,000 years ago.

Another classic document that has been mangled by modern politics is the *Supplex Libellus Valachorum*. Written in 1791, the *Supplex* was a petition sent by the Romanians of Transylvania towards the Habsburg monarchy, asking for what Hungarian nobles at the time believed to be an absurd demand: equal rights and representation with all of the other nationalities of Transylvania.[(Hitchins, 2001)] The petition buttressed its demand on, among other things, the idea that the Romanians were the descendants of the Roman colonists of Dacia and therefore the region's oldest inhabitants. The Hungarian historian André Du Nay claimed that this petition was the first time the Romanians were linked to the Roman colonization of Dacia[(André Du Nay, 1980)] and stated that "The study of Rumanian history and language was developed, in the first place, to be used in the struggle of Rumanian intellectuals for more political rights for their own people."[(André Du Nay, 1980)] Nothing could be further from the truth. Without exception, the major Romanian chroniclers of the 17th century, over 100 years prior to the *Supplex*, linked the origin of the Romanians to the Roman colonization of Dacia by Trajan.[(Verdery, 1995, pp. 31-32)] As an example, the foreword to the chronicle *Letopisețul Țărâi Moldovei* (*Chronicle of Moldova*), written by the boyar Miron Costin in 1675, asserted that:

"It has always been my thought, beloved reader, to write a history of our beloved country Moldova [Moldova] from its first foundation, which was made by Emperor Trajan who founded the beginnings of [our] history."[(Costin, cap. I)]

Miron Costin's position was that Romanian history in Moldova began with Trajan's colonization. Similar sentiments were expressed by the Moldovan prince Dimitrie Cantemir, who doubled in his spare time as a philosopher, ethnographer, historian, composer of music, linguist, and geographer. In his work *Descriptio Moldaviae* (*The Description of Moldova*) written from 1714 to 1716 he stated:

"After this people [the Dacians] lost their king *Decebal*, defeated by the brave *Nerva Trajan*, and were in part massacred, part dispersed here and there, the whole country which they occupied was made into a Roman province, the land being distributed to the Roman citizens.

...

This much is known: that the inhabitants of Moldova, who draw their origin from Italy saved their lives by fleeing into the mountains [of Transylvania] in the face of the barbarian invaders [throughout the Dark Ages], having their own kings and voievods."[(Cantemir, 1997, pp. 12, 58)]

Like many historians of his time, Cantemir took the word of ancient Roman authors at face value, believing that all of Dacia's natives were done away with and that Dacia's Roman colonists could only have come from Italy (the more realistic Balkan or Anatolian origin was seen as much too boorish). Nevertheless, Cantemir firmly acknowledged that the Romanians descended from Roman colonists in the region, a clear reflection of standard academic opinion at the time. Among Wallachian scholars, Constantine Cantacuzino's wrote in the mid-17th century:

"And then Trajan, due to his victory brought here many colonists and guards in this country from all over the world, from which even today the Romanians draw their origin.

...

That the Vlachs, as in the Romanians, as they are the remnants of the Romans brought here by Ulpius Trajan and as they draw their origins from them even today, is validated and proven by all the truthful and believable historians[a]..."(Cancatuzino, 1997, pp. 56, 62)

But what about Transylvanian intellectual thought? The chronicles cited above were written by educated men and humanists in Moldova or Wallachia, lands where Romanians ruled themselves. We therefore need to establish if what they wrote was reflective of the opinion of an average Romanian seventeenth century peasant. As the Romanians of Transylvania had neither a noble class to represent them nor much in the way of schooling, it is possible that they did not share the sentiments of the educated class from across the Carpathians.

Thankfully, there is one shining example of a Transylvanian Romanian intellectual from before the eighteenth century Enlightenment: his name was Nicolaus Olahus, or Nicholas the Romanian. Olahus was a Transylvanian Romanian humanist of the early sixteenth century who became the royal chancellor of the Bishop of Zagreb, later became the Archbishop of Esztergom in Hungary, wrote several works on the nations inhabiting Hungary, and exchanged letters frequently with the famed humanist Erasmus.(Louthan, 1997, p. 56) In other words: he did his homework. His writings thus are among the most advanced Romanian intellectual works of the sixteenth century. On the origin of the Romanians, Olahus wrote that:

"According to the tradition, Romanians are colonists of the Romans. This is proven by the fact that they have much in common with the Romans' language, people whose coins are abundant in these places [Transylvania]; undoubtedly, these are significant testimonies of the oldness of Roman rule here."(Pop, 2003)

Ignoring Olahus's simple arguments (though at the very least he used linguistics and archaeology) we find something of interest: Olahus informs the reader that it is "according to tradition" that the Romanians are the descendants of the Romans. Whether this tradition was held by the peasants of Transylvania and not just the aristocracy is, like all matters of public opinion at a time when most were illiterate, a question that will remain unanswered. What we can take away is that Olahus was a Transylvanian who asserted the Roman origin of the Romanians over 200 years prior to the *Supplex*, and his phrasing makes it clear this was the accepted opinion among scholars and possibly the populace as well. Olahus makes no political argument, not even a comment, on the

---

[a] The observant reader may notice that Cantacuzino is actually citing other historians who have demonstrated the origins of the Romanians. This is a far cry from Du Nay's claim that the Roman ancestry of the Romanians was invented by Romanians to gain a Renaissance equivalent of bragging rights.

rights held by the Romanians of Transylvania. As such his statement did not and still does not gain much attention from Hungarians: the Romanians could have their history so long as they did not demand equal rights.

More obvious manipulations are cases when historians leave out parts of texts, presumably because they were deemed irrelevant, though in reality because they were contradictory to the argument being made. The works of Anton Verantius (Antun Vrančić, Antal Verancsics), written in the sixteenth century, is one that has been targeted by such methods. Verantius was a Croatian-born humanist who also became the bishop of Esztergom and was a famous diplomat for the Habsburg monarchy. In what regards the Romanians, Hungarian scholars often quite the passage:

> "[Transylvania] is inhabited by three nations: the Szeklers, the Hungarians, and the Saxons; I would nevertheless add the Romanians, who easily equal their number... they are all commoners, bondsmen to the Hungarians and having no place of their own, spread everywhere, throughout the country, often in the mountains and forests with their sheep and lead a miserable life." (Verantius, 1857)

Hungarian scholars concluded from this fragment that the Romanians in the sixteenth century constituted barely 25 percent of Transylvania's population and that they arrived as shepherds into the region.(Köpeczi, 2002) This conclusion was deduced from, supposedly, basic math: since there were four major nations in Transylvania, and since the Romanians equal "their number", dividing 100 percent into four equal parts leaves the Romanians with only 25 percent of the total population. The glaring problem with this interpretation is that it requires that all four populations of Transylvania be roughly equal to each other. Yet Hungarian authors predictably make themselves the largest segment of Transylvania's Renaissance population, giving an overwhelming 47% share, while the Szeklers and Saxons supposedly constituted 13 and 16 percent of the population respectively. Such an interpretation would mean that the Romanians somehow "easily equaled" 13, 16, and 47 percent of the population in Transylvania at the same time. Unless we resign ourselves to such an illogical conclusion, we must admit that Verantius was instead suggesting that the Romanians formed the majority of Transylvania's population. More importantly, a telling section of the text was also left out:

> "[Transylvania] is inhabited by three nations, Szeklers, Hungarians, Saxons; I would nevertheless add the Romanians, who, though they easily equal their number, have no freedom, no aristocracy, no right of their own, besides a small number living in the Haţeg district, where they say Decebal's capital was, and who, during the time of Ioan of Hunedoara, born there, were granted aristocratic status because they had always taken part in the struggle against the Turks. The other [Romanians] are all commoners, bondsmen to the Hungarians and having no place of their own, spread everywhere, throughout the country, often in the mountains and forests with their sheep and lead a miserable life."(Pop, 2003)

Verantius highlights the lack of political rights of the Romanians, something often glossed over by Hungarians who wish to portray Romanians as settling in Transylvania for a better life.(Sozan, 1997) Verantius also argues in a different section of his work that the Romanians originate from the Romans colonized by Trajan in the region,(Verantius, 1857) another assertion that is inconvenient for some historians.

Yet sometimes, modern authors present a quote in its correct context only to use it to make the most hamstrung and convoluted interpretation, as is the case of the writings of the first Byzantine author to make reference to the origins of Vlachs:[b] the Byzantine general Kekaumenos. In his *Strategikon*, written around the year 1078, Kekaumenos gave a rather undiplomatic account of the Vlachs:

> "The race of the Vlachs is an altogether unreliable and corrupt group ... they fell into captivity after Emperor Trajan defeated and vanquished them; even their emperor was slaughtered. His name was Decebal and the Romans exhibited his head on a spear in the center of the town. These people are the so-called Dacians and Bessi. Earlier, they had been living near the Danube and Saos [Sava] rivers, where the Serbs live, in a fortified and inaccessible location. Relying on this haven, they pretended friendship for the Romans and submissiveness toward their late emperors, but they went off from their fortifications to plunder Roman provinces. Therefore, the Romans took umbrage and, as I said before, set out to destroy them. Thus, they left the area they inhabited and spread all over Epirus and Macedonia, but the majority settled in Hellas."(Vékony, 2000, p. 213)

While the link Kekaumenos makes between the Vlachs and the Dacians is indisputable, and while Kekaumenos also points out that the Vlachs migrated to Greece from the north, Hungarian author Michael Sozan used this exact passage as proof that Trajan's Dacia was a distant memory by late antiquity.(Sozan, 1997) Kekaumenos' ability to recall not only the Roman emperor who subdued the Dacians but also the obscure barbarian king he faced is however strong evidence that this was not the case. It is hard to believe Sozan's assertion given that Byzantine generals regarded the former Dacia as "Roman land"(Simocatta, VII, 7) even centuries after its evacuation, and some emperors tried to restore Dacia to the empire in the later centuries.(Lenski, 2002, p. 122)

Gabor Vekony, on the other hand, agrees that Dacia was not forgotten, but believes Kekaumenos only linked the Vlachs to the Dacians due to a Byzantine custom of giving names used in antiquity to contemporary inhabitants of the same land.(Vékony, 2000, pp. 213-214) Thus, Bulgarians were often referred to as *Mysians*, after the Roman province of Moesia. However, we should note that Kekaumenos made explicit

---

[b] In this case it should be noted we are speaking of Aromanians, a Romance-speaking people who still inhabiting the Southern Balkans. As the name indicates, these people are ethnically related to the Romanians but the precise date at which they separated as their own people remains uncertain.

references to Dacian history, rather than mere geography. Vekony concluded that Kekaumenos' text, one explicitly mentioning the Vlachs migrating to the south, indicates a Vlach migration to the north and that the Vlachs had barely reached northern Bulgaria at this time.

Vekony's explanation does not seem entirely sound. While Kekaumenos uses the relationship between the Vlachs and the Dacians to explain Vlach disloyalty to the Roman/Byzantine emperors as a historical constant,[Curta, 2006b, p. 175] and while Kekaumenos attributed the Sava region as the Dacian homeland because he was familiar with Vlach revolts in the area,[Spinei, 2009, p. 76] it would be an extraordinary coincidence if this alone resulted in the identification of Vlachs with the Dacians.[R. L. Wolff, 1949] It is too great of a coincidence for Kekaumenos to choose the Dacians over other tribes such as the Illyrians and Mysians, tribes that actually lived in the regions Kekaumenos describes, especially if we believe the archaic names are based on geography alone. Kekaumenos must have known something about Vlach history that made him choose the Dacians as ancestors of the Vlachs *in spite of* the geographical bias for other tribes.

More importantly: how does one reconcile Vekony's conclusion that Kekaumenos' passage serves as evidence of a Vlach migration northward when other sources affirmed a Vlach presence in the northern Balkans for a much longer period of time? Kinnamos, writing less than a century later, stated that the Vlachs near the Danube Delta were "colonists brought long ago from Italy."[Stephenson, 2000, p. 269] Unless we believe that "long ago" meant "about 100 years, give or take" to the medieval writers, we must conclude that the Vlachs must have been residing in the northern Balkans for a much longer period of time than Vekony's migration theory would allow.

Controversy also abounds in what sources, if any, can be considered as credible on the early history of the Romanians. Consider the *Anonymous Chronicle of Moldova*, written in the early sixteenth century by an anonymous Moldovan chronicler, and the *Gesta Hungarorum*, written most likely in the twelfth century by an anonymous Hungarian chronicler.

Like many medieval works covering early history, the first sections of the *Chronicle of Moldova* is historically worthless. Among other things, the chronicle states that:
1) Moldova was founded by two brothers, Roman and Vlahata, who came from a "fortress of Venice." The brothers' names were apparently derived from "Romanian" and "Vlach" respectively.
2) There was a split between the "Old Romans" and "New Romans" as well as the Romanians.
3) The Romanians were sent from Italy to Hungary to fight off the Mongol invasion in the thirteenth century.
4) The Romanians were settled in Northern Transylvania by the Hungarian king Vladislav, who lived in the eleventh century.

The last statement has received noted attention from Hungarian historians.[Vékony, 2000, p. 13] The chronicle states that the Romanians were settled in Maramureş by Saint Vladislav of Hungary, due to the valiant efforts of the Romanians in the wars against the Tatars. The glaring anachronism of having an eleventh century king defeat a thirteenth century invasion is ignored these historians, eager to find evidence of a Vlach migration into Transylvania. Some have tried in vain to identify the "King Vladislav" of the chronicle with king Vladislav the Cuman, who lived in the late thirteenth century, but that presents its own set of problems, not the least of which being that the Romanians are mentioned in Transylvania long before Vladislav the Cuman was even born.

Historians universally admit the inaccurate and confusing nature of the chronicle, but some argue that the chronicle contains an inkling of truth, in that it can be used to "deduce that Moldovan Rumanians had an awareness that they were newcomers, late settlers along in the territory framed by the Rivers Maros [Mureş], Tisza and Kõrös-es [Criş]."[Vékony, 2000, p. 14] It is interesting that Vekony supports the Moldovan chronicle as a valuable source while completely discrediting the *Gesta Hungarorum*, a text that has many similarities with the *Chronicle of Moldova*. Both texts were written by anonymous authors centuries after the events they described, but while Hungarian historians eagerly use the latter as evidence, they dismiss the chronicle as a work of fiction, especially the sections pertaining to the Magyars conquering Transylvania from the Vlachs. They justify the dismissal of the *Gesta Hungarorum* because the work was written at least two centuries after the events it describes and there are some known factual inaccuracies in the *Gesta*. Yet when we consider the *Anonymous Chronicle of Moldova*, a chronicle that is almost entirely fantasy, with two brothers founding Moldova à la Romulus and Remus, Hungarians fighting Mongols two centuries before the Mongol Invasion, and the Romanians settling in Transylvania at a time which everyone agrees is wrong, it seems an even more dubious source from which to draw any conclusions.

Both the *Gesta Hungarorum* and the *Chronicle of Moldova* were written centuries after the events they choose to describe and both have sections that are factually inaccurate. In spite of this, Hungarian historians dismiss the former as unreliable while attributing a reflective value on the latter. If the Moldovan chronicle can be considered to provide reflections on the awareness of the Romanians as being "latecomers", should we not deduce from the *Gesta Hungarorum* that the Hungarians had an awareness that they had taken Transylvania from the Romanians?

The *Gesta Hungarorum* is a critical source in the history of the Romanians. It is the earliest preserved chronicle written by the Hungarians and also the first to describe the Hungarian conquest of Transylvania. Its mention of the Romanians as the inhabitants of the region has become one of the most contentious subjects of the region's history, and Hungarian historians have tried to dismiss the chronicle by any means, while Romanian historians have been desperate to argue for its retention as a valid historical document. Clearly, anyone seeking to explain the origin of the Romanians will need to address the validity of this source.

Works Cited

Bodolai, Z. (1980). *The Unmaking of Peace: the fragmentation and subsequent destruction of Central Europe after World War One by the Peace Treaty of Trianon*. Melbourne, Australia: Committe for Human Rights in Central Europe.

Cancatuzino, C. (1997). *Istoria Tarii Romanesti*. Chişinău: Litera International.

Cantemir, D. (1997). *Descrierea Moldovei* (P. Pandrea, Trans.). Bucharest, Romania: Litera International.

Clark, H. (2000). *Civil Resistance in Kosovo*. London, UK; Sterling, VA: Pluto Press.

Costin, M. *Letopiseţul Ţării Moldovei*.

Curta, F. (2006). *Southeastern Europe in the Middle Ages: 500-1250*. Cambridge, UK: Cambridge University Press.

Hitchins, K. (2001). *The Idea of Nation among the Romanians of Transylvania, 1700-1849*. Paper presented at the Nation and National Ideology: Past, Present, and PRospects, Bucharest, Romania.

Köpeczi, B. (2002). History of Transylvania: from 1606 to 1830. In B. Köpeczi, L. Makkai & A. Mocsy (Eds.), *History of Transylvania, vol II: from the beginnings to 1606*. Boulder, CO; New York, NY: Social Science Monographs.

Kostovicova, D. (2005). *Kosovo: the politics of identity*. Abingdon, UK; New York, NY: Routledge.

Lenski, N. E. (2002). *Failure of Empire: Valens and the Roman state in the fourth century AD*. Los Angeles, CA: University of California Press.

Louthan, H. (1997). *The quest for compromise: peacemakers in counter-Reformation Vienna*. Cambridge, UK: Cambridge University Press.

Ludescu, S. (1998). *Letopiseţul Cantacuzinesc*. Chişinău, Moldova: Litera.

Malcolm, N. (1996). *Bosnia: a short history*. Washington Square, NY: New York University Press.

Nay, A. D. (1980). The Daco-Rumanian continuity Theory: Origins of the Rumanian Nation and Language. In L. L. Löte (Ed.), *Transylvania and the theory of Daco-Roman-Rumanian Continuity*. Rochester, NY: Committeee of Transylvania.

Oltean, I. (2007). *Dacia: Landscape, Colonisation and Romanisation*. New York, NY: Routledge.

Pop, I.-A. (2003). Nations and Denominations in Transylvania (13th-16th Century). In C. Levai & V. Vese (Eds.), *Tolerance and intolerance in historical perspective*. Pisa, Italy: Clioh's Workshop.

Simocatta, T. History.

Sozan, M. (1997). *Ethnocide in Romania*. Safely Harbor, FL: Simon Publications.

Spinei, V. (2008). The Cuman Bishopric: genesis and evolution. In F. Curta & R. Kovalev (Eds.), *The Other Europe in the Middle Ages: Avars, Bulgars, Khazars, and Cumans*. Leiden, Netherlands; Boston, MA: Brill.

Spinei, V. (2009). *The Romanians and the Turkic Nomads North of teh Danube Delta from the Tenth to the Mid-Thirteenth Century*. Leiden, Netherlands: Brill.

Stephenson, P. (2000). *Byzantium's Balkan Frontier: A Political Study of the Norhtern Balkans, 900–1204*. Cambridge, UK; New York, NY: Cambridge University Press.

Vekony, G. (2000). *Dacians, Romans, Romanians.* Budapest, Hungary: Corvinus Library.

Verantius, A. (1857). *Expeditionis Solymani in Moldaviam et Transsylvaniam libri duo. De situ Transsylvaniae, Moldaviae et Transalpinae liber tertius.* Pest: Eggenberger Ferdinand Akademiai.

Verdery, K. (1995). *National Ideology Under Socialism: identity and cultural politics in Ceausescu's Romania.* Berkeley, CA; Los Angeles, CA: University of California Press.

Wass, A. d. (1977). *Documented facts and figures on Transylvania.* Astor, FL: Danubian Press.

Wolff, R. L. (1949). The Second Bulgarian Empire: its origin and history to 1204. *Speculum, 24*(2), 167-206.

Wolff, S. (2004). *Disputed Territories: the transnational dynamics of ethnic conflict settlement.* New York, NY; Oxford, UK: Berghahn.

Xenopol, A. D. (1913). *Istoria Românilor din Dacia Traiană [The History of the Romanians from Trajan's Dacia]* (Vol. I). Bucharest, Romania: Librariei Şcoalelor.

2. THE GESTA HUNGARORUM AND ITS DISCONTENTS

For better or for worse, no book on the history of the Romanians would be complete without the *Gesta Hungarorum*. It is one of the most hotly debated books in Hungarian and Romanian historiography. As the first work to cover the Magyar conquest of Hungary and Transylvania in detail, it makes explicit mention of the battles the Magyars had with the Romanians, *or Vlachs [Blaci]*. The Vlachs were mentioned as inhabiting Pannonia(Anonymous, 2008, IX) as well as Transylvania(Anonymous, 2008, XXV) alongside Slavs, Khazars, and other ethnicities. The chronicler specifies three rulers in and around Transylvania: Gelu, Glad, and Menumorut. Of these three, the one ruling in Transylvania proper is Gelu, who is noted as being a Vlach, and the only ruler whose ethnicity is explicitly mentioned.(Anonymous, 2008, XXIV) Menumorut, on the other hand, ruled in Biharea to the north-west, and Glad was said to rule in Banat. Hungarian historians have, for slightly more than a century, considered the book to be nothing more than a work of fiction.(Makkai, 2002, p. 343) Romanian historians on the other hand have had a tendency to swear by the book on Romanian early history, often reaching dogmatic levels of belief. In spite of its controversial nature (or perhaps because of it), critical analyses of the text are few and far between. Thus, the question remains as to which side is correct in its evaluation?

So what exactly is the *Gesta Hungarorum*? Simply put, it is the oldest Hungarian chronicle in existence... sort of. There was supposedly an older chronicle, the *Gesta Ungarorum*(Makkai, 2002, p. 333) (also called the "Old Gesta"), but no copy of that book exists, and its contents are mostly vague and mythical.(Grzesik, 2003) The book's existence was only deduced from the fact that the *Gesta Hungarorum* and later chronicles contain very similar passages, pointing to a common source. There are contradictory arguments revolving around this issue, with some wishing to discredit its author by suggesting he did not use the Old Gesta, while others try to prove the older chronicle's existence by stating that Anonymous did use it!(Spinei, 2009, p. 73) Proving the "Old Gesta" existed involves an entirely new level of mental acrobatics, and we will opt to instead consider the *Gesta Hungarorum* as the oldest text on Hungarian history.

Unfortunately, the only Medieval copy of the *Gesta Hungarorum* that was discovered had its first page missing, and as a consequence, its author's identity remains nebulous, being known only as "Anonymous" to historians. The veracity of the *Gesta* however is dependent on the author, because that alone could explain how long after he wrote his work and whether he had access to earlier sources. Within the *Gesta* he only entitled himself as "P. Magister [chancellor]... of the late King Béla." Thus, we arrive at our first big question about the man: if he was the chancellor of King Béla, why do we not know his identity?

The problem lies in that there were four kings of Hungary named Béla, and choosing the right king greatly affects the chronicle's interpretation. The kings were Béla I (1060 – 1063), Béla II (1131 – 1141), Béla III (1172 – 1196), and finally Béla IV (1214 – 1270). The fourth Béla is out of the question as Anonymous makes no mention of the Mongol invasion in 1240, which completely ravaged Hungary. As Béla IV reigned in this time and Anonymous clearly mentions that his Béla had passed away, we can eliminate him from this list. Hungary after the Mongol Invasion certainly does not match Anonymous' description of his homeland as "happy Hungary, to which many gifts are given."

Much ink has been spilt on trying to determine which of the remaining three could be the Béla of Anonymous.(Curta, 2006b, p. 15) Arguments that he was the notary of Béla I include the fact that the *Gesta Hungarorum* does not describe any historical event after 1046, making it difficult to believe a century of history would be erased from his book for no reason had he lived in the time frame of 1150-1200. Others consider the mention of the "Duke of the Bulgarians" as a vassal to the Byzantine Emperor as evidence that the source was written before the foundation of the Second Bulgarian Empire in 1185. This would make Anonymous the notary of King Béla II, meaning he wrote his work around 1150.(Madgearu, 2005b) Still others have tried to identify the man with numerous personas of the late twelfth century, and attribute the chronicle's date to *c.* 1200, which is also the date of the earliest preserved manuscript.(Sugar, Hanák, & Frank, 1990, p. 53)

None of these three possibilities fit with the theory that Gesta's mention of Vlachs in ninth century Transylvania was a projection of the realities of thirteenth century Transylvania into the past. Hungarian historians that deny Romanian continuity in Transylvania argue that the Romanians only arrived in Transylvania in 1210, the date of supposedly the first document mentioning the Romanians in Transylvania.(Kosztin, 1997; Marácz, 1996, p. 88) However, the *Gesta Hungarorum* was likely written at the end of the twelfth century,(Illyés, 1992, p. 21) or around a decade before documents. This has caused the begrudging admittance by the aforementioned historians that the Vlachs could have inhabited Transylvania somewhat, or even much earlier than when that document was written, but nevertheless around the time in which Anonymous lived.(Illyés, 1992, p. 291; Makkai, 2002, p. 439)

The notion of a surreptitious Vlach migration into Transylvania that went unnoticed by Anonymous is nigh-unbelievable. Anonymous' position as chancellor as chancellor gave him unequaled access to court documents that would surely have documented such a migration.(Spinei, 2009, p. 76) He therefore would have been well-informed of any Vlach migration that supposedly took place during his lifetime, even if it had started decades before he wrote the *Gesta*. Anonymous' "mistake" of giving control of Transylvania to the Romanians and Slavs at the time of the Magyar conquest is thus inexplicable, unless it were not a mistake at all. It would equivalent to a modern British historian writing that the Battle of Hastings was fought between William the Conqueror and recent Polish immigrants. The implication that no document ever covered this Vlach migration(Moga, 1994) is hard to excuse were it to have occurred in the late twelfth and early thirteenth centuries, a time when the Vlachs had acquired great political importance due to the Vlach-Bulgarian rebellion of 1185.(Rady, 2000, p. 91)

More problematic to the theory of Vlach migration is Anonymous' failure to project the other ethnicities of Transylvania into the past as well. The Transylvanian Saxons, first invited into Transylvania in the mid-twelfth century[Hupchick, 1995, p. 56] and continued roughly to the end of the thirteenth century, dates that correspond very well with the supposed Vlach migration. Anonymous however, does not mention the Saxons, even though this would be expected had he been making uneducated projections into the past. The second group present in Transylvania was the Szeklers, border guards ethnically related to the Magyars whose origin is, to this day, hotly contested.[Engel, 2001, p. 116; Kristó, 1996, p. 73] Anonymous mentions that Szeklers joined the Magyars in their conquest of the region, and does get certain aspects of their history in Transylvania correct, though they would have been hard for him to guess. For instance he emphasizes that the Szeklers played a role in conquering the district of Biharea from Menumorut,[Anonymous, 2008, L] incidentally also the area where the Szeklers were first settled in Transylvania.[Pop et al., 2005, pp. 212-215] The Szeklers moved further into Transylvania in the twelfth century however, and by the first half of the thirteenth century they were moved to the Eastern Carpathians.[Wieczorek & Hinz, 2000, p. 135] That Anonymous does not blindly place the Szeklers in Eastern Transylvania indicates that he was not projecting the present into the past, and Anonymous indicates his familiarity with Transylvanian history by emphasizing their role in the region where they first settled.

The one group that has been used most damningly against Anonymous' credibility – other than the Romanians – is the Cumans, who were nowhere near Transylvania when the Magyars settled in Pannonia[Vásáry, 2005, p. 4] and would not reach the region until the eleventh century.[N. Berend, 2006, p. 69] Cumans are mentioned repeatedly in the *Gesta*, first described as fighting alongside the Russians [Ruthenians] against the Magyars near Kiev, then as joining the Magyars during their conquest of Hungary. Finally Glad's army was composed of "Cumans, Bulgarians and Vlachs."[Anonymous, 2008, XLIV] This was taken as particularly damning evidence as these three ethnicities were the principal trouble-makers during the Vlach-Bulgarian revolt in 1185.[Stephenson, 2000, pp. 288-300] The argument is thus that Anonymous took three ethnicities that cooperated militarily in the twelfth century, and supposedly just assumed they were doing so in the ninth century.[MacArtney, 2009, p. 79] In any case, the Cumans would be an anachronism in ninth century Transylvania.

Anonymous however had several reasons for mentioning "Cumans" in his chronicle, none of which throw a wrench into the timeline of Transylvania's history. Many historians have demonstrated that the word *Cumani* in the *Gesta Hungarorum* does not actually mean Cumans, as the Hungarian word *kun* for Cumans, translates by Anonymous into Latin as *Cumani*, designated not just the Cumans but Turkic nomads in general, like the Pechenegs and Khabars.[Spinci, 2009, p. 75] It is already widely admitted by historians that the "Cumans" that joined the Magyars were not an anachronism but in fact Khabars,[André Du Nay, 1996, p. 218] a tribe of the Khazars.[Toncilescu, 1996, p. 14] Though Hungarian historians still hold that the Cumans in Glad's army were actually intended to be Cumans and thus must be an anachronism, it is very likely that Anonymous was likely referring to the Pechenegs, Turkic nomads already in Wallachia by the tenth century,[(Brătianu, 1988, pp. 279-288)]when he used the term "Cuman." Confusion between the Pechenegs and Cumans was very common in thirteenth century documents, as the Pechenegs were conquered and assimilated by the Cumans in the twelfth century.[(Pop et al., 2005, p. 211)] Anonymous was therefore not wrong to mention the Cumans, as one Turkic nomad looked the same as another in his eyes, and his descriptions would thus match the ethnic realities of the early tenth century.[(Spinei, 2009, p. 75; Toncilescu, 1996, p. 11)] Anonymous portrayal of the duke of the Bulgarians and the Byzantine Emperor as allies[(Anonymous, 2008, XII)] certainly casts doubt on him using a Vlach-Bulgarian revolt against the Byzantines as inspiration.

One of the more interesting ethnic groups mentioned in Transylvania by the *Gesta* is the Khazars (*Cozari*), situating them in Menumorut's lands. While curious at first, a Khazar presence was attested both in Pannonia and in Biharea, within Menumorut's domain. The Khazars may have acted as catalysts for the formation of states in that area,[(Madgearu, 2004)] and therefore Anonymous's emphasis on them in the region, perhaps as a ruling elite, is justified. Thus, Anonymous was able to get the ethnic realities of Transylvania and its near-abroad relatively correct, even if he confused a few names here and there.

While this may be fine and dandy for the Khazars and the Cumans and other people that no longer exist in Transylvania, the pertinent question remains: what of the Romanians? There are several reasons why we should believe the *Gesta* even without critically analyzing it: the geographical correspondence between Dacia and the regions inhabited by the Romanians, the occurrence of the Romanians in the earliest documents in Transylvania's history (including the first to explicitly mention ethnicities), the exponential growth in the number of sources that mention the Romanians in the fourteenth century (indicating that the Romanians were not few in number), and the fact that the Romanians were the majority of Transylvania's inhabitants in all reliable census data from its later history.[(Engel, 2001, p. 117)] It is hard to believe that all of these facts would line up by coincidence.

One also should consider that the Romanians are typically recorded in Transylvanian documents as inhabiting the foothills and forests of Transylvania. Some see this as evidence of secondary habitation, as if the Romanians arrived after everyone else had already occupied the good farmlands and were relegated to infertile foothills.[(Engel, 2001, p. 118)] There is however another possible interpretation: the Romanians were pushed to the mountains and forests by the waves of barbarian invaders that took the fertile lands by force.[(Berry, 1919)] Were we to believe that occupancy of the foothills indicates "secondary habitation" and that the Romanians are a splinter group of the Balkan Aromanians, then we should find the Aromanians in possession of at least one fertile valley in the Balkans which would be the homeland of all of the Vlachs. This is however not the case: the Aromanians were always crowded into the foothills while the Slavs occupied the fertile valleys, even though the Romans (the ancestors of the Aromanians) lived in the Balkans long before Slavs arrived. Furthermore, a Romanian migration into Southern Transylvania from the Balkans does not explain why the mountainous northern-most part of Transylvania, Maramureş, was dominated by

Romanians, though it is easily explained if habitation of the foothills indicates that Romanians from central Transylvania's valleys were pushed north and south by the invading Slavs, Avars, and other newcomers.

Historical arguments aside, attempts to buttress the *Gesta* with archaeology have proven (predictably) contentious. Romanian archaeologists tend to attribute certain finds to the Romanian, while Hungarian archaeologists invariable attribute such finds to other groups.[Madgearu, 2001] This has resulted in an intellectual stalemate, as Romanian and Slavic remains from the ninth century are difficult to differentiate.[Madgearu, 2005c] How someone made their house or what sort of pots they used had very little impact on what language someone spoke, and it is easy to imagine how Bulgarian influences upon the Romanians and vice-versa (as well as the constant Byzantine influence) can make it difficult to determine whose remains one is looking at.

The argument has therefore shifted to the linguistic arena and (predictably) the interpretations are again contentious. Numerous place names were mustered to support Romanian continuity. Several names for rivers are known to be preserved since antiquity, including Criş, Gălpâia, Mureş, Olt (*Grisia, Gilpil, Marisia, Altinum*)[Jordanes, 1960, XXII, 113] and almost every major river in the area including the Someş, Barzava, and Bârsa.[Paliga, 2006] Names of Slavic origin shared exclusively between Romanians and Slavs but not with Germans or Hungarians may also act as evidence. The Târnava river name is but one example, where the Romanian version is clearly derived from Slavic, while the Germans and Hungarians use *Kokel* or *Küküllő*. Had the Romanians only arrived in Transylvania in the thirteenth century, when the Slavs were practically gone from the region, one would expect the Romanians to have derived such river names from the Hungarian version, as the Saxons evidently had done. There is even no reason to believe that a Slavic river name is of Slavic origin, as Slavic words permeate the Romanian language. Sometimes the Slavic river name is a translation of an earlier Romanian name, as in the case of the river *Bistriţa* ("swift river"), which goes by the Slavic name in the valleys formerly occupied by the Slavs while going by the Romanian name *Repedea* in the hills. The preserved meaning points to a time in which the Romanians and Slavs coexisted in Transylvania, which contrasts with the Hungarian and German names for the river that are only adaptations of the original Slavic name.[c]

But perhaps the most important argument against Anonymous projecting the Romanians into the past is that he would have no reason to do so. Had Anonymous been wrong and the Romanians only wandered into Transylvania as a handful of shepherds in the thirteenth century, they would have been demographically insignificant.[Kosztin, 1997, p. 28] Anonymous' whole purpose in writing the *Gesta* was not idle ethnography, but rather to portray the Magyars as valiant heroes with legitimate right to rule over their whole kingdom.[Grzesik, 2003; Madgearu, 2001] If Anonymous really had no idea about Transylvania's history and simply chose a convenient enemy for the ninth century Magyars to fight, the Romanians would probably have been the last people he would have chosen. There was

---

[c] *Beszterce* in Hungarian and *Bistritz* in German.

nothing valiant or heroic about fighting a bunch of shepherds, nor could defeating such a small segment of Transylvania's population have justified their rule over the region, and Anonymous easily could have chosen more worthy opponents. It must be concluded that Anonymous would never have chosen the Romanians as enemies had he simply invented the contents of his work.

As the *Gesta* was intended to justify the political control over Transylvania, it is important to discuss the political events in the work. The first issue is that of the Magyar's route of invasion, and it is here that the *Gesta* gets a surprising detail right. Though the "Old Gesta" claimed that the Magyars passed through Transylvania on their way to Pannonia, Anonymous had the Magyars crossing through the Verecke Pass in modern Transcarpathian Ukraine instead.[Anonymous, 2008, XI-XII] A few Hungarian historians claim Anonymous was wrong and that the Old Gesta was right, believing that "Anonymus turned history on its head; his Hungarians, instead of moving westward from Transylvania, are depicted as entering that region from the west."[Makkai, 2002, p. 337] Anonymous' credibility however, is substantially bolstered both by archaeology and by history.

As mentioned earlier, that the Verecke Pass is rich in early Magyar graves, and the only location that has graves belonging to Magyars born outside of the Carpathian arch.[Lazar, 1997, p. 28] The resettling of the Szeklers border guards eastward is yet more evidence, as they were initially settled in western Crişana and gradually moved to the eastern Carpathians. This implies that the border, which can be easily identified due to the use of *indagines* (strips of deserted land), was originally far to the west and the Magyars gradually moved into Transylvania from that direction with the Szeklers following the advancing border.[Pop et al., 2005, p. 211]

In general the silence of written sources on the Hungarian expansion into the region has prompted historians to use subtle archaeological changes for the purposes of chronology. In the 1100's, several key fortresses dating from the early 11th century were repaired by the Hungarians (of course, after being destroyed by the Hungarians),[Curta, 2001c] indicating a consolidation of Hungarian power in the region. The culture of the graves in the region changed with the introduction of Western European traditions and the relocating of Szeklers. By looking at coins from discovered at archaeological sites, in particular the monarchs that they depicted, one can date the settlements from the reign of Geza II (1130-1162) to the year 1200, suggesting that the Hungarian push into eastern Transylvania occurred in this time. This is corroborated by cemeteries on the eastern Carpathians that, to quote archaeologist Florin Curta: "bears testimony to the fact, otherwise not clearly attested in written sources, that by 1200 the Hungarian kingdom had established its frontiers firmly on the Carpathians."[Curta, 2006b, pp. 351-352]

More importantly, the Magyars did not have the luxury of conquering Transylvania so early, even if they had intended it. The Magyars had just witnessed a crushing defeat at the hands of the Pechenegs that saw them driven out of western Ukraine..[Róna-Tas, 1999, p. 283] A simultaneous Bulgarian attack from the south ensured that the beleaguered and fleeing Magyars could only go northward around the Carpathians and through the Verecke Pass, settling as far from their attackers as possible.[Madgearu, 2005c]

The Magyars first settling in Pannonia is backed by both political and archaeological evidence. Southern Transylvania was at that time controlled by the Bulgarian empire,[Róna-Tas, 1999, p. 335] and certainly the Magyars would not have tried to escape the Bulgarians by fleeing into Bulgarian lands. Furthermore the Byzantines, ever eager to convert the barbarians to Christianity, sent a mission to the Magyars in 953, and to date the only Byzantine coins and crosses associated with that mission were found between the Mureş, Tisza, and Criş rivers, while no such things are found in central Transylvania, likely because there were no Magyars there to convert.[Madgearu, 2008b] It was only the collapse of the Bulgarian Empire in the late tenth and early eleventh century that resulted in a power vacuum in Transylvania that could be filled by the Magyar tribes.

As for the rulers of the Romanians: they are an entirely different kind of problem. Both Menumorut and Gelu are not mentioned in any other documents, which is more than a little troublesome. Anonymous does mention Glad's supposed descendant, Ohtum (Ahtum, Ajtony), who is also mentioned in the *Legenda Sancti Gerhardi*, but even this hardly makes Glad a more believable character. In fact Glad's entire life in the *Gesta* is co-opted from Ohtum's story in the *Legenda* in an obvious display of plagiarism.[MacArtney, 2009, p. 71] In other words: there is no evidence that these personages ever existed.

Most Hungarian historians believe the three leaders, and other personages of the *Gesta*, were inventions by the chronicler based on place-names or a play-on-words.[Engel, 2001, p. 11] One leader's name, Zobor the duke of Nitra (modern Slovakia), is believed to derive from the word sobor, meaning "church" in Slavonic, likely after a Benedictine monastery founded near the city. Hungarian historians likewise claim Gelu is derived from the place name Gilău in central Transylvania. Many possible origins of the name Menumorut have been proposed, including that it derives from the Hungarian word for Moravian (Marot) or from the Hungarian word for stallion because (as the *Gesta* saucily claims) "he had concubines."[Spinei, 2006, p. 87] Anonymous inventing the names is fairly reasonable as it is hard to imagine how he could recall the names of obscure princes that lived more than two centuries prior.

Though Anonymous likely invented the names of individuals, there is some indication that Anonymous did not invent the characters behind the names. Interestingly, in spite Menumorut's promiscuous nature (or perhaps because of it), later residents of the region did bear his name. Hungarian royal registers from the thirteenth century mention the family *Marouth* as controlling vast estates in the same region where Menumorut supposedly ruled three centuries prior.[Madgearu, 2004] The presence of both Hungarian and Romanian personal names in the family's register indicate a mixed Romanian-Hungarian family, that corroborates the *Gesta Hungarorum*'s account that

Menumorut married his daughter to a Magyar chieftain, thereby continuing his family's ownership of the region.[(Anonymous, 2008, LI)]

As for Menumorut's political circumstances, when the Magyars demanded his lands he rebuked them by claiming his right to rule was guaranteed by the Byzantine Emperor,[(Anonymous, 2008, XX)] but can this vassal status be verified? The Magyars were used by the Byzantines as a counterweight to the Bulgarians, but by 897 the Byzantines and Bulgarians had signed a peace treaty,[79] removing the need to keep the Magyars as allies; the Magyars were shortly afterward listed in the book *Taktika* as potential enemies of the empire.[(Madgearu, 2005b, p. 42)] By the early tenth century the Magyars were fond of making their neighbors host their invasions, Byzantines included.[(Stokes, 1961)] Liutprand of Cremona, writing in the late tenth century, claimed that the Magyars had subdued both the Bulgarians and the Greeks, a statement that, in spite of being entirely wrong, showed the open hostility between the Magyars and their neighbors.[(Liutprand, II, 7)] It is therefore easy to imagine that the rulers of tenth century Transylvania would use the backing of the Byzantine Emperor to ward off a Magyar invasion, and thus Anonymous' *Gesta* accurately reflects the political realities of that time.

Gelu's existence has also been cast into doubt, but more recent evidence suggests Anonymous was surprisingly accurate. Some believe Gelu's name was derived from the place name Gilău, but the opposite story, that Gilău is named after Gelu, is just as likely.[(Madgearu, 2005b, p. 259)] There are many examples in Romania where certain locations bear the names of local rulers, for instance Cenad being named after the Magyar chief Csanád.[(Curta, 2001c, p. 144)] Another theory that claims Gelu derives from the Hungarian personal name "Gyula", is unlikely as Anonymous uses both personal names in his work. There is simply no strong argument against Gelu's existence.

More importantly, the political realities of Transylvania make the existence of Gelu, or at least someone like Gelu, very likely. The rich salt trade in Transylvania offered an opportunity for the rise of small Romanian and Slavic states, reflected in the *Gesta*'s claim that Gelu ruled over Romanians and Slavs. The *Gesta* also described Gelu's dukedom as being ravaged by Pechenegs,[(Anonymous, 2008, XXV)] something easy to imagine given the Pechenegs neighbored Transylvania at the time.[(Spinei, 2009, p. 90)]. The *Gesta* also makes it clear that the Magyars who confronted Gelu centered their attacks on the salt mines.[(Madgearu, 2005b, p. 140)] Many of the fortresses attributed to Gelu by archaeologists show signs of destruction and ravages dating from the beginning of the tenth century,[(Rusu, 1997, p. 436)] presenting compelling evidence for the events described in the *Gesta*. Gelu's political independence described in the *Gesta* is likewise supported by his realm being outside of the reach of the Bulgarian Empire.[(Madgearu, 2005b, p. 140)] Whether by coincidence or not, the historic facts are accurately reflected in the *Gesta*.

The last ruler left to talk about is Glad. His story appears to have been heavily influenced by that of his supposed descendant Ahtum from the *Long Life of St. Gerard*. Glad and Ahtum's stories match up so closely that some concluded the author of the *Gesta* knew nothing about Glad except for his descendant Ahtum.[(Curta, 2001c, p. 145)] It has also been argued that Glad's name was derived from the nearby village of Galád.[(Illyés,]

[1992, p. 20] Anonymous ascribes the conquest of Glad's realm to Árpád's officers, and while the earliest Magyar artifacts date from the first decades of the tenth century (after Árpád's death),[Spinei, 2006, p. 94] we should not forget that the author of the *Gesta* is known for short anachronistic projections because Anonymous wished to ascribe as much as possible to Árpád, the main hero his story.[Madgearu, 2001, pp. 23-26] His dating of the Magyar incursion of Banat, while still wrong, is not so inaccurate as to be an invention. Furthermore, Anonymous statement that the Magyar invasion of Banat lead to raids into the Byzantine Empire matches the historical record of the Magyars first raiding into Byzantine territory in 934.[Spinei, 2006, p. 94] The surprising accuracy of the *Gesta* thus supports Glad's existence.

At the very least the archaeological record shows that someone was running the show in Transylvania. More than 120 settlements were discovered in the combined domains of the three rulers, some of which appeared well fortified and suggest a large agrarian population.[Georgescu, 1991, p. 15] Menumorut's supposed fortress of Biharea was discovered and dated to the eighth or ninth or century, and incidentally shows continuous habitation from the Dacian times to Middle Ages.[Madgearu, 2005b, p. 44] Gelu's fortress of Dăbâca has similarly been discovered and dated to the ninth century. Still, one needs to be careful in interpreting such finds: we cannot be sure of the owner, or even the function, of such fortresses, and one cannot simply make archaeology the handmaiden of written texts.[Curta, 2001c, p. 152] "Text-driven archaeology" can lead even the most well-intentioned historian to fallaciously fit archaeological finds into the narrow narrative of chronicles. We cannot pick up every archaeological find from tenth century Transylvania and ascribe it to Gelu, Glad, or Menumorut, simply because the *Gesta* states they lived in the region. At the very least however, we can use it to confirm the presence of some central authority, whatever it may have been.[Rusu, 1997, p. 435]

While historians may disagree on the details, the fundamentals of the *Gesta* need to be considered in an entirely different manner. Anonymous' main goal in writing the *Gesta* was to legitimize the rule of the Árpád dynasty,[Madgearu, 2005b, p. 110] and inventing the Vlachs as adversaries of the early Magyars would not have served his purposes at all. Had the Vlachs only recently migrated into Transylvania, they would not have been numerous nor politically significant, and moreover, the absence of any formal colonization would have meant that these Romanians possessed no political rights. The earliest documents attesting the Romanians however, make very clear reference both to their nobles and to their equal political rights in Transylvania.[Seton-Watson, 1922] Anonymous simply would have had no reason to invent the Romanians, and such an invention would not match up with the political realities of his time. The *Gesta Hungarorum*'s second purpose, to explain the rights of conquered population of Transylvania, also argues against a Romanian migration into Transylvania. Anonymous portrayed the Romanians and Slavs as swearing an oath of loyalty to Tuhutum, their Magyar conqueror, analogous to the *Pacta Conventa* between the Croatians and Hungarians designed to preserve the rights and autonomy of the Croatians.[Sălăgean, 2005, p. 127] Had the Romanians been recent immigrants, they would have had no rights, and it would have made little sense for Anonymous to insist that the Magyar conquest of Transylvania was essentially by agreement with the locals.

It would be very hard to imagine Anonymous making *faux pas* after *faux pas* in his *Gesta*. If we are to believe that the Romanians were not in Transylvania and were statistically insignificant in the thirteenth century, then Anonymous' writing would have matched neither his present nor the past. The idea that a handful of shepherds would have their own prince to fight the Magyars would have gotten Anonymous laughed out of the royal court at best. It would have been neither truthful nor politically beneficial for the king.

Anonymous's work was highly ambitious in its nature. No other medieval chronicler would attempt to cover the Hungarian conquest of their new country in such detail. The legacy of his work however, lay not in the details, but in the big picture. The reality is that Anonymous's statue graces a prominent spot in Budapest City Park for a reason. A critical analysis of his work confirms that Anonymous was not a spinner of fairy tales. Rather, the majority of his narrative is corroborated by archaeology and other sources.

The writers following Anonymous would have noticed and corrected his mention of the Romanians if it were false. If, as modern Hungarian historians argue, the Romanian immigration into Transylvania continued throughout the Middle Ages, [Lipcsey, 2006] then Anonymous' "mistake" involving the Romanians would have become all-the-more evident. Anonymous' trial will therefore be decided by the jury of his peers, the other Hungarian chronicles that followed in his wake, and by what they wrote of the Romanians in Transylvania during this nebulous time.

Works Cited

Anonymous. (2008). *Gesta Hungarorum* (M. Rady, Trans.).

Berend, N. (2006). *At the Gate of Christandom: Jews, Muslims, and "pagans" in medieval Hungary.* Cambridge, UK; New York, NY: Cambridge University Press.

Berry, J. (1919). Transylvania and Its Relations to Ancient Dacia and Modern Rumania. *The Geographical Journal, 53*(3).

Brătianu, G. I. (1988). *Marea Neagră [The Black Sea]* (Vol. I). Bucharest, Romania: Meridiane.

Curta, F. (2001). Transylvania around A.D. 1000. In P. Urbanczyk (Ed.), *Europe Around the Year 1000.* Warsaw, Poland: Wydawnictwo DIG.

Curta, F. (2006). *Southeastern Europe in the Middle Ages: 500-1250.* Cambridge, UK: Cambridge University Press.

Engel, P. (2001). *The Realm of Saint Stephen: A History of Medieval Hungary, 895-1526.* London, UK: Tauris.

Georgescu, V. (1991). *The Romanians: a history* (A. Bley-Vroman, Trans.). Columbus, OH: Ohio State University Press.

Grzesik, R. (2003). Sources of a story about the murdered Croatian king in the Hungarian-Polish Chronicle. *Izlaganje sa znanstvenog skupa, 30.*

Hupchick, D. P. (1995). *Conflict and chaos in Eastern Europe.* New York: Palgrave.

Illyés, E. (1992). *Ethnic Continuity in the Carpatho-Danubian Area.* Hamilton, Canada: Struktura Press.

Jordanes. *Getica* (Vol. XI).

Kosztin, A. (1997). *The Daco-Roman Legend.* Hamilton-Buffalo: Matthias Corvinus Publishing.

Kristo, G. (1996). *Hungarian History in the Ninth Century.* Szeged, Hungary: Szegedi Középkorász Műhely.

Lazar, I. (1997). *Transylvania: a short history.* Safely Harbor, FL: Simon Publications.

Lipcsey, O. (2006). *Romania and Transylvania in the 20th Century.* Budapest, Hungary: Corvinus Library.

Liutprand. Antapodosis.

MacArtney, C. A. (2009). *The medieval Hungarian historians: a critical and analytical guide.* Cambridge, UK: Cambridge University Press.

Madgearu, A. (2001). *Rolul Crestinismului in Formarea Poporului român.* Bucharest, Romania: BIC ALL.

Madgearu, A. (2004). Voievodatul lui Menumorout în lumina cercetărilor recente" (The Duchy of Menumorout in the light of the recent researches). *Analele Universității din Oradea. Istorie-arheologie, 11.*

Madgearu, A. (2005a). *The Romanians in the Anonymous Gesta Hungarorum.* Cluj-Napoca: Center for Transylvania Studies.

Madgearu, A. (2005b). Salt Trade and Warfare: the rise of the Romanian-Slavic military organization in Early Medieval Transylvania. In F. Curta (Ed.), *East Central & Eastern Europe in the Early Middle Ages.* Ann Arbor, MI: University of Michigan Press.

Madgearu, A. (2008). The mission of Hierotheos: location and significance. *Byzantinoslavica*(1-2), 119-138.

Makkai, L. (2002). Transylvania in the medieval Hungarian kingdom (896-1526). In B. Köpeczi, L. Makkai & A. Mocsy (Eds.), *History of Transylvania, vol I: from the beginnings to 1606*. Boulder, CO; New York, NY: Social Science Monographs.

Marácz, L. s. K. r. (1996). *Hungarian Revival: Political Reflections on Central Europe*. Nieuwegein: Aspekt.

Moga, I. (1994). *Les Roumains de Transylvanie au Moyen âge*. Sibiu: Centrul de Studii şi Cercetări Privitoare la Transilvania.

Nay, A. D. (1996). *The Origins of the Romanians*. Toronto, Canada: Corvinus Library.

Paliga, S. (2006). *Etymological Lexicon of Indigenous (Thracian) Elements in Romanian*. Bucharest, Romania: Centrul Mass Media Evenimentul.

Pop, I.-A., Barbulescu, M., & Nagler, T. (2005). *The History of Transylvania, I (up to 1541)*. Cluj-Napoca: CTS, Romanian Cultural Institute.

Rady, M. C. (2000). *Nobility, Land and Service in Medieval Hungary*. Basingstoke; New York: Palgrave.

Róna-Tas, A. (1999). *Hungarians and Europe in the Early Middle Ages: an introduction to early Hungarian history*. Budapest: Central European University Press.

Rusu, M. (1997). Continuitatea Daco-Romana in Perioada 275-568 *Istoria Romaniei. Transilvania*. (Vol. I). Cluj-Napoca, Romania: George Baritiu.

Sălăgean, T. (2005). Dextram Dantes, Notes on the Specificity of the Relations Between the Hungarian Conquerors and the Local Population in Northern Transylvania in the 10th-14th Centuries. In Z. K. Pinter, I. M. Ţiplic & M. E. Ţiplic (Eds.), *Relatii interetnice in Transilvania (secolele VI-XIII)*. Bucharest: Departamentul pentru Relaţii Interetnice.

Seton-Watson, R. W. (1922). Transylvania (I). *The Slavonic Review, 1*(2), 306-322.

Spinei, V. (2006). *The Great Migrations in the East and South East of Europe from the Ninth to the Thirteenth Century*. Amsterdam: Hakkert.

Spinei, V. (2009). *The Romanians and the Turkic Nomads North of teh Danube Delta from the Tenth to the Mid-Thirteenth Century*. Leiden, Netherlands: Brill.

Stephenson, P. (2000). *Byzantium's Balkan Frontier: A Political Study of the Norhtern Balkans, 900–1204*. Cambridge, UK; New York, NY: Cambridge University Press.

Stokes, A. D. (1961). The Background and Chronology of the Balkan Campaigns of Svyatoslav Iogrevich. *The Slavonic and East European Review, 40*(94), 44-57.

Sugar, P. F., Hanák, P. t., & Frank, T. (1990). *A History of Hungary*. Bloomington: Indiana University Press.

Toncilescu, P. L. (1996). *Cronica Notarului Anonymus*. Bucharest, Romania: Miracol.

Vásáry, I. (2005). *Cumans and Tatars: Oriental military in the pre-Ottoman Balkans, 1185-1365*. Cambridge, UK: Cambridge University Press.

Wieczorek, A., & Hinz, H.-M. (2000). *Europe's Center Around 1000: Contributions to History, Art and Archaeology*. Stuttgart: Konrad Theiss Verlag.

3. A "MISTAKE" REPEATED BY EVERYONE

Cross-referencing is standard practice in any scholarly endeavor. One person arriving at the wrong conclusion – even if the person was as educated and well-positioned as Anonymous – is possible. It is harder to imagine the same mistake being repeated by numerous authors, let alone all of them. It is only fair that Anonymous be judged by the works his peers, those being the other great Hungarian chroniclers. By looking at their works, we can judge if Anonymous was alone in stating that the Romanians were in Transylvania at the arrival of the Magyars, or if this was commonly accepted in medieval Hungary?

Simon de Kéza is regarded by many as Hungary's most famous thirteenth century chronicler. His most famous work, entitled *Gesta Hungarorum et Hunnorum*, was written in 1282, and though the title may lead us to think he based his work off that of Anonymous, today it is known that Simon never considered Anonymous's work nor even Anonymous's sources.[Armbruster, 1972, p. 32] Instead, he based his account on a later work by a certain "Master Akos" dated to 1270, which has not survived to the present day.[Engel, 2001, p. 121] The first half of Simon's work takes us through a rollercoaster ride of early, often factually incorrect, Hunnish history. Simon links the Huns to the Hungarians in order to justify the Hungarian occupation of Pannonia, believing that the Magyars had only taken back what had belonged to them.[Kersken, 2003, pp. 194-195] Clearly territorial irredenta based on "we were there first" arguments is not just a modern phenomenon. Simon makes a curious statement when describing the exploits/ravages of the Huns in the Balkans:

> "The citizens of Pannonia, Pamphylia, Macedonia, Dalmatia, and Phrygia, who had been exhausted by repeated raids and sieges from the Huns… quit their native soil and crossed the Adriatic Sea to Apulia [Italy]; the Vlachs, however, who had been their shepherds and husbandmen, elected to remain behind in Pannonia."[Keza, 1999, XIV]

The citizens Simon is describing are the Romans, and are the forebears of the Italians. Simon subtly affirms a link between the Romanians and Italians by making the Vlachs the shepherds of the Romans, perhaps showing the author was aware their common ancestry. In addition to perfectly echoing Anonymous's statement that Pannonia was populated by, among others, the "shepherds of the Romans,"[Keza, 1999, IX] Simon makes it very clear that these shepherds were in fact Vlachs. His viewpoint is thus clearly stated: the Vlachs were not only in Pannonia when the Hungarians arrived, but had been there since the days of Hunnic rule.

As for Transylvania, Simon specifies in chapter 21 of his work:

> "The Szeklers are in fact remnants of the Huns, and when they found out that the Hungarians were returning to Pannonia, they came to meet them on the borders of Ruthenia, and then joined with them in the conquest of Pannonia and acquired part of the country. However, this was not in the

plains of Pannonia but in the mountains, which they shared with the Vlachs, mingling with them, it is said, and adopting their alphabet."[(Keza, 1999, XXI)]

This passage has several interesting things to note. Firstly, Kéza obviously places the Vlachs in Transylvania since the Szeklers do not have some hidden colony in the Tatra Mountains of Slovakia. Simon also unwittingly proved himself ignorant of Cyrillic alphabet used by the Romanians and the runic script used by the Szeklers when he claimed they were the same. However, that he believes the Szeklers adopted their alphabet from the Romanians that the Szeklers and Romanians had been living among each other for a considerable amount of time, certainly long before 1282.

Historians wishing to prove Anonymous' exceptional incompetence in mentioning the Romanians have unsurprisingly taken ire with Simon's statements as well. Those who tried to slander Anonymous were thus faced with the necessity of having to slander Simon as well. One way they have tried to solve the problem caused by Simon's statements was to simply argue that he never mentioned the Romanians at all! This argument, also levied against Anonymous, is mostly based on how one interprets the Latin word *Blaci* that was used for Romanians. Hungarian authors tried identifying the *Blaci* and *Blacki* of Anonymous and Simon with a Turkic tribe, the Bulaqs, who supposedly migrated to Europe with the Bulgarians in the seventh century.[(Rásonyi, 1979, pp. 129-151)] The problem with this interpretation is that there is no historical or archaeological evidence to back it up.[(Spinei, 2009, p. 79)] The identification of a Turkic tribe with the "shepherds of the Romans" is another hurdle that the proponents of this idea have tried to sidestep entirely. Even István Vásáry, a Hungarian historian who has little love for Romanian continuity in Transylvania,[(Curta, 2005c)] stated that the Bulaq theory "cannot be corroborated by any sound evidence, and every historical argument speaks against it... in the case of the term *Blaci*, we cannot but conclude that it was used to designate the Vlakhs."[(Vásáry, 2005, p. 29)]

With the Bulaq theory utterly rejected, some proposed the idea that the *Blaci* were actually Franks and not Romanians. That the Franks were never near Transylvania poses an obvious problem to this theory, one that most of its proponents have ignored. Instead, they attempted to buttress their interpretation by using a completely unrelated "Chronicle of Bygone Times", written in Russia in the mid-eleventh century.[(Magocsi, 1996, p. 52)] The version we are most familiar with was written by a monk named Nestor in the cave-monastery of Kiev (sadly, not the only book we know of written by people living in caves). The chronicle was rewritten, manipulated, and mangled repeatedly, as with any document of political significance, and its final revision was written in 1118.[(Róna-Tas, 1999, p. 62)]

As a religious man, Nestor decided the most accurate place to start his book was after Noah's flood and the division of the world among Noah's sons. It is also here that we see his first mention of "Vlachs", in chapter 1:[d]

"After the flood, the sons of Noah (Sem, Ham, and Japheth) divided the earth among them. … At the same [Varangian] sea Varangians are living as far to the east as Sem's lot, and in the west their area reaches to the Anglians' and Vlachs' [Волошской] land. Other descendants of Japheth are the Varangians, the Svear [Swedes], the Normans, the Götar [Gotlanders], the Rus, the Anglians, the Galicians, the Vlachs [волохи], the Romans, the Germans, the Carolingians, the Venetians, the Franks and other peoples who live in areas from the west to the east."(Nestor, 2003, I)

A brief interlude about the Tower of Babel follows, with an (incorrect) description of how the Slavs settled in Europe. In Nestor's perception, the Slavs were the original inhabitants of Pannonia as, unfortunately, there were no living Illyrians or Celts around to contradict him. The Poles (frequently called "Lechs" or "Leşi") were, according to Nestor, driven out of Pannonia by the Vlachs:

"For when the Vlachs attacked the Danubian Slavs, settled among them, and did them violence, the latter came and made their homes by the Vistula, and were then called Lechs [Poles]. Of these same Lechs some were called Polyanians, some Lutichians, some Mazovians, and still others Pomorians."(Nestor, 2003, III)

Nestor then claimed that the Magyars invaders found the Vlachs in Pannonia and drove them out from there:

"The Magyars passed by Kyiv [Kiev] over the hill now called Hungarian, and on arriving at the Dnipro, they pitched camp. They were nomads like the Polovcians [Cumans]. Coming out of the east, they struggled across the great mountains, and began to fight against the neighboring Vlachs and Slavs. For the Slavs had settled there first, but the Vlachs had seized the territory of the Slavs. The Magyars subsequently expelled the Vlachs, took their land, and settled among the Slavs, whom they reduced to submission."(Nestor, 2003, VIII)

The theory that the "Vlachs" were not actually Vlachs at first seems believable. It is true that some of Nestor's "Vlachs" were undoubtedly not the Romanians. The first reference to the Vlachs (*Voloshski*) situated them on the western border of the Viking realm, alongside countries such as English, and must obviously refer to the French. Nestor then recounts how the Vlachs attacked the Slavs and subdued them in Pannonia, which loosely matches the expansion of the Frankish Empire in Pannonia. The Frankish

---

[d] There have been a variety of translation issues with this excerpt, and the nationalities seem to change from source to source. Therefore, I have provided below the nations translated from the original Cyrillic text: Varangians [варяги], the Svear [шведы], the Normans [норманны], the Götar [готы], the Rus [русь], the Anglians [англы], the Galicians [галичане], the Vlachs [волохи], the Romans [римляне], the Germans [немцы], the Carolingians [корлязи], the Venetians [венецианцы], the Franks [фряги].

Empire was later called the "Holy Roman Empire", though Voltaire aptly indicated that it was "neither holy, nor Roman, nor an empire." The third mention recounts how the Hungarians drove out the "Vlachs", which roughly corresponds to the collapse of Frankish power in Pannonia at the arrival of the Magyars. Some historians have connected the dots in these interpretations and concluded that the "Vlachs" are therefore not Romanians, but Franks.(Kosztin, 1997, p. 27)

While this might seem believable, the theory becomes outlandish in its claim that Anonymous, who likely could not even read the Cyrillic Nestor used to write his chronicle, somehow acquired Nestor's chronicle, misinterpreted Nestor's "Vlachs" as Romanians and, through his supposedly characteristic incompetence, placed the Romanians in Pannonia.(Köpeczi, 2002) Finally, it requires for us to believe that Simon de Kéza was duped by Anonymous' chronicle and took it completely verbatim without even thinking of contradicting the "obvious mistake", resulting in him also placing the Vlachs in pre-Hungarian Pannonia. Thus, one small ambiguity by Nestor was propagated as a mistake in every single Hungarian chronicle that followed. If any chronicle thereafter mentioned the Romanians, they were just propagating Anonymous' error. Apparently, nobody bothered to check the facts.

The "Frankish Theory" is largely supported by the Slavs use of "Vlach" to describe a variety of people that spoke in a language derived from Latin. Thus, the first passage, referring to the Norman Vikings that settled in France in 911 and conquered England in 1066, obviously intended for the "Vlach land" to be France.(Nestor, 2003, p. 237f) There could be an argument that Nestor was referring Italy and the Normans of Sicily that arrived in the eleventh century, but Sicily, much like Romania, is prohibitively far from England, making France the most likely choice.

This is certainly not the first time that Nestor's vagueness has hindered gleaning historical fact from his text,(MacArtney, 2009, p. 73) and the meaning of "Vlach" in the next two passages are also open to interpretation. It is impossible to state for certain who the "Vlachs" were that drove out the Danubian Slavs.(Illyés, 1992, p. 22) To believe they were the Latin French is geographically impossible. To interpreted "Vlach" as meaning the Eastern Franks (i.e. the Germans) is possible, but highly unlikely. The Slavs never used the term "Vlach" or "Voloch" to designate Germanic people like the Franks, but rather used the word *Nemtsy* when referring to Germanic people, and Nestor used both *Nemtsy* and *Vlach* in his text.(Lind, 2001, pp. 481-500) Perhaps most concerning is that Nestor already mentioned the Franks and the Carolingians (i.e. the people of Charlemagne, Holy Roman Emperor) without actually calling them Vlachs. Nestor list of the people of Jafet included "the Vlachs, the Romans, the Germans, the Carolingians, the Venetians and the Franks."(Nestor, 1884, pp. 2-3) Nestor undoubtedly would not have used a completely different name for the same people *in the same sentence*.

Some believe Nestor could have been referring to actual Romans. It is interesting that Pannonia's Roman inhabitants survived into the Dark Ages in spite of its far greater exposure to barbarian invasions than Dacia. Burial sites at Keszthely (derived from the Latin *castellum*) and Pecs in Hungary show tell-tale signs of Late Eastern Roman or

Early Byzantine style,[Vida, 2008a, pp. 31-32] and the opulence of their burials signifies that these were hardly poor and oppressed prisoners of the barbarians.[Vida, 2008b, p. 37] They almost entirely disappeared by the eleventh century however, being assimilated by the Magyars. Nestor's unclear chronology on when the "Romans took over the lands of the Slavs" could mean that he was referring to the ancient Romans conquering Pannonia, wrongly concluding that the Romans conquered it from the Slavs instead of the Celts and Illyrians. Roman life in the region, still evidenced in the ninth century "Keszthely Culture", was finally snuffed out shortly after the arrival of the Magyars, likely not due to warfare but due to cultural assimilation into the Slavic and Magyar mass.[Madgearu, 2005b, p. 76]

Still another possibility is that Nestor's Vlachs were Italians, particularly Italian missionaries in Pannonia. The *Life of Methodius* for instance, speaks of the dissatisfaction the Slavs had with Catholic priests, who had come from "the Vlakhs, the Greeks and the Nemtsy." Historian John Lind identified the aforementioned Vlakhs with the Italians,[Lind, 2001, p. 490] an explanation more reasonable than having to invent a Vlach mission at a time when there was no organized religion in Romania. However, the Vlachs were described by Nestor as imperialistic and militant people, hardly fitting of the handful of missionaries that likely reached Pannonia from Italy. Missionary work may have been heavy-handed in the Middle Ages, but few could imagine a few venerable priests seizing lands from entire tribes as the Vlachs do in Nestor's work.

One other option remains: Nestor's Vlachs were Romanians. A number of Romanian place names have been discovered in medieval Hungary that date from the early eleventh to the late thirteenth century; documents even refer to a village known as *villa Vlach*![Madgearu, 2005b, pp. 77-80] While it is true that many chronicles did not explicitly mention the Romanians in Pannonia prior to Nestor, the same could also be said of the Keszthely Romans. Nevertheless, the Keszthely Culture is hard to deny given the preponderance of hard archaeological evidence. Furthermore, there is no evidence of a migration of the Romanians to Hungary after the Magyar arrival, so it is likely that the Romanians, like the Keszthely people, had remained in the region since Roman times.

Lastly, we cannot forget that Hungarian chronicles make the same reference to the Romanians. True, this argument would be circular if Anonymous' and Simon de Kéza's mention of the Romanians were based on a misinterpretation of Nestor's work, but there strong evidence that this is not the case.[Pop, 1996] Anonymous used many sources but Nestor was not among them. His education in Paris or Orleans[Anonymous, 2008] ensure that he knew many classical and Latin works of his time,[André Du Nay, 1980; Németh, 2003] not surprising for a man educated in Catholic Europe. His Paris-based education however, would have made it very unlikely that he knew of Cyrillic (the alphabet Nestor used), let alone any texts written in that script. Not only was Anonymous likely ignorant of Cyrillic, but there is also no evidence that Nestor's chronicle ever circulated in Hungary during his lifetime.[Pop, 1996, p. 78] We can safely use Anonymous' and Simon de Kéza's chronicles to cross-reference Nestor's work.

Some of the most imaginative arguments have been used to suggest that Anonymous used Nestor's work. László Makkai for instance claimed that the spelling of the word *Blach* in the *Gesta* came from the Nestor's chronicle,(Köpeczi, 2002, p. 340) claiming that if Anonymous used a Western source he would have written it as *Blac* instead. It is amazing that an entire argument can hinge on one letter. Yet there are numerous cases where Western writers used the spelling *Blach*: Pope Gregory IX in 1237 called John Asen II of Bulgaria "*dominus Blachorum et Bulgarorum.*"(Ahrweiler, 1998, p. 9) The cleric Ansbert that passed through Hungary during the third crusade called Emperor Peter of Bulgaria as "*Kalopetrus Blachorum dominus.*"(Vasiliev, 1958, p. 442) Even if we were to admit a direct Slavo-Byzantine influence in Anonymous's use of *Blachorum* (and there is no reason why we should, given the abundance of contemporary Latin chronicles using the same word), the term could just as easily have come from Nicetas Choniates, a Byzantine author living in the late twelfth century and who used the spelling *Blachi* (exactly matching Anonymous's spelling) repeatedly in his works.(Choniates, 1984, pp. 43, 46, 88, 154, 336, 429)

Makkai's second argument that, Anonymous must have used Nestor since both chronicles mention Slavs and Vlachs, is incredibly circular. According to Makkai, Anonymous mentioned Vlachs because he used Nestor's work, and Anonymous used Nestor's work because he mentioned Vlachs.(Köpeczi, 2002, pp. 240-241) In the end we must remember that the chronicles arose in two different cultural milieus, written in two different languages, with two different alphabets, and whose authors lived almost a century apart. All in all, there is no evidence that Anonymous had even heard of Nestor, and claims of Nestor influencing Anonymous remain unsubstantiated.

Simon de Kéza blindly copying what Anonymous had written is another tenuous idea. Simon built off of a new literary tradition established by Master Akos, ignoring the earlier *Gesta Hungarorum*. If Anonymous, as a writer from Central Hungary, could be considered ignorant Transylvania's demographic status due to his geographic distance, the same could not be stated of Simon. Simon was living in Transylvania when he compiled his work,(Brezeanu, 1999, p. 234) in essence putting him in the midst of the Romanians.(Armbruster, 1972, p. 32) He would have known if the Romanians were recent immigrants, yet he clearly repeated Anonymous's "mistake." That Simon never used Nestor's work is more than evidenced by his ignorance of the Cyrillic alphabet. Clearly then we are dealing with three independent authors who all support each other one the crucial argument: that the Romanians were in Transylvania (and in Pannonia) in 896.

Simon's work clearly was the inspiration of later chronicles. His words were repeated in the *Chronicon Pictum* written in 1358 in an almost word-for-word fashion.(Péter, 1992, p. 77) The Vlachs are again mentioned in chapter six as remaining in Pannonia after Attila's death, and in chapter ten when the Szeklers settle among them in Transylvania Three other sources also repeat Kéza's assertion: the *Chronicon Posoniense,* the *Chronicon Dubnicense,* and the *Chronicon Budense.*(Armbruster, 1972, p. 33) All three chronicles quote Simon almost verbatim.

Yet there is another source that describes the Magyar encounter with the Vlachs: the *Description of Eastern Europe* (*Descriptio Europae Orientalis*), composed in 1308 by an anonymous French monk. The text provides a very detailed and credible account of the pastoral way of life of the Balkan Vlachs.[Anonymous, 1916, IV] On the topic of the Balkan Vlachs, the author stated that they were formerly the shepherds of the Romans, settled in Pannonia, the pasture of the Romans, but were driven out by the Hungarians and sought refuge in Macedonia, Achaia, and Thessalonika. It is incredible that this corresponds so closely to Nestor's work, and yet it is very unlikely the two authors ever knew of each other. The author does not, for instance, mention that the Vlachs had subdued the Slavs in Pannonia, as Nestor did, and it is likely the anonymous author had taken the fact of a Vlach expulsion from a local tradition.

To what extend are the chroniclers after Simon de Kéza relevant to events that occurred more than four centuries before the texts were written? It should be remembered that fourteenth century saw an explosion of documentation in Hungary regarding the Romanians,[Engel, 2001, p. 117] and chroniclers of that time would have been more knowledgeable of the Kingdom's Romanian population, and of any possible immigration. If it were as Hungarian historians claim, that "the scale of Romanian settlements in the 14th century was far greater than in earlier times, and it cannot be attributed to natural increase in the Romanian community"[Köpeczi, 2002, p. 488] then it seems all the more bizarre that the Hungarian chroniclers would persist in their "mistake" of placing the Romanians in Transylvania before the Hungarians.

Only one conclusion is possible: these texts all corroborate each other in their mention of the Romanians. The statements made by Anonymous are echoed in Nestor's chronicle, in Simon de Kéza's work (including the chronicles that copied him), and in the *Description of Eastern Europe*. There is no explanation that would cause later chronicles to repeat Anonymous's "mistake" of placing the Romanians in Transylvania and Pannonia, unless it actually were not a mistake; otherwise, at least one chronicler would have noticed the glaring error. Certainly the chronicles written later, like the *Chronicon Pictum*, might have had a harder time reconstructing the past, but the growth in documentation throughout the fourteenth century would have produced a clerical class more knowledgeable of their present situation.[Molnár, 2001, pp. 47-49] It would take a veritable "conspiracy of ignorance" to produce a situation in which Romanians were continuously settling into Transylvania but every chronicler continued to ignore it, instead opting to repeat the notion that the Romanians were in Transylvania at the time of the Magyar arrival.

Of course, it was the Middle Ages, and accounts of the world could be truly fantastical. The *Descriptio Europae Orientalis* even claimed tigers and unicorns could be found in Bulgaria! This fantasy portrayal of the world however, largely disappeared with the Renaissance and the emergence of humanism. In general "humanist historians differed from their medieval predecessors especially in their newly won conviction that, if evidence was adequate, it could settle decisively even highly contentious matters."[Fryde, 1983, p. 5] It is therefore important to determine if this new way of thinking resulted in the dismissal of Romanian continuity in Dacia, or if it strengthened the conviction of writers in such an idea.

The first humanist to mention the Romanians was Poggio Bracciolini, writing in 1451 that the Romanians are the descendants of the Romans colonized by Trajan, likely receiving this information from hearsay.(Armbruster, 1972, p. 58) While some argue Bracciolini does not connect the Romanians to Dacia as he does not mention Dacia explicitly, it is not so hard to imagine what region Bracciolini was referring to since the only other regions Trajan conquered were in the Middle East, and Bracciolini could hardly have meant that the ancestors of the Romanians were Trajan's colonists in Mesopotamia. In any case, it would be only a short while later that Pope Pius II (1458 -1464) would explicitly state that the genesis of the Romanians was the result of Roman colonization in Dacia. (Vékony, 2000, p. 4)

Those texts, while technically still humanist in nature, did not draw upon the diverse array of evidence one associates with humanist histories. The first to truly apply a humanist method to Romanian history was Antonio Bonfini (1427-1502), a man that resided for his later life at the royal court in Hungary. He was the first to develop Romanian continuity in Dacia as a scientific theory.(Pascu, 1982, p. xxii) The crux of his argument was the Latinity of the Romanian language:

> "Because the Romanians are descendants of the Romans, a fact that even today is attested by their language, a language that, even though they are surrounded by diverse barbarian peoples, could not be destroyed.... even if all kinds of barbarian attacks flooded over the province of Dacia and the Roman people, we can see that the Roman colonies and legions that had been established there could not be annihilated."(Bonfinius, 1568, p. 542, III, 9; Treptow & Bolovan, 1995, p. 75)

Bonfini also used other arguments to demonstrate the continuity of the Romanians, including: the inscriptions and Roman ruins found in Transylvania, the Roman toponyms in the region, as well as the name of the Romanians.(Armbruster, 1972, p. 60) He believed the Romanians sprang from the fusion of Romans and Dacians in antiquity.(Kellogg, 1990, p. 15) The idea, with minor variations, was used by almost every other writer of the time. Of particular note is Francesco della Valle, who travelled at least twice through the Romanian principalities.(Armbruster, 1972, p. 80) He was undoubtedly surprised to discover the similarities between Romanian and Italian. Claiming to have learned of the origin of the Romanians from Orthodox monks in Wallachia, he states:

> "The emperor Trajan, after conquering this country, divided it among his soldiers and made it into a Roman colony, so that these [Romanians] are descendants, as it is said, of these ancient colonists, and they preserve the name of the Romans."(Armbruster, 1972, p. 82; Treptow & Bolovan, 1995, p. 135)

Some have tried to argue that Francesco was not retelling a local tradition, but rather claim that he used "a learned source, because a popular tradition would be about Oriental people, Greeks, *etc.* - not exclusively about Rome, from which only a very small part of the population of Dacia Traiana came."(Alain Du Nay, Nay, & Kosztin, 1997, p. 4) However, as the ethnic makeup of Dacia's colonists was only rediscovered in the nineteenth century, a much earlier local tradition could not have known about the multiethnic nature of the colonization. It is hard to imagine Romanian peasants walking around with copies of ancient Roman texts under their arms. Furthermore, Francesco's was not the most kind writer on the Romanians, often describing them as "corrupted" Romans, and therefore had no reason to invent a theory that would have glorified their ancestors. To date, there is no evidence that such a tradition, of Romanians hailing from Greeks and the like, even existed, and all other texts speak only of the tradition of Roman-Romanian continuity in Dacia. Neofit of Crete, the metropolitan of Wallachia and a Greek Orthodox monk not too dissimilar from those described by Francesco della Valle, confirmed the existence of a wide-spread folk tradition of Roman antiquity among the Romanians.(Năsturel, 1969)

Writers in the seventeenth and eighteenth century almost unanimously supported the Roman origin of the Romanian people. One example is Valentin Franck von Franckenstein (1643-1697), a Saxon writer from Transylvania, wrote that the Romanians were the oldest inhabitants of Transylvania and descended from the Trajan's colonists in Dacia.(Franckenstein, 1696, p. 26) Franckenstein used the full spectrum of evidence to support his argument, including the Romanian language, the Roman ruins and coins of Transylvania, as well as Trajan's Column.(Armbruster, 1972, p. 216) From the writings of Hungarian historian András Huszti in 1791(Huszti, 1791, pp. 135-137) to the famous *Decline and Fall of the Roman Empire* by the British historian Edward Gibbon, historians acknowledged Romanian continuity in Dacia as indisputable. Gibbon was aware of Emperor Aurelian's withdrawal from Dacia but concluded that the province had "a considerable number of its inhabitants [i.e. Romans] who dreaded exile more than a Gothic master."(Gibbon, 2004, p. 317) Though Gibbon was infatuated with the Romans, he certainly had little love for the Romanians, referring to the as "degenerate Romans", this did not stop him from assigning the Romanians a pure Roman ancestry. The consensus among Europe's intellectuals was summarized by Emperor Joseph II of Austria: the Romanians were "without doubt the oldest and most numerous inhabitants of Transylvania."(Sassu, 1973, p. 131)

This is not to say that the humanists were always right. Some aspects were undoubtedly too difficult to resolve using humanist methods, and thus resorted to myth. Pope Pius II for instance, failing to find a convenient explanation for the term "Vlach", invented a Roman general *Flaccus* from that gave the Romanians their name.(Kellogg, 1990, p. 14) In other cases history was manipulated and falsified in order to accommodate political realities. The Transylvanian Saxons sought to justify their political rights by pretending they descended from the Dacians, thereby making themselves ancient inhabitants whose rights were inalienable.

It is impossible, however, to suggest that the Roman ancestry of the Romanians was invented for political purposes. From the sixteenth century onward the very name "Romanian" became synonymous with "Orthodox" and "non-noble" in Transylvania.(Hitchins, 2001, pp. 85-86) It would make little sense for foreign historians to ascribe a glorious and noble ancestry to people lacking their own nobility, and it would almost have been inconceivable to suggest that non-Catholics could be Roman! Politics was clearly not a motivating factor in making the Romanians descended of the Romans. Rather, the theory was based on the sciences of the times. It is telling that the theory of Dacian origin of the Saxons was universally rejected by non-Saxons, while the Roman origin of the Romanians was universally supported, even by Hungarians.

We cannot help but notice the more scientific approach taken by the humanists. Linguistics, archaeology, and written classical sources were used to demonstrate that colonization had occurred in antiquity, and in general the application of a scientific method to history only strengthened the theory of Roman-Romanian continuity in Dacia. Even though authors had knowledge of the Latin populations in the Southern Balkans, the idea that the Romanians would have migrated northward during the Middle Ages, without anyone recording it, was rightfully seen as laughable.

So when did Hungarian historiography start to deny Romanian continuity in Dacia, and what had caused this divergence? Some Hungarian political publications (by lobbies like the "Committee for Transylvania") attempted to assert that the shift in theories was caused by the emergence of linguistics as a science and the fact that "Rumanian origins were not studied too in-tensely [sic]" and the Hungarian theory was a "fresh look upon a problem hitherto not studied by modern scientific methods."(Lötc, 1980, p. 14) Is such an explanation truthful, or is it more than coincidence that the attempt to refute Daco-Roman Continuity coincided with the emergence of nationalism and Austro-Hungary's attempts to save its multinational empire in the face of emerging nation-states?

Works Cited

Ahrweiler, H. (1998). Byzantine Concepts of the Foreigner: The Case of the Nomads. In H. Ahrweiler & A. LAiou (Eds.), *Studies on the internal diaspora of the Byzantine Empire*. Cambridge, MA: Harvard University Press.

Anonymous. (1916). *Descriptio Europae Orientalis*. Cracow, Poland: Gebethner.

Anonymous. (2008). *Gesta Hungarorum* (M. Rady, Trans.).

Armbruster, A. (1972). *Romanitatea Românilor: Istoria Unei Idei [The Romanity of the Romanians: the History of an Idea]*. Bucharest, Romania: Editura Academiei Republicii Socialiste Română.

Bonfinius, A. (1568). *Rerum Ungaricarum decades quatuor cum dimidia*.

Brezeanu, S. (1999). *Romanitatea Orientală în Evul Mediu : de la cetăţenii romani la naţiunea medievală [The Oriental Romanity in the Middle Ages: from Roman citizens to medieval nation]*. Bucharest, Romania: All Educational.

Choniates, N. (1984). *O City of Byzantium: annals of Nicetas Choniates* (H. J. Magoulias, Trans.). Detroit: Wayne State University Press.

Curta, F. (2005). Review of Cumans and Tatars: Oriental Military in the Pre-Ottoman Balkans, 1185-1365 by István Vásáry (Cambridge, 2005). *Canadian Journal of History, 40*.

Engel, P. (2001). *The Realm of Saint Stephen: A History of Medieval Hungary, 895-1526*. London, UK: Tauris.

Franckenstein, V. F. v. (1696). *Breviculus origines nationum et praecipue Saxonicae in Transylvania*. Sibiu: Cibinii Transylvanorum.

Fryde, E. B. (1983). *Humanism and Renaissance Historiography*. London, UK: Hambledon Press.

Gibbon, E. (2004). *The history of the decline and fall of the Roman Empire* (Vol. I). Holicong, PA: Wildside Press.

Hitchins, K. (2001). *The Idea of Nation among the Romanians of Transylvania, 1700-1849*. Paper presented at the Nation and National Ideology: Past, Present, and PRospects, Bucharest, Romania.

Huszti, A. (1791). *Ó és újj Dácia*: Diénes.

Illyés, E. (1992). *Ethnic Continuity in the Carpatho-Danubian Area*. Hamilton, Canada: Struktura Press.

Kellogg, F. (1990). *A History of Romanian Historical Writing*. Bakersfield, CA: C. Schlacks.

Kersken, N. (2003). High and Late Medieval National Historiography. In D. M. Deliyannis (Ed.), *Historiography in the Middle Ages*. Leiden, Netherlands: Brill.

Kéza, S. d. (1999). *Gesta Hungarorum*. Budapest: CEU Press.

Köpeczi, B. (2002). History of Transylvania: from 1606 to 1830. In B. Köpeczi, L. Makkai & A. Mocsy (Eds.), *History of Transylvania, vol II: from the beginnings to 1606*. Boulder, CO; New York, NY: Social Science Monographs.

Kosztin, A. (1997). *The Daco-Roman Legend*. Hamilton-Buffalo: Matthias Corvinus Publishing.

Lind, J. H. (2001). Scandinavian nemtsy and Repaganized Russians. The expansion of the Latin West During the Baltic Crusades and its Confessional Repercussions. In S. Hunyadi & J. Lászlóvszky (Eds.), *The Crusades and the Military Order:*

Expanding the Frontiers of Medieval Latin Christianity. Budapest, Hungary: CEU Press.

Löte, L. L. (1980). *Transylvania and the theory of Daco-Roman-Rumanian continuity*. Rochester, NY: Committee of Transylvania.

MacArtney, C. A. (2009). *The medieval Hungarian historians: a critical and analytical guide*. Cambridge, UK: Cambridge University Press.

Madgearu, A. (2005). *The Romanians in the Anonymous Gesta Hungarorum*. Cluj-Napoca: Center for Transylvania Studies.

Magocsi, P. R. (1996). *A History of Ukraine*. Toronto, Canada: University of Toronto Press.

Molnár, M. (2001). *A Concise History of Hungary*. Cambridge, UK: Cambridge University Press.

Murray, A. V. (2001). *Crusades and Conversion on the Baltic Frontier*. Aldershot: Ashgate.

Nasturel, P. S. (1969). *Les Journal des Visites Canoniques de Metropolite de Hongrovalachie Néophyte le Crétois*. Athens, Greece: Pepragmena Philologikos Syllogos.

Nay, A. D. (1980). The Daco-Rumanian continuity Theory: Origins of the Rumanian Nation and Language. In L. L. Löte (Ed.), *Transylvania and the theory of Daco-Roman-Rumanian Continuity*. Rochester, NY: Committeee of Transylvania.

Nay, A. D., Nay, A. D., & Kosztin, A. r. d. (1997). *Transylvania and the Rumanians*. Hamilton, Canada; Buffalo, NY: Matthias Corvinus Library.

Németh, G. (2003). The Origins of the Tale of the Blood-drinking Hungarians. In C. Levai & V. Vese (Eds.), *Tolerance and intolerance in historical perspective*. Pisa, Italy: Clioh's Workshop.

Nestor. (1884). *Chronique de Nestor* (L. Leger, Trans.). Paris, France: L'Ecole des Langues Orientales Vivantes.

Nestor. (2003). *Nestors krønike: beretningen om de svundne* (G. O. Svane, Trans.). Højbjerg, Denmark: Wormianum.

Pascu, Ş. (1982). *A History of Transylvania*. New York, NY: Dorset Press.

Péter, L. (1992). *Historians and the history of Transylvania*. Boulder, CO: East European Monographs.

Pop, I.-A. (1996). *Românii şi maghiarii în secolele IX-XIV: Geneza statului medieval în Transilvania [The Romanians and Magyars in the 9th-14th centuries: the genesis of the medieval state in Transylvania]*. Cluj-Napoca, Romania: Centrul de Studii Transilvane.

Rásonyi, L. (1979). Bulaqs and Oguzs in Medieval Transylvania. *Acta Orientalia Academiae Scientiarum Hungaricae, 33*, 129-151.

Róna-Tas, A. (1999). *Hungarians and Europe in the Early Middle Ages: an introduction to early Hungarian history*. Budapest: Central European University Press.

Sassu, C. (1973). *Rumanians and Hungarians: historical premises*. Bucharest, Romania: P. Georgescu-Delafras.

Spinei, V. (2009). *The Romanians and the Turkic Nomads North of teh Danube Delta from the Tenth to the Mid-Thirteenth Century*. Leiden, Netherlands: Brill.

Treptow, K. W., & Bolovan, I. (1995). *A History of Romania*. Iaşi, Romania: Center for Romanian Studies.

Vásáry, I. (2005). *Cumans and Tatars: Oriental military in the pre-Ottoman Balkans, 1185-1365*. Cambridge, UK: Cambridge University Press.

Vasiliev, A. (1958). *History of the Byzantine Empire, 324-1453* (Vol. 2). Wisconsin: University of Wisconsin Press.

Vekony, G. (2000). *Dacians, Romans, Romanians*. Budapest, Hungary: Corvinus Library.

Vida, T. (2008a). Conflict and Coexistence: the local population in the Carpathian Basin under Avar Rule (sixth to seventh century). In F. Curta & R. Kovalev (Eds.), *The Other Europe: Avars, Bulgars, Khazars and Cumans*. Leiden, Netherlands; Boston, MA: Brill.

Vida, T. (2008b). Conflict and Coexistence: the local population of the Carpathian Basin under Avar rule (sixth to seventh century). In F. Curta & R. Kovalev (Eds.), *The Other Europe in the Middle Ages: Avars, Bulgars, Khazars, and Cumans*. Leiden, Netherlands; Boston, MA: Brill.

4. THE (AUSTRO-HUNGARIAN) EMPIRE STRIKES BACK

The principle "never build on a bad foundation" is as applicable to history as it is to architecture. The writers and historians from the eleventh to the eighteenth century had created a substantial foundation, if not a complete edifice, for the theory of Daco-Roman-Romanian continuity. From Britain to the Ottoman Empire, historians were in agreement that the ancestors of the Romanians were the Romans of Dacia. They were aware of Aurelian's abandonment of Dacia, but they concluded that moving all of the Latins out of Dacia was impossible, especially given that a Latin population still inhabited Transylvania. Why then, did Hungarian historians almost unanimously abandon this theory in the late nineteenth century?

To be fair, the idea that Roman Dacia was completely evacuated by the Romans was expressed prior to that time, predictably by a Hungarian humanist: István Szamosközy (1570-1612). Studying in Italy, he is considered by some to be Hungary's first archaeologist. He had published a work on the Roman ruins of Dacia in 1593, and concluded that Transylvania, Moldova, and Wallachia were all inheritors of a Dacian patrimony. Szamosközy's work dealt mainly with the vestiges of the Romans, adding rather poetically that the Romans had left not only lifeless, but also living remnants. In his opinion, their colonists had become the Romanians, this being evident from the fact that Romanian was related to the other Latin languages.[Zamosius, 1598, p. 12]

Szamosközy completely reversed his opinion on the matter a few years later, when he wrote his work *On Hungarian Origins* (*De Originibus Hungarorum*) around 1600. Far from the glorious past ascribed to the Romanians in his previous work, Szamosközy claimed in his new publication that the Romans were not the ancestors of the Romanians, for the Emperor Gallienus settled all of Dacia's Romans South of the Danube when he evacuated the province. Szamosközy became the first historian to question the continuity of the Romans in Dacia.[Georgescu, 1991, p. 300] Instead of the Romans, Szamosközy instead decided the Romanians were far too barbaric, and made the Dacians ancestors of the Romanians. He concluded that the Dacians had learned Latin from the Romans, such that those Romanized Dacians would become the Romanians.[5]

What could possibly have happened from the time frame 1593 to 1600 that could so have shaken Szamosközy's faith in his own words? One is almost led to believe he had unearthed a Roman inscription saying "I came, I saw, I left." Szamosközy's motives behind making this new theory become evident from his circumstances. The period from 1593 to 1601 witnessed the reign of a man who was to become one of Romania's national hero: Michael the Brave. Michael's contemporaries, both in Transylvania and in Austria, were more than happy to sing praises to him and his people so long as he was busy fighting the Ottomans.[Xenopol, 1914, pp. 173-224] Michael however, had bigger plans. He invaded Transylvania in 1599 on the pretext of restoring it to the Austrian emperor, but rather had himself crowned its ruler. Michael's tumultuous reign would end in an uprising by the Hungarian nobility, backed by a veritable Habsburg conspiracy; he was even assassinated by the Habsburg soldiers sent to help him!

Szamosközy appears to have suffered much under Michael's reign, for his work spares no expense in the insults hurled at Michael, referring to him as a "barbarian" and a loathed and hateful tyrant.(Daniel Prodan & Lăzărescu, 1971, p. 89) Szamosközy's hatred for the Romanians was however, placed at odds with his education: how could he reconcile the supposed "barbarian" nature of the Romanians with their noble Roman pedigree? The solution was simple: the Romanians must descend from Romanized barbarians! To seal the deal, Szamosközy made the argument that all the actual Romans had been evacuated from the province.

Szamosközy in many ways echoed the words of Kekaumenos. Both authors had a bone to pick with the Vlachs, and both satisfied their vendettas by assigning them ignoble, barbarian ancestry. The only problem was that while Kekaumenos did not need any evidence to make his claims, Szamosközy had to explain the language of the Romanians, whose Latin character was well-known by the seventeenth century. Szamosközy therefore concluded that the Dacians had all been Romanized. It was a strange idea to propose during the height of the Renaissance, and it won Szamosközy few admirers. The German historian Toppeltinus referred to the theory as "ridiculous",(Armbruster, 1972, p. 140) and no historian until the late eighteenth century adopted the idea that Dacia was evacuated.

Some have tried to argue that Szamosközy was a forebear to the theory held by many modern Hungarian historians that the Romanians originated in the Balkans and only migrated to Transylvania after the Magyars had settled there.(Rady, 1988, p. 483) Upon closer inspection however, one realizes the only aspect Szamosközy's text has in common with the modern Hungarian theory is the idea that the Romans had completely evacuated Dacia. Szamosközy however, did not believe the Romanians withdrew with them! He certainly didn't believe the Romanians had come to Transylvania at a later date. He tried distancing the Romans from the Romanians, but the idea of separating the Romanians from Dacia was ridiculous. Ironically, Szamosközy's "Romanizing the locals" idea was more akin to Daco-Roman Continuity than the other theories that argued for "pure Roman blood". It is impossible, therefore, to claim Szamosközy was a forebear for the modern Hungarian theories.

It was only in the late eighteenth century when the Roman continuity would again be contested, this time by a Swiss-born Austrian: Franz Josef Sulzer.(Boia, 2001b, p. 47) Sulzer's career was mostly in the military and in law and he is remembered as an amateur historian.(Ellis, 1998) His three volume work *The History of Transalpine Dacia*, written in 1781, proposed a novel theory on the origin of the Romanians. In his opinion the Romanians were not descended of the Roman colonists of Dacia, for the Romans had evacuated in 271 AD, nor even from the Romanized Dacians. Instead, the Romanians had formed South of the Danube, in Moesia and Thrace, and only moved North of the Danube in the twelfth and thirteenth centuries.(Părăușanu, 2008, p. 109)

Sulzer's theory was politically motivated.(T. Diaconescu, 2000) The Romanians of eighteenth century Transylvania did not have any nobility or political rights, and to the eighteenth century mind of Sulzer, "serf" and "Roman origin" did not mix. Scholars of the time were aware of this "contradiction," and many theories were brought about to explain it. András Huszti, a Hungarian contemporary of Sulzer, proposed the exact opposite argument: the Romanians were serfs precisely because they were Romans! Unlike the colonized populations of Transylvania, that had been granted privileges by the Hungarian kings, Huszti saw the Romanians as long-time residents of Transylvania that the Hungarians conquered by force, and consequently lacked rights. To substantiate this claim he (erroneously) postulated that the Hungarian word for Romanian – oláh – derived from the Turkic word for slave.(Huszti, 1791, pp. 135-137)

This historical problem became a political problem when the Romanians began to ask themselves the same question. The Romanian "national awakening" started with the formation of a Romanian Greek-Catholic church in Transylvania in 1698. The Romanians could continue to practice all of their tangible Orthodox Christian rites and traditions. The only demand was to accept a few theoretical Catholic additions, including the *Filioque* clause, the concept of purgatory, and the supremacy of the Pope.(Barta, 2002) In exchange, the Romanians were allowed to attend schools, including Jesuit academies, and would no longer be considered second-class citizens. In typical Italian fashion, the Papacy had made the Romanians an offer they could not refuse.

The Romanians who accepted this offer would play a fundamental role in the rise of Romanian nationalism. Transylvania's Romanians had up to that point been overwhelmingly rural and uneducated. The Transylvanian Romanians who accepted the union, and were consequently educated in Jesuit academies and enjoyed political rights, assumed political leadership of their co-nationals by default.(Hitchins, 1996, p. 199) The graduates of Greek-Catholic schools formed a cohesive Romanian intellectual circle, the first to raise fundamental questions regarding Romanian nationhood and the status of Romanians in Transylvania.(Hitchins, 2001)

The first of such influential activists was Inocenţiu Micu-Klein. Micu-Klein's studies led him to question the position of the Romanians in Transylvania's social fabric and began a long (though fruitless) campaign for equal rights for the Romanians. He submitted numerous petitions to the Imperial court in Vienna, asking for the fulfillment of equal rights for the Romanians, repeating his words before the Transylvanian Diet in 1744 as the sole representative of the Romanians; one representative for the majority of Transylvania's population! Klein's arguments for equal rights were astonishingly fundamental:

> "The Romanian nation is inferior to no other nation, neither in its character, nor in its culture. ... For we since the time of Trajan, even before the entry of the Saxon nation in Transylvania, were the owners of this regal land and up to today we own entire towns, even though we are oppressed by thousands of miseries and tasks from the stronger [nations]... Not only are the Romanians by far the oldest inhabitants of the hills and valleys of Transylvania, but they are also the most numerous."(Bunea, 1900, p. 123; Roc, 2005, pp. 114-115)

The Transylvanian Diet was taken aback; they were unwilling to accept a Romanian nation even existed, let alone grant them rights! The Romanians were only ever referred to as "Vlach plebeians."(Tóth, 1998, pp. 89-90) In a world defined largely by medieval principles, the idea of "nation" was inherently linked to possessing a nobility, which the Romanians sorely lacked.(Hitchins, 2001) This presented a curious challenge, as the Romanians could not be granted rights and "nation" status since they had no nobility, and the Romanians could not gain a nobility since they had not rights as a "nation." Micu-Klein's demands were seen as disturbing to the peace in Transylvania. He was forced into exile in Rome, where he died. Though he never saw the fruition of his dream, his efforts inspired many that followed in his wake.

Micu-Klein's efforts were not entirely in vain, but the issue of Romanian rights was far from solved. He had succeeded in granting the Romanians a noble class (the Uniate clergy) with equal rights, but Romanians were still not viewed as equals. The "Romanian problem" persisted through a whole new generation of Romanian scholars spearheaded by Samuil Micu (1745-1806), Gheorghe Șincai (1754-1816), and Petru Maior (1760-1821). They lead what became known as the "Transylvanian School", a group of Romanian intellectuals who lobbied for the recognition of the Romanians as a nation in Transylvania, often using history to buttress their demands.(Hitchins, 2002) The Saxons and Hungarians, worried about the fate of civil order in the province if the Romanians got any brash ideas, turned to attacking the root of the problem: the origin of the Romanians. The Hungarians and Germans would secure political and territorial hegemony in Transylvania indefinitely if only they could erase the past of the Romanians.(Romocea, 2004, p. 163) It is here where Sulzer, a man married to a Transylvanian Saxon noble, entered the arena.

The arguments Sulzer used to deny Romanian continuity were at best semi-scientific. They included: (Xenopol, (1884) 1998, p. 11)

1) Romanian lacks words of Hungarian origin or from other languages, which it should have contained had they been continuously present in Transylvania.
2) The similarity of Romanian and the languages of the Balkan Vlachs.
3) The Romanian Orthodox faith must have formed south of the Danube. Had they been in Transylvania, the Magyars would have converted them to Catholicism.
4) The lack rights and liberties among the Romanians, and also lack their own nobility, is unnatural were they the descendants of Romans.
5) The absence of documents referring to the Romanians in Transylvania throughout the Dark Ages.

Sulzer concluded that the Romanians formed South of the Danube, in Moesia, Thrace, and Macedonia, as a result of mixture of the Thraco-Moesians, the Romans, and the Slavs.(Ionescu, 2002) In his theory, the Romanians only migrated onto their present territory in the twelfth and thirteenth centuries. Since these exact same arguments were used by later partisans of this theory, and even persist to modern day, it is important to spend a brief amount of time on each before accepting or rejecting them.

In short: most of Sulzer's arguments do not support his conclusion. The fifth argument, while still universally maintained by Hungarian scholars,[Rady, 2000, p. 91] is a logical fallacy. The absence of documents cannot be turned into documentation of absence. Sulzer made several mistakes in his analysis of documents as well, when he tried to create the impression of a Romanian migration in the thirteenth century. For instance, he chosen to use the Diploma of the Knights of Saint John written in 1247, claiming that the territories mentioned therein that were "hitherto" (*hactenus*) controlled by the Romanians, were under Romanian control for at most two years prior, rather than the much longer timeframe implied.[Ionescu, 2002] Given Sulzer's inexperience in history, it is to this date not sure if Sulzer had done this on purpose or unwittingly.

On the absence of sources, it is telling that Sulzer and modern partisans of the Immigration Theory never explain why the Romanians are similarly absent from documents in the Balkans up until the tenth century. Here it must be pointed out that an absence of Romanians from documents north of the Danube could at least seem plausible since for much of the Dark Ages the region was inhabited by illiterate barbarian tribes. It is by far harder to reconcile the absence of Romanians from documents were they to have been south of the Danube, in the heart of the Eastern Roman Empire. As British historian Robert Seton-Watson pointed out: "the very theorists who have banished the Roumanians from Transylvania for lack of records, are driven to admit an even more complete and far more perplexing lack of records regarding the Roumanians in their alleged Balkan home."[Seton-Watson, 1934, p. 13] The ethnographer T.J. Winnifrith, in his study on the Balkan Vlachs, concluded that "above all we can place little reliance on any argument from silence to prove that no Vlachs were present",[Winnifirth, 1987, p. 39] an argument equally applicable north and south of the Danube. Sadly this form of argumentation is, as already mentioned, universally used by modern Hungarian historians on this subject.

The fourth argument betrays Sulzer's motivation. In his mind, the Romanians did not have rights because they were recent immigrants, and they could not be granted rights because of their supposed status as recent immigrants! This however runs counter to the historical evidence. The Romanians had representative landowning nobility well into the thirteenth century in Transylvania, one that was gradually diminished and displaced by a Magyar aristocracy. The position of the Romanian nobility, and of all Orthodox Christians, diminished with the draconian edicts issued by King Louis I of Hungary in the late fourteenth century. The systemic exclusion of the Romanians from the nobility of Transylvania was formalized in 1437, with the establishment of the *Unio Trium Nationum* ("Union of Three Nations"), an alliance by the Hungarian, Szekler, and Saxon nobilities. The Hungarian nobility assimilated what remained of the Romanian nobles and the Romanians were left without any political representation.[Sedlar, 1993, p. 64]

Two types of Romanian nobles existed due to these policies: one which was ennobled due to valorous deeds in the Ottoman wars, retaining feudal control of their lands, and the other, which became a subordinate middleman between the Romanian serfs and the Hungarian nobility. The former converted to Catholicism and were assimilated into the Hungarian nobility, noted names including the Hunyadi and Dragffy families. The knezi which were middlemen and remained Orthodox Christians gradually lost even their residual powers. Sulzer's argument is therefore historically incorrect.

The third argument is easily disproven by the Byzantine missions north of the Danube throughout the early Middle Ages. The ruler of Transylvania in the early eleventh century, Gyula, is known to have been an Orthodox Christian, and the existence of several Greek and Bulgarian monasteries are confirmed in Hungary throughout the early Middle Ages.[Molnár, 2001, p. 19] Therefore, the conversion of the Romanians could just as easily have happened north of the Danube. Hungary also possessed a large Orthodox Ruthenian population, one that has no ethnic link to the Balkans.

What we do know is that Catholic proselytism in Transylvania intensified primarily in the fourteenth century,[Pop, 2003] after the Romanians would have supposedly settled there. Antonius Bonfini wrote that by 1380 only one third of the Hungarian kingdom was Catholic, even after substantial and heavy-handed Catholic proselytism. Sulzer's settlement of the Romanians in Transylvania still prior to this point would not have spared them of these efforts.

By far Sulzer's strongest arguments were (1) and (2), both based on linguistics. Balkan linguistics was a recent field, pioneered by Swedish philologist Johann Thunmann. Thunmann was the first to link Albanian and Romanian via a common linguistic substratum – a basal language that influenced the two modern descendants – publishing the idea in 1774.[Thunmann, 1774, pp. 169-366] His theory was supported by Bartholomeus Kopitar, who concluded that the common elements between the two languages could be derived from a Thracian-Dacian-Illyrian base, transmitted to the Albanians and inherited by the Romanians. Thunmann was familiar with an Aromanian scholar, Teodor Cavallioti, a forerunner in comparative linguistics, and even reproduced Cavallioti's trilingual dictionary (in Greek, Albanian, and Aromanian; a veritable Balkan Rosetta Stone).[Friedman, 2000] In addition, Thunmann gained was further aided by a Macedoromanian student.[Tanaşoca, 2001] Thunmann pioneering academic investigation into Romanian origins[Brezeanu, 1984, p. 64] concluded that the Romanians had formed north of the Danube while the Macedoromanians had formed separately to the south. More importantly, Thunmann's detachment from the region's politics meant he had no ulterior motive behind his investigation.

Sulzer's motives can be understood by the political climate in which he published his work. In 1781 Emperor Joseph II of Austria proclaimed equality between the Romanians and the other nations of Transylvania.[Stoicescu, 1980, p. 76] The good days of medieval feudalism were drawing to a close, but the magnates of Transylvania were not going to relinquish their political stranglehold easily. It was difficult to justify keeping the "sons of Rome" in shackles... but it could have seemed more palatable to the imperial court in Vienna if the Romanians were rebranded as latecomers or illegal immigrants, and Sulzer thus used Thunmann's findings to make the completely opposite conclusion.

Given the political nature of Sulzer's work, Hungarian historians have tried to find an antecedent for the theory; a conception untainted by politics. An attempt was made to credit John Lucius with the theory's inception in 1666.(Vékony, 2000, pp. 19-20) Lucius's writings however, bear only cursory similarity to the modern Immigration Theory. While Lucius was the first author to note the silence of sources on the Romanians north of the Danube, he did not conclude that the Romans evacuated Dacia. Rather, the Romanians traced their origin, according to him, from the Romans left behind by Aurelian in Dacia and Romanized people brought north of the Danube by the Bulgarians in the seventh to ninth centuries.(Brezeanu, 1984, p. 39) Lucius was only stating that the number of Romanians increased due to immigration to the north caused by the Bulgarians at a date before the arrival of the Magyars.(Stoicescu, 1980, p. 18) This can only loosely be regarded as a precedent to the theories supported by today's Hungarian academics.

Sulzer was the first to completely deny Roman continuity in Dacia, but he was not the founder of the modern Immigration Theory. Sulzer's work did not find acceptance among Europe's historians, and it was either ignored or discredited, (Părăuşanu, 2008, p. 110) in spite of claims otherwise by modern Hungarian historians.(Vékony, 2000, p. 22) Only two writers supported Sulzer's theory: Carol Eder and Johan Christian Engel.

Eder's work was a polemical response to a Romanian petition to the imperial court, the *Supplex Libellus Valachorum*, that asked for the Romanians to be granted equal status with the other nations, "to the same place it held... in the year 1437 [before the *Unio Trium Nationum*]."(Trencsényi & Kopeček, 2006, p. 281) It called for the end of anti-Romanian discriminatory practices in Transylvania.(Hupchick, 2001, p. 204) The authors of the *Supplex* are unknown but likely included the leading figures of the "Transylvanian School." The *Supplex*'s use of history to support its demands is evident:

> "The Romanian nation is by far the oldest of all nations in today's Transylvania, because it is a certain and proven thing based on historical evidence – of a tradition that was never discontinued, of the similarity of languages, traditions and customs that spring from the Roman colonies brought here to Dacia, at the beginning of the second century by the Emperor Trajan."(Trencsényi & Kopeček, 2006, p. 279)

The *Supplex* was diplomatically phrased and stressed the military and strategic value of the Romanians as the largest ethnic group in the region, but the opposition of the Transylvanian Diet was unrelenting. Eder, a Transylvanian Saxon, joined the uproar. His response was a direct reproduction of the *Supplex* with an "addendum" of 59 points – longer than the *Supplex* itself – criticizing the historical argumentation for the demands. Eder largely reiterated Sulzer's thesis, but also attempted to discredit the *Gesta Hungarorum* of Anonymous, of which Sulzer was not aware. Eder spared no expense when it came to insults, and his work had started a whirlwind polemic between the Hungarians and Saxons on the one side, and the Romanian intellectuals on the other.(Daniel Prodan & Lăzărescu, 1971, pp. 95-96)

The other man who genuinely accepted the withdrawal of the Roman population from Dacia in 271, J.C. Engel, did not fully believe Sulzer's argumentation in light of the *Gesta Hungarorum*. Engel's instead promoted his own theory in 1794, where he tried to reconcile Sulzer's theory with the newly discovered *Gesta*. He took the work of John Lucius in 1666, erased the inconvenient parts regarding the remnant Roman colonists in Dacia, and concluded that the Romanians descended from the Roman-Byzantine and Slavic prisoners of the Bulgarians who were settled North of the Danube in 818.[Kellogg, 1990, p. 18] His evidence included the Greek words in Romanian as well as the name Vlach, which he erroneously believed derived from the Volga river in central Asia, the homeland of the Bulgars. Engel erased the Roman-Romanian link but also placed the Romanians in Transylvania early enough to fight the Magyars, as was recorded in the *Gesta*. His theory posed a problem to Hungarian aristocrats as it gave the Romanians chronological precedence.

No one else adopted Sulzer's theory for almost a century. The furious attempt to erase the Roman-Romanian connection resulted in arguments approaching the absurd. Márton Bolla proposed that the Romanians arrived in Transylvania from the Volga after the Hungarians,[Brezeanu, 1984, p. 61] by suggesting that the nomadic way of life of the Vlachs could only have arisen there. Such absurd theories continued even into the twentieth century, when a Croatian historian proposed that the Vlachs were descended from Trajan's African cavalrymen![Malcolm, 1996, p. 75] For the opponents of continuity, it did not matter where the Romanians hailed from, so long as it was from *somewhere else* and their arrival was after everyone else.

Sulzer's theory was convenient, but it was unbelievable even to those who wished it were true. Several prominent Hungarian historians dismissed the idea: Stephen Katona, József Benkő, Mathias Peter Katancsich, Count Joszef Kemeny, and András Huszti all denounced the idea. Continentally, Sulzer's theory did not even produce a ripple, but not because people were unaware of it, as Sulzer was a member of the "St. Andrew" Masonic lodge, an organization renowned for spreading ideas in the Age of Enlightenment.[Ionescu, 2002] The reason why the theory was rejected was it did not make any sense. In the battle between Sulzer and Thunmann, historians like Theodor Mommsen, Leopold von Ranke, and Heinrich Kiepert all sided with Thunmann. Charles Upson Clark succinctly put it that "Mommsen, Ranke and Kiepert came to Thunmann's rescue" and Romanian continuity in Dacia "is to-day generally agreed (outside of Hungary!)"[C. U. Clark, 1932, p. 38]

It was only in 1871 that a new writer, Robert Rösler, revived the theory of Romanian migration in his work *Romanian Studies* (*Romänische Studien*). Rösler's was a highly educated individual, being a philologist trained in Vienna, Graz, and Lvov. His work however, blatantly vilified the Romanians and dismissed their demands for equal rights; his writings "thereby crossed a subtle border from the writing of academic history to the writing of history for political purposes."[Ellis, 1998] It was after Rösler's publication that international academia became divided on the issue of Romanian continuity.

Rösler's motives for resurrecting the argument become clear when we consider his political circumstances. In 1867 the Austrian government conceded to Hungarian demands for equal representation, resulting in the creation of the Austro-Hungarian Empire; a state where not one, but two nations dominated the national minorities of Slavs and Romanians. Austria's strategy with the Hungarians was simply summarized by Austria's prime minister: "you manage your hordes and we'll manage ours."[(Wawro, 2000, p. 206)] Robert Seton-Watson gave the most apt description of what followed:

> "The settlement of 1867, which left the Magyars in complete political control of their half of the Dual Monarchy (subject only to Croatia's autonomous position, which lies outside my present scope) went to their head like strong wine. With almost complete unanimity their statesmen and politicians set before themselves the Magyarisation of Hungary as the supreme aim of the state, and to this fatal end, equally undesirable and impossible of attainment, they devoted a very large part of their energies during the fifty years that followed."[(Seton-Watson, 1925)]

The Hungarians feared that if they could not somehow Magyarize all of the kingdom's inhabitants in a very short time, then the whole kingdom was going to collapse in the face of the emerging nation-states. Of course we know they were right: Magyarization largely failed – even though it was vigorously pursued[(Neamțu & Cordoș, 1994, p. 54)] – and the kingdom collapsed in 1920. It may however, also be the case that the alienation of national minorities caused by the policies of cultural suppression is exactly what caused the state's collapse. One thing was clear from the new policies: the Romanians, by their very culture, were the enemy of this new state. To top it all off, the Romanians had not ceased their demands for equal rights, but had moved on to a more practical level of emphasizing the demographic majority of the Romanians in Transylvania, as well as the fact that they paid the most taxes, but historic arguments were not abandoned either.[(Jelavich, 1989, p. 328)]

The Magyars saw themselves as the "civilizing light" for their lowly subjects. The political nature of Rösler's book is evidenced in almost every paragraph. Rösler even went so far as to state that Romanian desires for equal rights were "hilarious… stemming from the hybrid and heated mentality of small people."[(Rösler, 1871, p. 140)] The compromise of 1867 was also significant because it erased Transylvania's autonomous status, making it directly subordinate to Budapest. This nullification turned the Romanians from a regional demographic majority into a minority of a much larger state. It should not come as a surprise that Rösler's publication came about at a time when the Romanians were very vocal in their displeasure at the loss of Transylvania's territorial identity.

Rösler's arguments were much the same as Sulzer's but more developed, given his high level of education. Rösler believed the Romanians came from an unspecified region south of the Danube.[(Bulei, 2005, p. 16)] The same argument from silence was used as evidence for the absence of Romanians in Transylvania and played a central role in Rösler's work, as was acknowledged even by positive reviewers of his time.[(Leskien, 1872, p.]

33) Rösler also focused on the lack of old Germanic words in Romanian, which supposedly would be unexpected had the Romanians lived under Gothic occupation north of the Danube. Rösler was able to use the relation between the Albanian and Romanian languages to suggest that this relation could only have developed if the Albanians and Romanians lived in a common homeland throughout the Dark Ages, which Rösler believed was close to Albania and as far away from Transylvania as possible. Rösler also necessarily dismissed the *Gesta Hungarorum*, throwing a plethora of *ad hominems* in Anonymous's direction.

Seeing as Rösler's ghost has survived to the present day, it is important that we give his arguments some consideration. The argument from silence is a logical fallacy, though a rather persistent one in Hungarian history books. The linguistic arguments however, pose a different problem. The lack of "Old Germanic" words in Romanian is perplexing and has received much attention. It continues to be a staple of advocates of the Immigration Theory[Illyés, 1992, p. 260; André Du Nay, 1996, p. 243] though several linguists and philologists were able to identify thirty Romanian words of Old Germanic origin,[Poruciuc, 2008, p. 221] though some debate the etymology.[Sala, 2005, p. 18] The number may be small, but then again, so is the number of words relating Romanian to Albanian, which is at most 150, so it something significant to consider.

More importantly, Rösler's theory does not explain the absence of Germanic words in Romanian as placing the Romanians South of the Danube would have not spared them from Germanic influence. It is actually easier to explain if one keeps the ancestors of the Romanians in Dacia, given that the Goths largely ignored the former Roman province and only settled in Trajan's Dacia after 375 AD.[A. Diaconescu, 2004; Madgearu, 2001, p. 34] In contrast, Gothic raids in the Balkans date from the middle of the third century, even killing the Roman Emperor Decius in 251 near Odessus (modern day Varna, Bulgaria). Raids into the Balkans continued throughout the third century and the fourth century saw the establishment of a permanent Gothic presence in the Balkans, when Roman authorities resettled the Goths that were driven out of Moldova by the Huns in the fourth century. The Gothic refugees in the Balkans were so numerous that Roman officials even remarked "who wishes to know this [their number] would wish to know how many grains of sand are on the Libyan plain."[Marcellinus, XXI, 3, 6] The move proved to be a strategic disaster, culminating in the Goths defeating the Roman army at the battle of Adrianople in 378. Endless Gothic uprisings forced the Romans to concede lands for permanent Gothic settlement in the empire. It was a humiliating circumstance, but Roman spin doctors did their best to paint it otherwise, suggesting that it was better to conquer the Goths by friendship and fill Thrace with Gothic labourers than useless Gothic corpses.[P. Heather, 1996, pp. 135-137; Themistius]

The Goths soon spread all over the Balkans, reaching the Southern tip of Greece in 396, and would remain a strong presence for more than a century. Gothic influence in the Balkans only ended in 496 when the Ostrogoth leader Theodoric defeated Odovacar, the Germanic king of Italy that deposed the Western Roman Emperor in 476. Theodoric had thereby established a Gothic kingdom in Italy, and most of the Goths would leave the Balkan Peninsula after this date, preferring life in their own kingdom.[Fine, 2000, p. 22]

146

The Gothic presence in the Balkans lasted well over a century or even two centuries if we consider raiding and trade, and it stands to reason that if the Romanians adopted any words from the Goths, they could just as easily have done so south of the Danube frontier. Rösler's proposal to move the Romanians south would not have spared the Romanians of Germanic influence. This argument is unfortunately still echoed by modern Hungarian historians.

Rösler's Romanian-Albanian connection is even more contentious because the origin of the Albanians is in itself controversial. The Illyrian origin of the Albanians is often assumed by modern historians, but it came under fire from linguists in the twentieth century. Vladimir I. Georgiev, a prominent Bulgarian linguist, pointed out that the only reason Albanian is considered to originate from Illyrian is because Albanian does not have anything in common with the other Balkan languages: "the Albanians have often been regarded as the heirs of the ancient Illyrians, although there are no other data supporting such a claim. In the same way, the Bulgarians might be considered as Thracians [the ancient inhabitants of Bulgaria] if other Slavonic peoples and languages were not known."[(Georgiev, 1966)] Georgiev instead proposed that the Albanians were of Daco-Mysian origin, their homeland being in northern Bulgaria or Serbia. He presented several arguments that against an Illyrian origin, including:

1) The geographical names of Illyrian origin in Albania show a Slavic intermediary.
2) The Albanian words borrowed from Latin show characteristics typical of Eastern Balkan Latin as opposed to Western Balkan Latin, namely a the lack of Italian influence. The Albanians therefore did not borrow these words when residing in territories corresponding to modern day Albania.
3) All Albanian maritime terminology is borrowed from other languages, indicating that the Adriatic coast was not a part of their original homeland.
4) The lack of ancient Greek loan words in Albanian indicates they originated in the northern Balkans, away from Greek influence.
5) The Albanians are not mentioned in written documents until the ninth century even though texts referring to regions in modern day Albania existed since the fourth century. Georgiev adds that this is different from the case of the Romanians in Dacia since after Aurelian's withdrawal Dacia became a proverbial *terra incognita*, the first place names in Romania being mentioned only in the tenth century.
6) The Latin words in Albanian are of proto-Romanian origin.
7) The words shared between the Albanians and the Romanians are inherited from a Dacian substratum also found in Romanian.[(Georgiev, 1966)]

Jean W. Sedlar added to the arguments against Illyrian-Albanian continuity. Place names in Albania suggest the presence of a Slavic population in the area in early Middle Ages, but place names of Albanian origin are missing altogether from that period. The earliest uncontested document referring to the Albanians dates from the eleventh century, adding once again that the absence of documentation is not comparable to that of the north-Danubian Romanians since Albania (unlike Dacia) lay well within the Roman Empire. He assessed that "these facts strongly suggest that the ancestors of the Albanians could not have been present in their present country since the days of the Roman Empire."(Sedlar, 1993, p. 7)

Linguistics has only strengthened Georgiev's argument, revealing Albanian and Illyrian are not even part of the same linguistic branches of Indo-European. There are two language groups of Indo-European, *centum* and *satem*, named after the way members of both groups state the number "one hundred", though they differ in other features as well. Latin, for instance, is a *centum* language since the Latin term for one hundred is, well, *centum*. This division causes some problems for an Illyrian-Albanian connection, as Illyrian was a *centum* language while Albanian is a *satem* language. The *satem* nature of the Albanian language could be explained by making it a descendant of Thracian or Dacian, both of which exhibited *satem* characteristics.(Boardman, 1982, p. 848) While modern Romanian has preserved the word *sută* for one hundred from the Dacians,(Paliga, 2006, p. 182) Romanian became a member of the *centum* family by grace of the cultural annihilation the Romans inflicted upon the Dacians. This provides a logical explanation for how, in the case of Romanian, a *centum* language was able to develop out of a *satem* substratum. There is however no explanation by which Albanian could have crossed the divide in the opposite direction. The only way to explain the *satem* nature of Albanian is to consider it a descendant of Daco-Mysian or Thracian.

Historical facts also make an Albanian migration into the southern Balkans more believable than a Romanian migration in the opposite direction, especially when one considers that the barbarian invaders of the Roman Balkans all came from the north. The Morava valley in particular served as the primary invasion route for the barbarians, and was thus a region from which an indigenous population would have fled.(Fine, 2000, p. 11) This gives the Albanian migration something completely lacking for a hypothetical Romanian movement in the opposite direction: a motive. The Albanians' ancestors were (in such a scenario) forced south by the Goths and Slavs who took over their homeland in the northern Balkans. On the other hand, a migration of the Romanians towards lands already occupied by other people does not make a lot of sense. Georgiev's arguments thus have strong historical backing and require careful consideration.

Even if we were to ignore all of these arguments and believe in an Illyrian origin of the Albanians and Romanians, this still would not be reason to believe the Romanians originated in Albania. The Illyrians were quite widespread and inhabited the entire Western Balkan peninsula, not just Albania, stretching all the way north to Dalmatia and Pannonia.(Wilkes, 1995, p. 183) Though there has been a tendency by historians and linguists to refer to anything non-Celtic in the Western Balkans as "Illyrian", it still cannot be denied that the borders of ancient Illyria far exceeded those of modern Albania, and likely stretched to the Morava valley bordering Romania and the Adriatic coast in Dalmatia (modern Croatia).(Pounds, 1973, p. 51) Roman rule in the Balkans had forced the Illyrians even further east. The Illyrian relocation began with the reign of Emperor Augustus, who moved Illyrian tribes to the Danube in the first century AD.(Wilkes, 1995, p. 82) Trajan even settled entire Illyrian communities in Roman Dacia.(Wilkes, 1995, p. 224) Even if the Romanian words shared with Albanian are of Illyrian origin – a hypothesis that goes against all evidence – the Romanians would not need to go on an elaborate millennium-long journey to explain these words. They could just as easily have learned them from the Illyrians in and around Dacia.

Lastly, we should remember that the Dacians, Thracians, and Illyrians were very similar and distinguishing one barbarian from another was a confusing ordeal to most of the ancient authors. There was constant intermingling between the Thracians and the Illyrians,(Wilkes, 1995, p. 86) and archaeologists have not been able to definitively identity even major tribes in this region as either Illyrian, Thracian, or even Celtic. Not one verifiable inscription has survived in the Illyrian language.(Woodard, 2008, p. 8) Only five inscriptions in Dacian exist, and no lengthy texts in Dacian or Thracian have been discovered.(Price, 2000, p. 120) The inability to distinguish between the three groups based on scant linguistic evidence has resulted in a slew of confusing conjugations by modern linguists and historians, including Thraco-Illyrian,(Jordan-Bychkov & Jordan-Bychkov, 2002, p. 132) Thraco-Dacian,(Schulte, 2009, p. 234) Daco-Illyrian,(Pei, 1976, p. 158) Daco-Moesian,(Woodard, 2008, p. 9) Thraco-Moesian,(Cunliffe, 2001, p. 377) and even the almost offensive Thraco-Daco-Illyrian.(Olmsted, 2001, p. 57) Rösler's adamant support for an Illyrian origin for 150 Romanian words shared with the Albanians is even more contentious when we consider that modern linguists have difficulty distinguishing between the various Balkan tribes.

It is unlikely that the Romanians picked up the terms they share with the Albanians through contact with them in the Balkans. The few words the two languages have in common are too weak a relation to support the claim that the Romanians and Albanians shared a homeland in the ninth century. Recent linguistic evidence indicates Albanian and Romanian split apart for some time, probably before the Roman era.(Quiles & López-Menchero, 2009, pp. 94-95) It is entirely possible that the Albanian language originated from Illyrian and that Romanian originated from the Romanization of the similar Dacian language. This is all the more likely given that some of the substratum words preserved in Romanian do not exist in Albanian.

Rösler's Albanian argument requires several assumptions. Firstly, one must assume the contentious Illyrian origin of the Albanians. Secondly, one has to believe the Albanians formed in or very near to modern Albania, which goes against the linguistic evidence. Thirdly, one must assume that the words shared between Romanian and Albanian result from direct borrowing from Albanian due to cohabitation rather than simply being carryovers from a substratum language. None of these assumptions have any uncontestable evidence and some go against the evidence. While speculatory linguistics was in vogue in the nineteenth century, today's scholars are hard-pressed to utter Rösler's conclusions with the zealous certainty he displayed. In the case of the Romanians, the linguistic evidence is overwhelmingly in favor of a Dacian origin in the northeastern Balkans.(Price, 2000, p. 383)

Rösler's argumentation, in spite of its political nature, proved convincing for a significant number of his contemporaries. His writing made a big impact both in Austro-Hungary and abroad, for the first time dividing intellectuals on the origin of the Romanians. The overwhelming majority of European scholars still supported Daco-

Roman Continuity[Brezeanu, 1984, p. 79] but there was a significant school of intellectuals, linguists in particular, which supported Rösler. Wilhelm Tomaschek, a Czech orientalist, is one example, often noted by modern Hungarian and Romanian scholars,[Brezeanu, 1984, p. 80; Vékony, 2000, pp. 25-27] of someone who originally supported Romanian continuity in Dacia but changed his opinion in light of Rösler's work. Nevertheless, Tomaschek's opinion was based on a very poor understanding of the relation between Thracian and Illyrian,[Polomé, 1987] and his considerations thankfully did not bring an end to a debate that was otherwise incomplete.

There were a few Romanian linguists who also questioned Romanian continuity in Dacia, the most prominent of these being Ovidiu Densusianu. He was the disciple of Gaston Paris, one of Rösler's advocates, and studied the Romanian language extensively. In his work *Histoire de la Langue Roumaine* (1902) he placed the origin of the Romanians not in Dacia but rather in Illyria, south and west of the lower Danube.[Boia, 2001a, p. 118] Hungarian authors have never missed the opportunity to refer to Densusianu in order to suggest that Daco-Roman continuity was denied by Romanian intellectuals with "a sincere, almost passionate desire for finding the truth."[André Du Nay, 1980, pp. 24-36] This is however performing a sin of omission, as Hungarians rarely mention when Densusianu believed the Romanian migration back into Transylvania took place. A closer inspection of Densusianu's work reveals that he would not have supported the modern Immigration Theory. He did believe that the Romanians formed in Illyria, but this was on tenuous research at a time when little was understood on the relation between Thracian, Dacian, and Illyrian. Furthermore, though Densusianu moved the center of Romanian ethnogenesis in Illyria he never denied a continuity of the Romans in Dacia and was vocal against such ideas. He flatly stated that "though we affirm the center of the formation of Romanian was in Illyria, we are in no way excluding the conservation of a Latin element, probably quite important, in Dacia and in Moesia."[Densusianu, 1901, P. 289] Densusianu also used the far better understood linguistic evidence involving Slavic borrowings in Romanian to conclude that that the Romanians had already migrated back into Dacia by the sixth or seventh century.[Brezeanu, 1984, p. 78] Densusianu stated that Rösler's version of the Immigration Theory, which held that the Romanians had arrived in Transylvania only in the thirteenth century, "could not be reconciled with the linguistic facts" that pointed to a much earlier migration.[Densusianu, 1901, p. 306] It would be intellectually dishonest to portray him as a supporter of the Immigration Theory currently held by Hungarian historians.

It was not long before Rösler's work garnished a significant backlash. The Romanian historian A.D. Xenopol dedicated an entire book, *Rösler's Theory: Studies Upon the Perseverance of the Romanians in Dacia Traiana*, to systematically refuting all of Rösler's arguments. Xenopol used plenty of scientific evidence, but he did not hesitate in pointing out the illogical nature of Rösler's thesis. The key weaknesses included the impossibility that the Romans exterminated an entire people[Xenopol, (1884) 1998, pp. 22-23] and the unlikeliness that a settled population would just flee its homeland due to an invasion,[Xenopol, (1884) 1998, pp. 38-39] as Rösler suggested the Romans would have done in the third century. More importantly, Xenopol pointed out the impossibility of a Romanian migration north of the Danube in the thirteenth century. This would have happened at a time when the Vlachs would have had their own empire – the "Empire of the Bulgars and Vlachs" or Second Bulgarian Empire – south of the Danube. Xenopol flatly asked "how can we imagine that the Vlachs would have abandoned their country [i.e. Bulgaria/Moesia] exactly at a time when, having established their own independent state, they would have enjoyed every right, and for what purpose would they have done so?"(Xenopol, (1884) 1998, p. 49) Although these are very fundamental considerations, to this date they have no adequate response.

Foreign specialists also voiced their concerns with Rösler's theory. If Xenopol could be accused of personal bias, the same could not be said of Jung's defense of Daco-Roman continuity. Julius Jung, a German historian, was concerned by the evident political undertones of Rösler's work.(Jung, 1878, pp. 238-239, 273-274, 312-314) Jung argued for continuity of the Romanians both north and south of the Danube using archaeological and linguistic evidence. More importantly, Jung was far more knowledgeable than Rösler in the matter of Roman history.(Stoicescu, 1993, p. 35) Jung's counterattack was quickly joined by many other eminent academics, including Josef L. Píč, Leopold von Ranke, and Wilhelm Meyer-Lübke.(Brezeanu, 1984, p. 80)

A special note must be placed on a man who, though he had no interest in the debate, discovered a significant counter-argument to Rösler's theory: Konstantin Jireček. While undertaking his studies of the region of Dalmatia, Jireček discovered a distinct cultural divide in the ancient Balkans: inscriptions, coinage, and ancient milestones all indicated a strong division of the region into Latin-speaking North and Greek-speaking South.(Stoianovich, 1994, p. 129) This line that divides the two regions has come to be known as the Jireček line and runs from the Adriatic, through northern Albania, Kosovo, and across the middle of Bulgaria all the way to the Black Sea. The people north of this line were Romanized and spoke Latin, while those to its south were Hellenized and spoke Greek.(Stoianovich, 1994, p. 123)

When one combines the Jireček Line with the east-west divide of Balkan Latin, one is left with four quadrants of Balkan linguistics, and with the conclusion that the Romanians must have formed in the northeast Balkans, in northern Bulgaria (Moesia) and Romania.(Friedman, 1986, p. 288) To this one needs to keep in mind two facts: firstly, trade and population transfers were common across the Danube between the two provinces,(Fletcher, 1999, p. 70) and secondly, that Romanization was more intense north in Romania than in the rest of the Balkans. The British historian and diplomat Sir Ignatius Valentine Chirol, provides a summary of such a point:

> "It must be recollected that the number of Roman colonies established in the Balkan Peninsula was not considerable; and though through them Latin obtained as the official language a footing in the country, it may well be doubted whether their influence was sufficient to Romanize the whole population of Thrace. There are, in fact, many proofs to the contrary: the Greek colonies along the shores of the Aegean preserved their nationality throughout the days of Roman rule; the survival of the old Illyrian tongue in Albania shows that in that part of the peninsula Roman influences were

never paramount; the fact that many Thracian tribes preserved their national organization under their own rulers up to the third century also tends to prove that Thrace was never completely Romanised. On the other hand, on the northern bank of the Danube, in the province of Dacia Trajan, the California of the ancients, which attracted colonists from all parts of the empire, the Roman element must have rapidly acquired a complete preponderancy, and absorbed the native population."(Chirol, 1881, pp. 154-155)

Some modern Hungarian historians have tried to rework the Immigration Theory to cope with the ever-increasing body of evidence against it, producing increasingly elaborate narratives on the Vlach migration. For instance, now it is argued that the Vlachs were Romanized north of this line, but ended up migrating south of the Jireček line in an early period.(Illyés, 1992) This migration was, again, completely undocumented, a flaw brought up almost eighty years ago(Seton-Watson, 1934, p. 13) and still unanswered to this day. This brings up the whole question of parsimony: if the whole of Dacia was Romanized, and if there is no evidence for a later Vlach migration, why not believe the Romanians had always resided there instead of making increasingly elaborate counter-theories?

Such considerations did not stop Hungarian historians from championing Rösler's new theory, beginning with Paul Hunfalvy.(Bucur & Costea, 2009, p. 278) Hunfalvy was profoundly contemptuous towards the Romanians. He even threatened the Romanians in the Hungarian parliament with the words "do not provoke us to employ towards the other nations the methods of total extermination employed by the Anglo-Saxons towards the Red Indians of North America."(Brezeanu, 1984, p. 74) The historian Rudolf Bergner described him as a man who "no longer speaks as a scientist accepting the truth but rather as a representative of Magyar chauvinism who excelled in his blind fury against the Romanians."(Réthy, 1884)

Numerous other Hungarian historians adopted Rösler's thesis, but their works were profoundly unscientific.(Karácsonyi, 1912) László Rethy for instance claimed that the Romanians were nomad shepherds from central Italy who then migrated into the Balkans and only came north of the Danube in the thirteenth century.(Spinei, 2009, p. 80) Janos Karacsony claimed that not only did the Romanians originate in Italy but they had only migrated into Transylvania in 1526! Janos Peisker even suggested that the Romanians were descended from Tatars and Mongolians who settled in northern Bulgaria, were Romanized by the locals there, and then moved into Transylvania.(Livezeanu, 1995, p. 148) These are among the two more outlandish theories produced at the time.

All of these theories had one thing in common: they justified Magyar dominance over the Romanians and presented the Romanians not only as late arrivals but also as culturally inferior. The emphasis was always placed spitefully on the "shepherd" nature of the Romanians. Reviewers commented on Peisker's work: "[to him] their language is a secondary fact; their nomadic habits of life are the fundamental fact."(Bury, 1920) It was, like in Sulzer's time, not important to resolve the actual home of the Romanians. All that mattered was proving that the Romanians were late arrivals in Transylvania and to show the timeless inferiority of their culture. These authors figured that the Romanians would have willingly become Magyars, if only they knew of the inferiority of their maternal culture.

The Romanians did not prove receptive to Magyarization by these means. Ironically, the centuries of persecution the Romanians faced resulted in the very introverted, conservative Romanian culture in Transylvania that made their Magyarization impossible.(Hitchins, 1996, p. 233) Exclusion from the urban and learned class produced a high level of illiteracy that ironically protected their nationhood from Magyarization. Magyarization in schools did not produce patriots, but rather created resentful minorities that supported separatist, national movements of their own.(D. B. Heather, 2004, p. 202) Portraying the cruel policies of Magyarization as cultural charity fooled few international observes as well.

These factors culminated in drastic consequences for the Kingdom of Hungary at the end of World War One. The peace treaty of Trianon signed by the Entente and Hungary in 1920 dismembered the kingdom and ended centuries of Hungarian domination of the Transylvanian Romanians. Greater Hungary ceased to exist, Transylvania became a part of Romania, and by all measures Rösler's theory should have become politically useless. It should have ceased to find support both in Hungary and abroad. Unfortunately, it did not, and a debate which belonged in the nineteenth century continues to dominate Hungarian-Romanian historical discourse.

Works Cited

Armbruster, A. (1972). *Romanitatea Românilor: Istoria Unei Idei [The Romanity of the Romanians: the History of an Idea]*. Bucharest, Romania: Editura Academiei Republicii Socialiste România.

Barta, C. (2002). Unirea cu Roma: fundamentarea teologico-dogmatică. Un exemplu: Catehismul lui Iosif de Camillis. *Annales Universitatis Apulensis Series Historica, 6*(I), 75-79.

Boardman, J. (1982). *The Prehistory of the Balkans, and the Middle East and the Aegean World, tenth to eight centuries B.C.* Cambridge, UK: Cambridge University Press.

Boia, L. (2001a). *History and Myth in the Romanian Consciousness*. Budapest, Hungary: Central European University Press.

Boia, L. (2001b). *Romania: Borderland of Europe*. London, UK: Reaktion.

Brezeanu, S. (1984). *Daco-Romanian Continuity: Science and Politics*. Bucharest, Romania: Editura Ştiintifică şi Enciclopedică.

Bucur, I.-M., & Costea, I. (2009). Transylvania between Two National Historiographies. Historical Consciousness and Political Identity. In S. G. Ellis, R. Esser, J.-F. Berdah & M. Řezník (Eds.), *Frontiers, Regions and Identities in Europe*. Pisa, Italy: Plus-Pisa university press.

Bulei, I. (2005). *A Short History of Romania*. Bucharest, Romania: Meronia.

Bunea, A. (1900). *Din Istoria Românilor. Episcopul Ioan Inocenţiu Klein (1728–1751)*. Blaj.

Bury, J. B. (1920). Review of Peisker, J. Die Abkunft der Rumdnen wirtschaftsgeschichtlich untersucht. *The English Historical Review, 35*(140).

Chirol, I. V. (1881). *'Twixt Greek and Turk, or, Jottings during a journey through Thessaly, Macedonia, and Epirus*. London, UK; Edinburgh, UK: William Blackwood and Sons.

Clark, C. U. (1932). *United Roumania*. New York, NY: Dodd, Mead and Company.

Cunliffe, B. (2001). *The Oxford illustrated history of prehistoric Europe*. Oxford, UK: Oxford University Press.

Densusianu, O. (1901). *Histoire de la Langue Roumaine* (Vol. I). Paris, France: Macon & PRotat.

Diaconescu, A. (2004). The towns of Roman Dacia: an overview of recent research. In W. S. Hanson & I. P. Haynes (Eds.), *Roman Dacia: the Making of a Provincial Society*. Portsmouth, RI: Journal of Roman Archaeology.

Diaconescu, T. (2000). Historia Augusta: Una Nuova Lezione dei Testi di Vopisco. *Studia Antiqua et Archaeologica, VII*, 155-170.

Ellis, L. (1998). Dacia Terra Deserta: Populations, Politics, and the [de]colonization of Dacia. *World Archaeology, 30*(2).

Engel, J. C. (1794). *Commentatio de expeditionibus Trajani ad Danubium et origine Valachorum*. Vienna, Austria.

Fine, J. v. A. (2000). *The Early Medieval Balkans: a critical survey from the sixth to the late twelfth century*. Ann Arbor, MI: University of Michigan Press.

Fletcher, R. A. (1999). *The Barbarian Conversion: from Paganism to Christianity*. Berkeley, CA: University of California Press.

Friedman, V. A. (1986). Linguistics, Nationalism, and Literary Languages: A Balkan Perspective. In P. C. Bjrakman & V. Raskin (Eds.), *The Real-World Linguist: Linguistic Applications in the 1980's*. Norwood, NJ: ABLEX.

Friedman, V. A. (2000). After 170 years of Balkan Linguistics: Whither the Millennium? *Mediterranean Language Review, 12*, 1-15.

Georgescu, V. (1991). *The Romanians: a history* (A. Bley-Vroman, Trans.). Columbus, OH: Ohio State University Press.

Georgiev, V. (1966). The Genesis of the Balkan Peoples. *The Slavonic and East European Review, 44*(103), 285-297.

Heather, D. B. (2004). *A History of Education for Citizenship*. London, UK; New York, NY: Routledge.

Heather, P. (1996). *The Goths*. Cambridge, MA: Blackwell.

Hitchins, K. (1996). *The Romanians, 1774-1866*. Oxford, UK: Claredon Press.

Hitchins, K. (2001). *The Idea of Nation among the Romanians of Transylvania, 1700-1849*. Paper presented at the Nation and National Ideology: Past, Present, and PRospects, Bucharest, Romania.

Hitchins, K. (2002). Romanian Intellectuals and the Enlightenment in Transylvania. *Annales Universitatis Apulensis Series Historica, 6*(I), 99-105.

Hupchick, D. P. (2001). *The Balkans : From Constantinople to Communism*. New York, NY: Palgrave Macmillan.

Huszti, A. (1791). *Ó és újj Dácia*: Diénes.

Illyés, E. (1992). *Ethnic Continuity in the Carpatho-Danubian Area*. Hamilton, Canada: Struktura Press.

Ionescu, P. (2002). Interferențe culturale germano-romǎne în epoca iluministǎ: Franz Joseph Sulzer. *Annales Universitatis Apulensis Series Historica, 6*(I).

Jelavich, B. (1989). *History of the Balkans: Eighteenth and Nineteenth Centuries* (Vol. I). Cambridge, UK: Cambridge University Press.

Jordan-Bychkov, T. G., & Jordan-Bychkov, B. (2002). *The European Culture Area: a systematic geography*. Lanham, MD: Rowman & Littlefield.

Jung, J. (1878). *Römer und Romanen in der Donaulandern*. Innsbruck, Germany: Historisch-ethnographische Studien.

Karacsonyi, J. (1912). *Die Ansiedlung der Rumänen auf dem linken Donauufer*. Kolozsvar.

Kellogg, F. (1990). *A History of Romanian Historical Writing*. Bakersfield, CA: C. Schlacks.

Leskien, A. (1872). Review of Romanian Studies. *The Academy and Literature, 3*(40).

Livezeanu, I. (1995). *Cultural Politics in Greater Romania: Regionalism, Nation Building, & Ethnic Struggle*. Ithaca, NY: Cornell University Press.

Madgearu, A. (2001). *Rolul Crestinismului in Formarea Poporului romǎn*. Bucharest, Romania: BIC ALL.

Malcolm, N. (1996). *Bosnia: a short history*. Washington Square, NY: New York University Press.

Marcellinus, A. Rerum Gestarum.

Molnár, M. (2001). *A Concise History of Hungary*. Cambridge, UK: Cambridge University Press.

Nay, A. D. (1980). The Daco-Rumanian Theory of Continuity: Origins of the Rumanian Nation and Language. In L. L. Lőte (Ed.), *Transylvania and the theory of Daco-Roman-Rumanian Continuity*. Rochester, NY: Committeee of Transylvania.

Nay, A. D. (1996). *The Origins of the Romanians*. Toronto, Canada: Corvinus Library.

Neamţu, G., & Cordoş, N. (1994). *The Hungarian Policy of Magyarization in Transylvania: 1867-1918*. Cluj-Napoca, Romania: Center for Transylvanian Studies and the Romanian Cultural Foundation.

Olmsted, G. S. (2001). *Celtic art in transition during the first century BC : an examination of the creation of mint masters and metal smiths, and a analysis of stylistic development during the phase between La Tene and Provincial Roman*. Innsbruck: Inst. für Sprachen u. Literatur.

Paliga, S. (2006). *Etymological Lexicon of Indigenous (Thracian) Elements in Romanian*. Bucharest, Romania: Centrul Mass Media Evenimentul.

Părăuşanu, T. (2008). *Instituţiile juridice în procesul de formare a poporului român*. PhD., Universitatea de Stat din Moldova, Chişinău, Moldova.

Pei, M. (1976). *The Story of Latin and the Romance Languages*. New York, NY: Harper & Row.

Polomé, E. C. (1987). Tradition and Development in Indo-European Studies. *The Journal of Indo-European Studies, 15*(3), 225.

Pop, I.-A. (2003). Nations and Denominations in Transylvania (13th-16th Century). In C. Levai & V. Vese (Eds.), *Tolerance and intolerance in historical perspective*. Pisa, Italy: Clioh's Workshop.

Poruciuc, A. (2008). An Opening to Remember: Meyer-Lübke's Outlook on the Old Germanisms in Romanian. In T. Khan (Ed.), *Das rumänische und seine Nachbarn*. Berlin, Germany: Frank & Timme.

Pounds, N. J. G. (1973). *An historical geography of Europe, 450 B.C.-A.D. 1330*. Cambridge, UK: Cambridge University Press.

Price, G. (2000). *Encyclopedia of the Languages of Europe*. Malden, MA: Blackwell.

Prodan, D., & Lăzărescu, M. (1971). *Supplex Libellus Valachorum: or, the political struggle of the Romanians in Transylvania during the 18th century*. Bucharest, Romania: Editura Academiei Republicii Socialiste România.

Quiles, C., & López-Menchero, F. (2009). *A Grammar of Modern Indo-European*. Badajoz, Spain: Indo-European Association (DNGHU).

Rady, M. C. (1988). Review of Köpeczi, Béla (ed.), Erdely tortenete. 3 vols. Akademiai kiad6, Budapest, 1986. *The Slavonic and East European Review, 66*(3).

Rady, M. C. (2000). *Nobility, Land and Service in Medieval Hungary*. Basingstoke; New York: Palgrave.

Réthy, L. (1884). *Daco-Roumains ou Italo-Roumains? Études historiques et philologiques*. Budapest: Impr. "Magyar Nyomda, 1897.

Roe, P. (2005). *Ethnic Violence and the Social Security Dilemma*. London, UK; New York, NY: Routledge.

Rösler, R. (1871). *Rumänische Studien: Untersuchungen zur älteren Geschichte Rumäniens*. Leipzig.

Romocea, C. G. (2004). Reconciliation in the ethnic conflict in Transylvania: theological, political and social aspects. *Religion, State and Society, 32*(2), 159-176.

Sala, M. (2005). *From Latin to Romanian: the historical development of Romanian in a comparative Romance context*. Oxford, MS: University of Mississippi Press.

Schulte, K. (2009). Loandowrds in Romanian. In M. Haspelmath & U. Tadmor (Eds.), *Loanwords in the World's Languages: A Comparative Handbook*. Berlin: De Gruyter Mouton.

Sedlar, J. W. (1993). *East Central Europe in the Middle Ages, 1000-1500*. Seattle, WA: University of Washington Press.

Seton-Watson, R. W. (1925). IV. Transylvania since 1867. *The Slavonic Review, 4*(10), 101-123.

Seton-Watson, R. W. (1934). *A History of the Roumanians*. Cambridge, UK: Cambridge University Press.

Spinei, V. (2009). *The Romanians and the Turkic Nomads North of teh Danube Delta from the Tenth to the Mid-Thirteenth Century*. Leiden, Netherlands: Brill.

Stoianovich, T. (1994). *The Balkans: the first and last Europe*. Armonk, NY: Sharpe.

Stoicescu, N. (1980). *Constituirea Statelor Feudale Românesti*. Bucharest, Romania: Editura Academiei Republicii Socialiste România.

Stoicescu, N. (1993). *O falsă problemă istorică: discontinuitatea poporului român pe teritoriul strămoşesc*. Bucharest, Romania: Editura Fundatiei Culturale Romane.

Tanaşoca, N.-Ş. (2001). Aperçus of the History of Balkan Romanity. In R. Theodorescu & L. C. Barrows (Eds.), *Politics and Culture in Southeastern Europe*. Bucharest, Romania: UNESCO.

Themistius. Oration.

Thunmann, J. (1774). *Untersuchungen über die Geschichte der östlichen europäischen Völker*. Leipzig.

Tóth, Z. n. (1998). *Az erdélyi román nacionalizmus elso"százada*. Csíkszereda: Pro-Print könyvk.

Trencsényi, B., & Kopeček, M. (2006). *Discourses of Collective Identity in Central and Southeast Europe (1770-1945)*. Budapest, Hungary: Central European University Press.

Vekony, G. (2000). *Dacians, Romans, Romanians*. Budapest, Hungary: Corvinus Library.

Wawro, G. (2000). *Warfare and Society in Europe: 1792-1914*. London, UK; New York, nY: Routledge.

Wilkes, J. (1995). *The Illyrians*. Oxford, UK; Cambridge, MA: Blackwell.

Winnifirth, T. J. (1987). *The Vlachs: the History of a Balkan People*. New York, NY: St. Martin's Press.

Woodard, R. D. (2008). *The Ancient Languages of Europe*. Cambridge, UK: Cambridge University Press.

Xenopol, A. D. (1914). *Istoria Românilor*. Bucharest, Romania: Institutul de Arte Grafice si Editura "LIBRARIEI SCOALELOR" C. SFETEA.

Xenopol, A. D. ((1884) 1998). *Teoria lui Rösler: Studii asupra stăruinţei Românilor în Dacia Traiană*. Bucharest, Romania: Albatros.

Zamosius, S. (1598). *Analecta lapidum vestutorum et nonullarum in Dacia antiquatorum*. Francofurit ad Moenum.

5. RÖSLER'S CURTAIN CALL

Rösler's theory, born out of political considerations, should have perished once it became politically useless. Even if the theory somehow justified Magyar domination of the Romanians, a situation in which no Romanian had been appointed to the office of governor in any county since 1870,(Seton-Watson, 1925) that no longer mattered once Transylvania became a part of Romania. Rösler's theory should have become useless.

Yet the debate about Romanian continuity persisted for a variety of reasons. Firstly, in spite of its political nature, Rösler's theory brought to light some considerations on Romanian continuity that needed to be explored and explained. His conclusion can no longer be accepted in light of modern evidence and arguments, but the facts he highlighted in order to reach that conclusion were in many cases real and prompted further study in the field both by Romanians and by foreign specialists. The political aspects of the debate tended to die off among third-party (non-Hungarian and non-Romanian) historians. The second and main reason why Rösler's theory was kept alive among Hungarian historians was because it had been adapted to serve a new political purpose: to justify Magyar territorial irredenta. It is almost impossible to understand the effect Trianon had on Hungarian society. Flags were flown at half-mast throughout Hungary for the eighteen years that followed the treaty. Revisionism of the treaty and reacquisition of the lost territories became a staple goal for an entire generation of lawmakers, politicians, and historians.(Pearson, 1996, p. 95) This single goal dominated politics for the next twenty years, and still has strong reverberations today.

The Hungarian nationalists of Austro-Hungary had, in some respects, succeeded in their goals. They desired to transform Hungary from a multi-ethnic empire into a homogenous Magyar nation-state. The Treaty of Trianon was ironic in this regard, since the much smaller Hungary which remained was ethnically homogenous. Only nine percent of Hungary's 7.6 million inhabitants were non-Magyars in the post-Trianon borders, whereas the percentage of non-Magyars in pre-Trianon Hungary of 1910 reached 51 percent.(Rothschild, 1992, p. 193) It is doubtful that this gave any solace to the Hungarian politicians who witnessed the dissolution of their empire.

Given that Magyarization did not produce Magyar patriots out of the minorities, but rather virulent separatists, it might have been a fair assumption that a more tolerant Hungary would have weathered the storm better. Instead, the exact opposite lesson was drawn by the Hungarians: Hungary's failure was not its oppression of the minorities or its Magyarization policies, but rather, its inability to pursue such policies with sufficient vigor. It was believed that a more intense policy of Magyarization would have resulted in an ethnically homogenous country that could have prevented Trianon.(Bideleux & Jeffries, 2007, p. 254)

The lesson Hungarian historians took from Trianon was that Hungary had failed in public relations. The British had a profound, almost irrational sympathy for Hungarians in the late nineteenth century,(Bátonyi, 1999, p. 71) but this was gradually eroded by growing awareness of the Magyarization policy. Robert Seton-Watson and Henry

Wickham Steed are two examples of prolific writers who at first opposed national self-determination in Hungary but became sympathizers of the minorities after witnessing the policies of Magyarization.(Cornwall, 2004, pp. 2-3) H. W. Steed wrote of the Hungarians in 1905: "my friends the Magyars who, after all, have a certain sense for progress and liberalism as we understand it."(Steed, 1914, pp. 284-285) His perspective changed significantly after having witnessed "Magyar liberalism." In his work *The Habsburg Monarchy*, published in 1914, he stated in no uncertain terms that:

> "From the standpoint of the internal cohesion of the Monarchy, the Magyar State has acted as a repellent force, powerless for good, powerful for evil; and, pending proof to the contrary, students of Hapsburg affairs are constrained to regard the Magyars rather as a liability than as an asset of the Crown. The instinct of self-preservation might perhaps work a miracle at the twelfth hour had not the present generation of Magyars been so steeped in chauvinism as to have lost all sense of their real position in Europe."(Steed, 1914, pp. 284-295)

Hungarian historians campaigned to prove the injustice of Trianon and win back foreign opinion. To do this, the Magyars launched a public relations campaign by setting up historical research institutes in numerous European capitals.(Brezeanu, 1984, pp. 82-83) Science became submerged by politics as Hungarian historians tried to paint a caricature of Hungarian and Balkan history, consequently resuscitating the Immigration Theory. The principle was to create a contrast between the Hungarians as representatives of European civilization, and the Romanians and Slavs who represented Balkan barbarism. Transylvania was presented as a citadel of this European civilization which had been surrendered to the "Balkan savages."(Halmos, 1982, p. 9) In their eyes the Romanians should have been grateful for the "civilization" the Magyars bestowed upon them.

Unfortunately this argument continues to enjoy substantial popularity among Hungarian historians. The idea that the Romanians "owe their civilization" to the Hungarians was widely published in the late twentieth century, especially by the Hungarian diaspora. Phrases akin to "primitive Wallach serfs" became all-too-common. It was argued that "the uncultured Vlachs, instead of being assimilated or oppressed, received their first Bible translations from the Hungarian [people]."(Balogh, 2006, p. 6) Endre Haraszti's work *The Ethnic History of Transylvania* (1971) is almost a caricature of this argument:

> "The Transylvanian Vlach peasant and shepherd did not wish to imitate his Magyar or Saxon neighbours although the Anjou kings offered them opportunities for this. Nevertheless, in the light of the brilliant Kingdom, they gradually transformed themselves. Their life-standard, their homes, Greek-Orthodox churches, their personal looks became bette[r], more cultured."(Haraszti, 1971, p. 62)

This pressed forward the issue of why the Romanians had become serfs in Transylvania, given all of this Magyar "generosity." Hungarian historians concluded that only the Romanians could be held accountable for their own plight. Though the Magyars had tried to civilize them, the Romanians either refused civilization and "remained some sort of 'Balkanic' community in the heart of Transylvania"[Haraszti, 1979, p. 125] or remained uncivilized out of their own incompetence.[c] They were just "culturally too primitive and socially too underdeveloped to assume responsibility for themselves."[Endrey, 1986, p. 61] Even academic works written by Hungarian authors and published by Western institutions express this sentiment. István Vásáry, in a book published in 2005 by Cambridge University Press, stated that "The Balkans have yet to find the key and meaning of their historical existence and to decide whether they want to belong to the mainstream of European development or to insist on their Byzantine and Ottoman autocratic traditions."[Vásáry, 2005, p. 167] The message is clear: the Romanians had chosen to remain backward and refuse Hungary's civilizing light.

There are a multitude of problems with such an idea, and it is tragic that it has remained in force for so long. Not only is the argument downright chauvinistic but factually incorrect as well. It is similar to the early twentieth century concept of the "White Man's Burden", which turned European imperialism and colonialism of the nineteenth century into a "noble duty of diffusing the benefits of civilization amongst the lesser races."[Parchami, 2009, p. 105] The culturally deficient subordinates should have felt honored to receive civilization, even if this "civilization" was ultimately based on exploiting the indigenous people. The idea of a "Hungarian Man's Burden" is also inaccurate given that the Hungarian crown was largely uncaring about the state of (under)development of its various ethnic groups. Rather than somehow pushing for the "education" of the Romanians, the crown saw them more as an obstacle to the expansion of its holdings or those of the Hungarian nobility. Sadly, the idea of a "Hungarian Man's Burden" is still seen as valid in Hungary.

Hungarian loanwords in the Romanian language were used to substantiate this idea of "civilizing Magyars." One example is the Romanian word "oraş" for city, believed to be derived from the Hungarian "varos." It was claimed that "the Wallachians / Vlachs / Roumanians, who had migrated north of the Danube had borrowed Old Hungarian waras 'town' along with masses of Hungarian words pertaining to a relatively high level of societal life, proves once more the hollowness of the Daco-Roman continuity theory."[Kazar & Makai, 2001, p. 35] In essence, since the Romans were (according to the same source) famous for their urban life, the Romanians could not be their descendants since they appear to have re-learned urbanity from the Hungarians.

The idea that the Hungarians civilized the Romanians is not only wrong, but ironic since it works against an Immigration Theory. Firstly it must be pointed out that regardless of where one places them the Romanians still descend from Roman colonists;

---

[c] One would wonder why only the Transylvanian Romanians were incompetent in administration given Moldova and Wallachia managed to survive as territorial entities that were populated and run by Romanians. Not only did Wallachia and Moldova not collapse under their own weight due to the "primitive nature" of their Romanian inhabitants, but they proved able to resist the onslaught of the much larger Hungarian, Ottoman, and Polish states that surrounded them.

the language alone is evidence enough. Secondly, the Balkans hosts several large Roman cities that survived since antiquity, many in close proximity to the supposed homeland of the Vlachs. Such cities included Naissus (Niš), Scopium (Skopje), Dyrrachium (Durrës), Philipopolis (Plòvdiv), and Thessalonica. The Romanian word for "city" should have been preserved from Latin or come from Greek had the Romanians formed south of the Danube. The Aromanians for instance use the Greek-derived term *poli*, but the word is indicatively absent in Romanian. This absence is easier to explain had the Romanians formed in Dacia: urban life largely disappeared in the province in the fifth century with the arrival of the Huns.[(Pop et al., 2005, pp. 230-231)] The loss of the Latin term and absence of a Greek term for city becomes readily explainable if one admits the Romanians continued to reside in the ruralized, former Roman province. The word would simply have fallen out of use with the end of urban life.

All things considered, Hungarian interference did not produce a "civilizing effect" on the Romanians but rather stunted their social development. The Hungarian crown's actions largely led to the absorption or dissolution of the Romanian nobility and administration. The case of the dukedoms mentioned in the *Gesta Hungarorum*, which were dissolved or incorporated into the Magyar aristocratic system, provide a prime example. The destruction of Litovoi's voievodship in 1273 is another example of retarding Magyar interference,[(Rădvan, 2009, pp. 45-46)] since no mention is made of a Romanian state in the area afterwards until 1324. It is telling that the only Romanian states that emerged later were all on the margins of the Hungarian kingdom, outside of direct Hungarian influence.[(Treptow & Bolovan, 1995, pp. 63-66)] Only with the internal chaos caused by the end of the Árpád dynasty as well as the Tatar raids of 1285-1293 that the Romanians would establish their own state, Wallachia, at the turn of the thirteenth century.[(Rădvan, 2009, p. 46)]

The Hungarian crown had a disastrous effect on Romanian holdings and the knezial system within the kingdom. The Romanian nobles, at least the those who had not been assimilated by the Hungarians, were "simply dispossessed, despoiled eventually of their land, reduced to utter poverty and even to servitude."[(Stratilescu, 1906, p. 46)] Lands and fortresses were stripped "from the hands of the schismatic Vlachs" (*de manibus Vallachorum (et) schismaticorum*) starting in the early thirteenth century.[(Pop, 2002, pp. 64-65)] Marginalization is noted in the very first Hungarian documents regarding Transylvania's Romanians. King Andrew II's charter of 1222 granted the Teutonic Knights the right not to pay customs when travelling through the "the Vlach land" (*terra Blacorum*).[(Hurmuzaki, 1887, p. 75, LIV)] Economical marginalization was shortly followed up by expropriation, as in 1223 King Andrew II made a donation of land to the monastery of Cârţa, land that had been taken from the Vlachs (*erram quam prius eidem monasterio contuleramus exemptam de Blaccis*).[(Hurmuzaki, 1887, p. 79, LVII)]

As an aside, Hungarian historians use these texts as evidence that the Vlachs had arrived in Transylvania in the thirteenth century,[(Alain Du Nay et al., 1997, pp. 51-52)] but this is in contradiction to the actual content of the documents. None of them refer to Vlachs settling in Transylvania and yet all the documents indicate that Vlachs were proprietors of lands which could be identified by their ethnic character. This indicates that the

Vlachs were residing in these regions earlier than when these documents were written, most likely for as long as anyone could remember. Such a conclusion is corroborated by the Hungarian chroniclers like Anonymous and Simon de Kéza who gave the Vlachs chronological precedence in Transylvania.

The pressure on the Romanians grew throughout the centuries, with their gradual decline in social status easy to follow. In 1234 King Béla IV swore an oath to Pope Gregory IX that he would do everything in his power to subdue the "heretics" and "root out the false [Orthodox] Christians of our country"[(Hurmuzaki, 1887, p. 128)] The Decree of Turda, issued in 1366 by Louis I of Hungary, officially made the knezes of the Romanians equal to commoners, save for the few whose rights were conferred by royal charters. In addition, the Hungarian nobles reserved the right to "exterminate from this country malefactors belonging to any nation, especially the Vlachs [*Olachorum*]."[(Pop, 2003, pp. 122-123)] The Romanians were formally and completely excluded from Transylvanian politics by the *Unio Trium Nationum*.[(Georgescu, 1991, p. 41)] By the time the Approved Constitution of Transylvania was written in 1635 the status of the Romanians deteriorated to such an extent that their presence in Transylvania was "merely tolerated", the constitution stating that "the Vlachs of the Greek [Orthodox] rite are temporarily allowed to stay in the country as long as this is agreeable to the princes and inhabitants of the country."[(Bod, 1890, p. 344, XVI; Giurescu, 1969, p. 89)] So long as they could be used for cheap labor they could stay, and their subordinate position was strictly enforced.

Even this cursory glance at Transylvanian history indicates that the status of the Romanians had deteriorated not out of their own blundering but rather due to specific policies employed by the Hungarians. The Romanians were being driven down Transylvania's social pyramid or out of Transylvania in general, their positions to be taken up by more loyal, Catholic colonists. This conclusion did not escape foreign commentators on Hungary's history, as an article in the 1863 London Quarterly Review stated:

> "The degeneracy of this people [the Romanians] is attributable to prolonged Magyar tyranny, which kept them for centuries in a state of abject helotry. A Rouman [Romanian] was obliged to wear sandals instead of shoes; he was not permitted to wear an embroidered coat or a hat; his house was not to be furnished with windows that looked into the street, nor was it allowed to be constructed with a chimney. Much has been done of late by the Austrian Government to elevate this long-depressed people."[("The Resources and Future of Austria," 1863, p. 34)]

The Immigration Theory needed to explain a demographic conundrum as well: when and by what means had the Romanians become the majority in Transylvania? The number of Romanians in Transylvania must have already been significant in the thirteenth century, since the Romanian principalities of Moldova and Wallachia were founded by Romanian emigrants from Transylvania around 1290 and 1345. The Romanian population in Transylvania must have been sufficiently large to repopulate Wallachia and Moldova after the Mongol devastation of the thirteenth century.[(Jordan, 1998,]

p. 184) It seems plausible that the Romanians were two-thirds of Transylvania's population in 1241, just prior to the Mongol Invasion.(Sedlar, 1993, p. 9) A Romanian majority in Transylvania in the thirteenth century obviously made any claim that the Romanians had arrived only a few decades prior an absurdity.

It was understandable that Hungarian historians tried to minimize the historical demographic presence of the Romanians, as well as to present the growth of the Romanian population as more gradual. Various historical documents were manipulated in this regard. Another example involves the use of Catholic tithes to approximate populations. The ratio of names recorded on tithe registers could, supposedly, be used to approximate the ethnic makeup of the entire province. Supposedly the small number of the Vlach population was shown "on the papal tithing lists of between 1332 and 1337… [showing that] in all of Transylvania 310,000 Hungarian and Szekely Catholics, 21,000 catholic Saxons, and 18,000 orthodox Vlachs were manifest."(Kosztin, 2006, p. 12) Unfortunately, such registers only recorded Catholic inhabitants, and as most Romanians were Orthodox Christians, they went unrecorded.(Lazar, 1997, p. 64) Those present on the tithe listings must have belonged to the far less numerous Catholic Romanians. If even as much as one quarter of the Romanians were Catholic, this leaves a massive body of Romanians in Transylvania which easily discredits any notion that they had arrived only a century prior to Transylvania.

Similar manipulation was performed on a Romanian Uniate Church document from 1701 that claimed 200,000 Romanians converted to the Uniate (Greek Catholic) faith.(Bethlen, 1971, p. 21) Hungarian historians claimed this document proved that "in Transylvania, one-fourth of the population, amounting to about 800,000 souls, was Rumanian at the time."(David Prodan, 1996, p. 29) However, the document clearly only refers to Romanians that converted to Greek Catholicism. Furthermore, we know that only a minority of Transylvania's Romanians had accepted the Union with Rome,(Treptow & Bolovan, 1995, p. 108) meaning that one would have to at least double the figure to reach the true Romanian population. Therefore, the document proves that the Romanians in 1700 represented over half of Transylvania's population. An official, religious-based census conducted in 1733 in Transylvania confirms this, as it recorded 677,308 members of the Romanian faiths (Greek Orthodox and United) representing 63.5% of the population. Most historians today consider it indisputable that the Romanians formed the majority of Transylvania's population by the mid-sixteenth century at the latest,(Sugar, 1977, p. 144) regardless of what one makes of Transylvania's ethnic composition prior to this time.

Hungarian historians have insisted on the Romanians first arriving into Transylvania in the thirteenth century had to explain how the Romanians became the demographic majority in such a short amount of time. One explanation came in the argument that Romanian immigration into Transylvania accelerated after the thirteenth century. Similarly, the argument continues that the sixteenth century saw "a massive migration of Rumanians continued… from the Rumanian principalities (Wallachia, Moldova) because of extreme social oppression and the uncertain political situation there."(Lazar, 1997, p. 64) This migration continued up until the eighteenth century, when the Romanians "flooded Transylvania and the eastern parts of the Hungarian Plain."(Bethlen,

163

1971, p. 28) Thus the Romanians, due to continuous immigration, became a majority in the eighteenth century, coincidentally the time when the first reliable censuses were performed in the region.

There are significant problems with such an argument, the first of which being that Wallachia and Moldova were always less populous than Transylvania. It was estimated that mid-fourteenth century Wallachia had a population of 500,000; Moldova of 400,000 (though some have argued as low as 84,000); and Transylvania had an overwhelming 900,000 inhabitants. Constant warfare had reduced the populations of the principalities, while the population of Transylvania continued to grow. By the early sixteenth century, Wallachia's population had been reduced to 300,000-400,000, and Moldova's to roughly 300,000 as well. A census in Moldova in 1591 recorded 46,860 families, which, if we plug in five people per family, results in only 234,300 inhabitants. By the eighteenth century Wallachia was inhabited by only 800,000 people, Moldova had 500,000 inhabitants, while Transylvania's population, well-protected by the other two principalities and by the Habsburg army, had grown to roughly 2,000,000.(Georgescu, 1991, p. 21; Spinei, 2009, p. 194) The counter-argument is obvious: even if *all* of Wallachia's and Moldova's Romanians moved to Transylvania, they still would not have been enough to create a Romanian majority in the region.

The second problem for such an argument involves the abundance of evidence and documentation for a Romanian exodus from Transylvania. It is telling that Wallachia's founding legend revolves around a Transylvanian Romanian noble named Negru Vodă escaping from Transylvania and settling in Wallachia.(Ludescu, 1998, 1, 4) Moldova was likewise founded by a Romanian noble originally from Transylvania, called Bogdan and medieval sources even refer to how he "lead his Romanians from that region, to the lands of Moldova... which had been depopulated due to the nearby Tatars."(Thuroczy, 1766, III, 49) The fourteenth century saw the acceleration of Romanian flight from the region, largely due to economic pressure and extensive Catholic proselytism.(Spinei, 1986, p. 139) Religious persecution continued to force an exodus of Romanians from Transylvania. Hussites, a branch of Christianity founded in Bohemia, as well as Orthodox Christian Romanians continued to flee to Moldova throughout the fifteenth century. In 1692 the Transylvanian Diet (government) notified Leopold I that they were having trouble stemming the flow of Romanians to Wallachia and Moldova.(Georgescu, 1991, p. 22) Similarly, the German ambassador to Transylvania wrote that over 24,000 families had fled from Transylvania to Wallachia and Moldova in 1764.(Ciolan, Voicu, & Racovițan, 1993, p. 27) Social oppression was not a motivator for Romanian flight into Transylvania, but rather for a Romanian exodus from it. The eye-witness testimony of the Habsburg General Preiss in the late eighteenth century leaves no doubt in this regard:

> "Unfortunately, a large number of Romanians from Transylvania emigrate to Wallachia and Moldova every year. But it is quite seldom that one may see Romanians emigrating from those countries to Transylvania. The reason for it is easily found if one considers the fact that the former Romanian Prince Constantin Mavrocordat did away with serfdom. ... *The*

Romanians do only moderate unpaid work for their masters and what they have to pay every year is again a *moderate* sum of money. The result of all this is the fact that, if they are not ravaged by war and invading enemies, these two neighbouring countries have a plentiful life; by the industrious, but not exhaustive cultivation of land, the generous nature offers plenty of rich products; the peasant is content and always in high spirits; he works for his own good and, knowing it, he becomes quite productive and, therefore, has not the slightest intention to emigrate."(David Prodan, 1996, p. 213)

A variety of smaller but no less fundamental problems also plague this theory. Firstly, it the Romanians would not have migrated to a region where they were "socially and economically oppressed, brutalized, and enserfed."(Evans, 2006, p. 163) Furthermore, the Ottoman conquest of the Hungarian kingdom resulted in a large flight of Hungarians from Central Hungary to Transylvania,(Roc, 2005, p. 114) one which would surely have counter-balanced any Romanian immigration. Furthermore, the outright absence of documentation for Romanian settlement in Transylvania is perplexing if their settlement were truly "the outcome of a deliberate settlement policy on the part of the monarch and the local landowners."(Petrovics, 2009, p. 72) How could it be explained that none of these landowners, not even the king himself, had bothered to write of this colonization? Again, one should not take it as mere coincidence that this supposed demographic takeover of Transylvania had rather conveniently been completed by the time reliable censuses of the eighteenth century.

Since immigration was not a convincing explanation for the Romanian majority in Transylvania, Hungarian historians looked for other reasons. The most frequent explanation was that the Romanians had been shielded from the harsh realities of war at the expense of the Hungarians. It was argued that "the Magyars died on the battlefields, or were exterminated during the Mongol Conquest. The Wallachians hid themselves well; reappeared after the danger, and invited new groups of their nationality from Wallachia and Moldova."(Haraszti, 1971, p. 55) Thus, the Romanians, masters of subterfuge, had not only entered Transylvania so stealthily that no one noticed their arrival, but they had also managed to evade all the Mongol and Turkish invaders. This contrast of "brave Hungarian warriors" and "elusive Romanians" persists even in recent literature:

"The Romanians who immigrated to Transylvania belonged to the mass of outcast peasants who did not contribute to defending the land. Therefore they were not included in the alliance of the three Transylvanian nations (Hungarians, Szeklers, Saxons) founded in 1437. It was the Hungarians, together with the Transylvania Saxons, who defended Transylvania from enemy attacks and paid a high price in blood, while the Romanians contributed practically nothing to military defense for a century."(Holló, 2007, p. 176)

This theory is also at odds with historical evidence. Ironically, the very first mention of Romanians in Hungarian documents in 1210 portrays them as warriors in the Hungarian army,(Curta, 2006b, p. 385) and were even recorded as fighting as far away as

Bohemia.(Boczek, 1841, p. 286, CCXCV) The Mongol invasion of 1241 did not spare the Romanians, who engaged the Mongols in several battles both outside and inside of the Transylvanian Carpathians,(Papacostea, 1993, p. 95; Pop, 1996, p. 163) and there is evidence that Romanians also participated at the disastrous battle of Mohi.(Epure, 2011) The Mongols were also engaged by the Romanians during retreat from Hungary in 1242 and, if we are to believe the chronicler Philippe Mousket, "the king of the Vlachs[f] defeated the Mongols at the passes."(Reiffenberg, 1838, p. 681) A second Mongol invasion, in 1285 met with stiff resistance from the Romanians and Szeklers, who had managed to seal off the mountain passes,(Binder, 1996) and Romanians continued to defend Transylvania throughout the fourteenth century.(Nicolle & McBridge, 2004, p. 11)

The Romanians were also much-noted participants in the struggle against the Ottomans. Firstly, the principalities of Wallachia and Moldova served as buffer regions for the Kingdom of Hungary and Poland. Furthermore, Transylvanian Romanians repeatedly won renown in the wars against the Ottomans. Numerous Romanian families were ennobled in the fifteenth century as a result of the anti-Ottoman struggle.(Köpeczi, 2002, p. 493) The most famous of these Romanian nobles was John Hunyadi, who would eventually become Regent of Hungary. Perhaps the most famous general in Hungarian history, it is no coincidence that the Romanian nobility experienced great social mobility throughout his reign as a result of their outstanding military contributions.(Dragan, 2008, pp. 177-178) Jehann de Wawrin is an important source on the Romanians fighting against the Ottomans under the banner of Hunyadi:

> "The Grand Turk [the Ottoman Sultan] assembled a huge army numbering a hundred thousand men commanded and led by Beirlabey. With this great army he crossed the River Danube and entered Wallachia. When the Vlachs knew that it had come, they assembled as many men as they could and appointed a captain called Johannes de Hognac [John Hunyadi], a great lord of that realm whose domains were in Transylvania, stretching between Hungary and Wallachia."(Imber, 2006, p. 108)

The Romanian nation had by this time earned renown as a warrior nation. Pope Pius II, a contemporary of John Hunyadi, stated that John's "Dacian" (i.e. Romanian) ancestry was evidenced by his military valor.(Fejér, 1844) Some Hungarian contemporaries of the time even regarded Transylvania's army as a predominantly Romanian institution.(Pop, 2003, pp. 114-115) The Romanians were the majority of Transylvania's population and were well represented in the army, as joining the army was a popular method by which one could escape serfdom. One of the most violent Romanian peasant

---

[f] It must be noted that the identity of this supposed "king" is still debatable but much evidence suggests he was the Emperor of Bulgaria. Dimitri Korobeinikov noted that the chronicle of Mousket matches an Arab description of the Emperor of Bulgaria as the "king of Vlachia" (*malik awalaq*). There are some historians (Pop, 1996. p. 163) that doubt this interpretation, especially due to the geographical description, and believe Mousket is writing of a Romanian cneaz in the Carpathians. Whatever the case may be, Mousket's source is yet another document which illustrates that the Romanians did not "hide themselves well" but rather fought both north and south of the Danube.

revolts in Transylvanian history, the revolt of Horea in 1784, was caused by Emperor Leopold I abolishing voluntary military enrollment.(Karpat, 2002, p. 404) It seems evident then that the Romanians were not "protected at the expense of the Hungarians" but rather proved ever-ready to join armies and campaigns. War proved more appealing to the Romanians than the miserable existence on the lowest rung of Transylvania's social ladder. They formed a vanguard of Transylvania's defense as the gate-keepers of the Carpathians, along with the Szeklers.

Hungarian historians also attempted to discredit the Daco-Roman theory by presenting it as an invention of Romanian nationalists in the eighteenth and nineteenth century. The claim was that "in the nineteenth century, in the Age of Romanticism, the myth of the Daco-Roman origin of the Romanians was created."(Botos, 1999, p. 78) The theory had simply been invented for political gain, as "Rumanian nationalism was fueled by a relatively new historical theory"(Sisa, 1990, p. 190) which was used to justify their demands for equal rights. It was argued that the Romanians, and not the Austrians or Hungarians, had broken from the established theories of European historiography and had invented something for political gain. The theory therefore should not be taken seriously by modern academics as it was invented for political purposes. The Transylvanian School is usually credited as being the mastermind behind this intrepid conspiracy:

> "Also during this initial stage, the theory of the so-called Daco-Roman continuity emerged at the end of the eighteenth century and served as a foundation of the romantic Romanian national identity. Samuil Klain-Micu, working in Hungarian-ruled Transylvania, and Petru Maior, operating in the Ottoman-dominated Romanian Principalities around the turn of the eighteenth and nineteenth centuries, rediscovered early myths about the glorious origins of the Romanians people."(I. Berend, 1998, p. 57)

From all we have read on the controversy up to this point, this argument is almost ironic. The Daco-Roman Continuity Theory has a large number of historical precedents, the first writers to make such claims being Byzantines during the High Middle Ages. Daco-Roman Continuity was then propagated, in one form or another, by Renaissance humanists. Lastly we have the numerous writers from the Baroque period and onward who continued to bring forward new evidence and arguments for the theory. It is arguable then that the theory of Daco-Roman Continuity is nine centuries old if we consider Byzantine sources. It cannot be considered a new invention made by Romanian historians for political purposes.

The irony is that the Immigration Theory that was invented in the nineteenth century was adopted by Hungarians out of national interest. Daco-Roman continuity had been an accepted fact until then. When Micu-Klein used historic arguments to justify the expansion of Romanian civil liberties, he was simply repeating what he had learned in the Western Jesuit schools! Clearly Daco-Roman Continuity must have been generally accepted for Micu-Klein to even consider it as a political weapon. When the Austrians and Hungarians had seen the headache a little bit of education in history could make, they decided the best policy was to nip the problem in the bud. The Immigration Theory was thus invented to silence the Romanian national awakening and counter their claims for political equality.

The Immigration Theory has remained stagnant for the better part of a century. The arguments used in Hungarian publications today are mostly the same as those used nearly a century ago. Some new arguments were introduced, but this was done by making the conclusion first and finding the evidence later. Romanian historians have also not been innocent of using the same methodology, but at the very least the Daco-Roman Continuity theory was not always politically motivated.

Critical questions have still not been resolved by the Immigration Theory. Where the Romanians would have formed is still not clarified. No logical motive for why the Romanians migrated to Transylvania has been produced, and likely never will be. The basic yet fundamental question of where so many Romanians came from has never been answered, and it relies on the spontaneous generation of "Vlach refugees" from the Balkans that were never recorded. Some of these questions were asked in the 1930's in Robert Seton-Watson's *A History of the Roumanians*[Seton-Watson, 1934, p. 15] and they still have no convincing answer.

The Immigration Theory has failed to answer any historical questions. It was a politically-motivated invention with numerous inconsistencies that has only mystified and obscured Romanian history. It was from its inception merely designed to contradict the central tenets of Daco-Roman Continuity. If Daco-Roman Continuity argued that a Dacian element continued in Dacia after the Roman conquest, then the Immigration Theory countered that the vast majority of the Dacians were exterminated.[Vékony, 2000, p. 105] If the Daco-Roman theory then argued that the Dacians left in the Roman province were Romanised, the Immigration Theory retorted that Romanising the Dacians in 165 years would have been impossible... even though according to the same theory the Dacians were already exterminated. While, indeed, it would be pretty hard to teach Latin to the dead, this is clearly not the argument of the Immigration Theory. Put it simply, the Immigration Theory is the product of a dishonest method of studying history.

The Daco-Roman Continuity theory is supported by modern historians, both in Romania and abroad, not for any political purposes but rather because it a logical thesis. The claim that the Daco-Roman theory is used by the Romanians to justify their rule in Transylvania is disingenuous. Romanian rule in Transylvania is justified by the fact that the Romanians form the absolute demographic majority, a situation that likely has not changed for over 1,000 years. Historical precedence is meaningless in an era where demographic representation is used to justify self-determination. Rather, it is the Hungarians, who do not make up the ethnic majority, that require historical precedence as a weapon of last resort to prove "rightful ownership."

If Romanian historians reject Rösler's theory, it is not because it is "anti-Romanian" but rather because, as historian Florin Curta pointed out, "it is not supported by any shred of evidence."[Curta, 2006a] Rudolf Windisch provided a review of Rösler's theory one hundred years after it had been conceived, taking into account the progress made in archaeology and linguistics since then. His conclusion was telling: "in essence we consider that the Röslerian thesis – especially in the dogmatic, obstinate form represented by Rösler himself – can no longer be maintained."(Windisch, 1981, p. 415) Or, to put it in the words of Coriolan H. Opreanu:

"Still, nowhere else has anyone defied reason by stating that a Latin people, twice as numerous as any of its neighbors of different ethnic-linguistic origins, is only accidentally inhabiting the territory of a former Roman province, once home to a numerous and strongly Romanized population, but to which the contemporary inhabitants are allegedly not related in any way. Those attempting to scientifically demonstrate the absurd are free to do so. It is not our duty… to respond by demonstrating the absurdity of the absurd."(Opreanu, 2006, p. 108)

Works Cited

Balogh, S. (2006). Separating Myths and Facts In the History of Transylvania *Hungarian history, 1100 years of success*. Budapest, Hungary: Corvinus Library.

Bátonyi, G. (1999). *Britain and Central Europe, 1918-1933*. Oxford, UK: Oxford University Press.

Berend, I. (1998). *Decades of Crisis: Central and Eastern Europe before World War II*. Berkeley, CA: University of California Press.

Bethlen, I. (1971). *The Treaty of Trianon and European peace*. New York, NY: Arno Press.

Bideleux, R., & Jeffries, I. (2007). *A History of Eastern Europe: crisis and change*. Abingdon, UK; New York, NY: Routledge.

Binder, P. (1996). Antecedente şi consecinţe sud-transilvănene ale formării voievodatului Munteniei (sec. XIII-XIV). *Acta Historiae, 2,* 265-279.

Boczek, A. (1841). *Codex diplomaticus et Epistolaris Moraviae* (Vol. III). Olomucii: Typographia Alousii Skarnitzl.

Bod, P. t. (1890). *Historia Hungarorum Ecclesiastic* (Vol. III). Lugduni-Batavorum.

Botos, L. (1999). *The Road to the Dictated Peace*. Cleveland: Árpád.

Brezeanu, S. (1984). *Daco-Romanian Continuity: Science and Politics*. Bucharest, Romania: Editura Ştiintifică şi Enciclopedică.

Ciolan, I. N., Voicu, C., & Racoviţan, M. (1993). *Transylvania: Romanian history and perpetuation, or, what official Hungarian documents say*. Bucharest, Romania: Military Pub. House.

Cornwall, M. (2004). Great Britain and the Splintering of Greater Hungary: 1914-1918. In L. Péter & M. C. Rady (Eds.), *Proceedings to the conference on British-Hungarian Relations Since 1848*. London, UK: University College London; Hungarian Cultural Centre.

Curta, F. (2006a). Response to István Vásáry's Response to Curta's review of Cumans and Tatars. Oriental Military in the Pre-Ottoman Balkans (1185-1365) (Cambridge: Cambridge University Press, 2005). *The Medieval Review, 06.04.03.*

Curta, F. (2006b). *Southeastern Europe in the Middle Ages: 500-1250*. Cambridge, UK: Cambridge University Press.

Dragan, I. (2008). The Romanian Nobility of Transylvania in the Time of the Hunyadis *Matthias Corvinus' Personality and Time*. Cluj-Napoca, Romania: Babeş-Bolyai University Press.

Endrey, A. (1986). *The Other Hungary: the history of Transylvania*. Melbourne: The Hungarian Institute.

Epure, V.-A. (2011). Invazia Mongolă în Ungaria şi in spaţiul românesc [The Mongol Invasion in Hungary and the Romanian space]. *ROCSIR Revista RomâROCSIR Revista Româna de Studii Culturale (pe Internet)*.

Evans, R. J. (2006). *Austria, Hungary, and the Habsburgs: essays on Central Europe, c. 1683-1867*. Oxford, UK; New York, NY: Oxford University Press.

Fejér, G. (1844). *Genus et incunabula Joannis, regni Hungariae Gubernatoris*. Buda: Magyar Orszagos Leveltar.

Georgescu, V. (1991). *The Romanians: a history* (A. Bley-Vroman, Trans.). Columbus, OH: Ohio State University Press.

Giurescu, C. C. (1969). *Transylvania in the History of Romania: an historical outline.* London, UK: Garnstone.

Halmos, M. (1982). *The Truth about Transylvania.* Youngstown, OH: The Author.

Haraszti, E. (1971). *The Ethnic History of Transylvania.* Astor Park, FL: Danubian Press.

Haraszti, E. (1979). Origin of the Rumanians. In A. F. Sannborn & G. W. de Czege (Eds.), *Transylvania and the Hungarian-Rumanian Problem.* Astor Park: Danubian Press.

Holló, L. (2007). Thinking God in National and Religious Conflicts: The Case of Romania. In N. Nintersteiner (Ed.), *Naming and Thinking God in Europe Today: theology in global dialogue.* Amsterdam, Netherlands; New Yor, NY: Rodopi.

Hurmuzaki, E. (1887). *Documente Privitoare la istoria românilor [Documents relevant to the history of the Romanians].* Bucharest, Romania: Academia Româna.

Imber, C. (2006). *The Crusade of Varna, 1443-45.* Aldershot, UK Burlington, VA: Ashgate.

Jordan, P. (1998). Romania. In C. B. Paulston & D. Peckham (Eds.), *Linguistic Minorities in Central and Eastern Europe.* Clevedon: Multilingual Matters.

Karpat, K. H. (2002). *Studies on Ottoman Social and Political History: selected articles and essays.* Leiden, Netherlands: Brill.

Kazar, L., & Makai, J. (2001). *Transylvania, in search of facts.* Linfield, Australia: Trianon Forum.

Köpeczi, B. (2002). History of Transylvania: from 1606 to 1830. In B. Köpeczi, L. Makkai & A. Mocsy (Eds.), *History of Transylvania, vol II: from the beginnings to 1606.* Boulder, CO; New York, NY: Social Science Monographs.

Kosztin, Á. (2006). *Chronicle of Cruelties: Romanian mistreatment of the Hungarian minority in Transylvania.* Toronto, Canada: Corvinus Library.

Lazar, I. (1997). *Transylvania: a short history.* Safely Harbor, FL: Simon Publications.

Ludescu, S. (1998). *Letopiseţul Cantacuzinesc.* Chişinău, Moldova: Litera.

Nay, A. D., Nay, A. D., & Kosztin, A. r. d. (1997). *Transylvania and the Rumanians.* Hamilton, Canada; Buffalo, NY: Matthias Corvinus Library.

Nicolle, D., & McBridge, A. (2004). *Hungary and the Fall of Eastern Europe, 1000-1568.* Oxford, UK: Osprey.

Opreanu, C. H. (2006). The North Danube Regions from the Roman Province of Dacia to the Emergence of the Romanian Language. In I.-A. Pop, I. Bolovan & A. Susana (Eds.), *History of Romania: Compendium.* Cluj-Napoca, Romania: Romanian Cultural Institute.

Papacostea, Ş. (1993). *Românii in Secolul al XIII-lea: între Cruciată şi Imperiul Mongol [The Romanians in the 13th Century: between the Crusade and the Mongol Empire].* Bucharest, Romania: Editura Enciclopedică.

Parchami, A. (2009). *Hegemonic Peace and Empire: the Pax Romana, Britannica and Americana.* Abingdon, UK; New York, NY: Routledge.

Pearson, R. (1996). Hungary: a state truncated, a nation dismembered. In S. Dunn (Ed.), *Europe and Ethnicity: World War I and contemporary ethnic conflict.* Florence, KY: Routledge.

Petrovics, I. (2009). Foreign Ethnic Groups in the Towns of Southern Hungary in the Middle Ages. In D. Keene & B. Nagy (Eds.), *Segregation – Integration – Assimilation*. Farnham, England; Burlington, VA: Ashgate.

Pop, I.-A. (1996). *Românii şi maghiarii în secolele IX-XIV: Geneza statului medieval în Transilvania [The Romanians and Magyars in the 9th-14th centuries: the genesis of the medieval state in Transylvania]*. Cluj-Napoca, Romania: Centrul de Studii Transilvane.

Pop, I.-A. (2002). Unele urmări în plan confesional ale cruciadei a IV-a (1204) în Centrul şi Sud-Estul Europei. In M. Dobre (Ed.), *Istorie şi Ideologie: omagiu profesorului Stelian Brezeanu la 60 de ani*. Bucharest, Romania: Editura Universitară Bucureşti.

Pop, I.-A. (2003). Nations and Denominations in Transylvania (13th-16th Century). In C. Levai & V. Vese (Eds.), *Tolerance and intolerance in historical perspective*. Pisa, Italy: Clioh's Workshop.

Pop, I.-A., Barbulescu, M., & Nägler, T. (2005). *The History of Transylvania, I (up to 1541)*. Cluj-Napoca: CTS, Romanian Cultural Institute.

Prodan, D. (1996). *Transylvania and Again Transylvania: a historical expose*. Cluj-Napoca, Romania: Centrul de Studii Transilvane, Fundaţia Culturala Română

Rădvan, L. (2009). Considerations Regarding the Urbanization Process in Wallachia (13th-15th Centuries). In L. Pilat (Ed.), *Medieval and Early Modern Studies for Central and Eastern Europe*. Iasi, Romania: Alexandru Ioan Cuza University.

Reiffenberg, A. F. d. (1838). *Chronique Rimée de Philippe Mouskes* (Vol. II). Brussels, Belgium: Commission Royale d'Histoire.

The Resources and Future of Austria. (1863). *The Quarterly Review, 114*, 34.

Roe, P. (2005). *Ethnic Violence and the Social Security Dilemma*. London, UK; New York, NY: Routledge.

Rothschild, J. (1992). *East Central Europe between the two World Wars*. Seattle, WA: Univ. of Washington Press.

Sedlar, J. W. (1993). *East Central Europe in the Middle Ages, 1000-1500*. Seattle, WA: University of Washington Press.

Seton-Watson, R. W. (1925). Transylvania (IV) Transylvania since 1867. *The Slavonic Review, 4*(10), 101-123.

Seton-Watson, R. W. (1934). *A History of the Roumanians*. Cambridge, UK: Cambridge University Press.

Sisa, S. (1990). *The Spirit of Hungary: a panorama of Hungarian history and culture*. Toronto, Canada: Rákóczi Foundation.

Spinei, V. (1986). *Modlova in the 11th-14th Centuries*. Bucharest, Romania: Editura Academiei Republicii Socialiste România.

Spinei, V. (2009). *The Romanians and the Turkic Nomads North of teh Danube Delta from the Tenth to the Mid-Thirteenth Century*. Leiden, Netherlands: Brill.

Steed, H. W. (1914). *The Habsburg Monarchy*. London, UK: Constable & Company.

Stratilescu, T. (1906). *From Carpathian to Pindus*. London, UK: T. Fisher Unwin.

Sugar, P. F. (1977). *Southeastern Europe under Ottoman Rule: 1354-1804*. Seattle, WA: University of Washington Press.

Thuroczy, J. d. (1766). *Chronica Hungarorum*. Vienna.

Treptow, K. W., & Bolovan, I. (1995). *A History of Romania*. Iași, Romania: Center for Romanian Studies.

Vásáry, I. (2005). *Cumans and Tatars: Oriental military in the pre-Ottoman Balkans, 1185-1365*. Cambridge, UK: Cambridge University Press.

Vékony, G. (2000). *Dacians, Romans, Romanians*. Budapest, Hungary: Corvinus Library.

Windisch, R. (1981). Teza lui Robert Roesler – o sută de ani mai târziu. In W. d. Gruyter (Ed.), *Logos Semantikos. Studia in honorem Eugenio Coseriu* (Vol. I). Madrid, Spain; Berlin, Germany: Gredos/Walter de Gruyter.

Part 2 Figures

a) The original regions of Romanian habitation according to the *Cantacuzino Chronicle*, described as being bound by the Olt, Mureş, Danube, and Tisza rivers, matches the boundaries of the ancient Roman colony of Dacia.

b) The political map of Transylvania on the eve of the Magyar conquest, as drawn by James Berry in 1919. The names of states are coupled with the rough date of their supposed existence, though Berry's attempt to cover three centuries in one image makes the map slightly confusing. Menumorut's, Glad's, and Gelu's holdings are shown in Transylvania.

c) Innocentiu Micu-Klein, one of the leaders of the Transylvanian School and the Romanian enlightenment. His active, if unsuccessful, political overtures were buttressed by established historical knowledge of the time, making Daco-Roman Continuity a political issue.

d) Hungarian historians until the nineteenth century widely admitted that the Romanians were present north of the Danube before the thirteenth century. This ethno-political map of Europe in the tenth century, from a Hungarian encyclopedia published in 1893, situates the Romanians (*Vlachok*) north of the Danube.

e) An ethnic map of Austro-Hungary dating from 1892. Notably, the Hungarians (white) were only a majority in the central part of the kingdom and in the eastern fringe of Transylvania. The rest of the Transylvanian landscape was demographically dominated by the Romanians.

a)

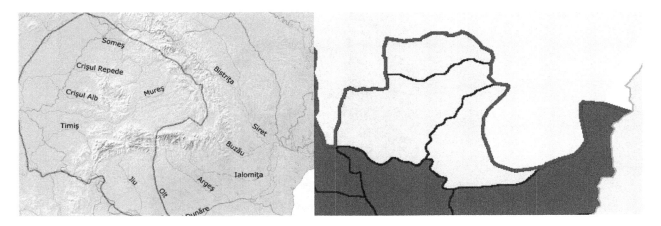

b)

175

c)

d)

e)

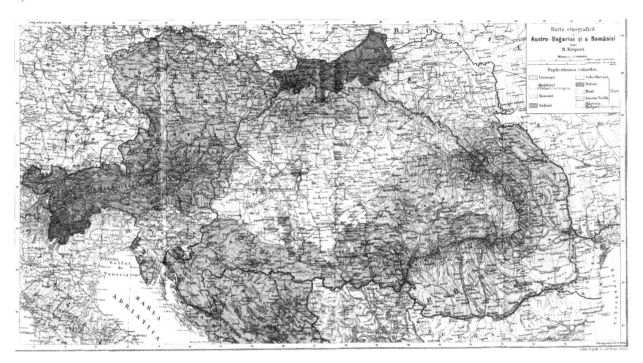

COMPLETE BIBLIOGRAPHY

Ahrweiler, H. (1998). Byzantine Concepts of the Foreigner: The Case of the Nomads. In H. Ahrweiler & A. LAiou (Eds.), *Studies on the internal diaspora of the Byzantine Empire*. Cambridge, MA: Harvard University Press.

Al-Nadim. (1970). *The Fihrist. A Tenth-Century Survey of Muslim Culture*. New York, NY: Columbia University Press.

Ambrose. Expositio evangelii secundum Lucam.

Angold, M. (1997). *The Byzantine Empire, 1025-1204: a political history*. London, UK ; New York , NY: Longman.

The Annals of Fulda. (T. Reuter, Trans.). Manchester, UK: Manchester University Press.

Anonymous. (1916). *Descriptio Europae Orientalis*. Cracow, Poland: Gebethner.

Anonymous. (2008). *Gesta Hungarorum* (M. Rady, Trans.).

Ansbert. (2010). *Historia de expeditio Frederici Imperatoris*. Farnham, UK Burlington, VT: Ashgate.

Ardevan, R. (2007). *On the Latest Inscriptions of Roman Dacia*. Paper presented at the 13th International Congress of Greek and Latin Epigraphy, Oxford, UK.

Armbruster, A. (1972). *Romanitatea Românilor: Istoria Unei Idei [The Romanity of the Romanians: the History of an Idea]*. Bucharest, Romania: Editura Academiei Republicii Socialiste România.

Arvinte, V. (1983). *Român, Românesc, România [Romanian people, Romanian, Romania]*. Bucharest, Romania: Editura Ştiinţifică şi Enciclopedică.

Augustus. Res Gestae.

Băcueţ-Crişan, D. (2005). Depresiunea Silvaniei în secolele VII-XI. *Bibliotheca Septemcastrensis, XII*.

Bakker, P., & Kiuchkov, K. (2000). *What is the Romani Language*. Hatfield, UK; Paris, France: University of Hertfordshire Press Centre de recherches tsiganes.

Balogh, S. (2006). Separating Myths and Facts In the History of Transylvania *Hungarian history, 1100 years of success*. Budapest, Hungary: Corvinus Library.

Barta, C. (2002). Unirea cu Roma: fundamentarea teologico-dogmatică. Un exemplu: Catehismul lui Iosif de Camillis. *Annales Universitatis Apulensis Series Historica, 6*(I), 75-79.

Bátonyi, G. (1999). *Britain and Central Europe, 1918-1933*. Oxford, UK: Oxford University Press.

Bejan, A. (1995). *Banatul in secolele IV-XII [Banat in the 4th to 12th centuries]*. Timisoara: Editura de Vest.

Bejan, A. (1998). *Dacia Felix: Istoria Daciei Romane*. Timisoara, Romania: Editura Eurobit.

Bennett, J. (1997). *Trajan Optimus Princeps: A Life and Times*. London, UK New York, NY: Routledge.

Berend, I. (1998). *Decades of Crisis: Central and Eastern Europe before World War II*. Berkeley, CA: University of California Press.

Berend, N. (2006). *At the Gate of Christandom: Jews, Muslims, and "pagans" in medieval Hungary*. Cambridge, UK; New York, NY: Cambridge University Press.

Berry, J. (1919). Transylvania and Its Relations to Ancient Dacia and Modern Rumania. *The Geographical Journal, 53*(3).

Berza, M., & Pascu, Ş. (1977). *Documenta Romaniae Historica*. Bucharest, Romania: Academia de Ştiinţe Sociale şi Politice a Republicii Socialiste România.

Bethlen, I. (1971). *The Treaty of Trianon and European peace*. New York, NY: Arno Press.

Bideleux, R., & Jeffries, I. (2007). *A History of Eastern Europe: crisis and change*. Abingdon, UK; New York, NY: Routledge.

Binder, P. (1996). Antecedente şi consecinţe sud-transilvănene ale formării voievodatului Munteniei (sec. XIII-XIV). *Acta Historiae, 2*, 265-279.

Boardman, J. (1982). *The Prehistory of the Balkans, and the Middle East and the Aegean World, tenth to eight centuries B.C.* Cambridge, UK: Cambridge University Press.

Boczek, A. (1841). *Codex diplomaticus et Epistolaris Moraviae* (Vol. III). Olomucii: Typographia Alousii Skarnitzl.

Bod, P. t. (1890). *Historia Hungarorum Ecclesiastic* (Vol. III). Lugduni-Batavorum.

Bodolai, Z. (1980). *The Unmaking of Peace: the fragmentation and subsequent destruction of Central Europe after World War One by the Peace Treaty of Trianon*. Melbourne, Australia: Committe for Human Rights in Central Europe.

Boia, L. (2001a). *History and Myth in the Romanian Consciousness*. Budapest, Hungary: Central European University Press.

Boia, L. (2001b). *Romania: Borderland of Europe*. London, UK: Reaktion.

Bonfinius, A. (1568). *Rerum Ungaricarum decades quatuor cum dimidia*.

Bosch, E., Calafell, F., González-Neira, A., Flaiz, C., Mateu, E., Scheil, H.-G., . . . Comas, D. (2006). Paternal and maternal lineages in the Balkans show a homogeneous landscape over linguistic barriers, except for the isolated Aromuns. *Annals of Human Genetics, 70*(4), 459-487.

Botos, L. (1999). *The Road to the Dictated Peace*. Cleveland: Árpád.

Brătianu, G. I. (1988). *Marea Neagră [The Black Sea]* (Vol. I). Bucharest, Romania: Meridiane.

Braund, D. (1984). *Augusts to Nero: a sourcebook on Roman history, 31 BC-AD 68*. London, UK: Croom Helm.

Breza, M., & Pascu, Ş. (1977). *Documenta Romaniae Historica*. Bucharest, Romania: Academia de Ştiinţe Sociale şi Politice a Republicii Socialiste România.

Brezeanu, S. (1984). *Daco-Romanian Continuity: Science and Politics*. Bucharest, Romania: Editura Ştiinţifică şi Enciclopedică.

Brezeanu, S. (1999). *Romanitatea Orientală în Evul Mediu : de la cetăţenii romani la naţiunea medievală [The Oriental Romanity in the Middle Ages: from Roman citizens to medieval nation]*. Bucharest, Romania: All Educational.

Brezeanu, S. (2001). A Byzantine Model for Political and State Structure in Southeastern Europe between the Thirteenth and Fifteenth Centuries. In R. Theodorescu & L. C. Barrows (Eds.), *Politics and Culture in Southeastern Europe*. Bucharest, Romania: UNESCO.

Brezeanu, S. (2003). The Lower Danube Frontier during the 4th-7th Centuries. An ambiguous Notion. *Annuario, Instituto Romeno di cultura e ricerca umanistica, 5*.

Bryant, D., Filimon, F., & Gray, R. D. (2005). Untangling our past: Languages, Trees, Splits and Networks.

Bucur, I.-M., & Costea, I. (2009). Transylvania between Two National Historiographies. Historical Consciousness and Political Identity. In S. G. Ellis, R. Esser, J.-F. Berdah & M. Řezník (Eds.), *Frontiers, Regions and Identities in Europe*. Pisa, Italy: Plus-Pisa university press.

Bulei, I. (2005). *A Short History of Romania*. Bucharest, Romania: Meronia.

Bunea, A. (1900). *Din Istoria Românilor. Episcopul Ioan Inocenþiu Klein (1728–1751)*. Blaj.

Burdrick, W. L. (2003). *The Principles of Roman Law and Their Relation to Modern Law*. Clark, NJ: Lawbook Exchange.

Burger, M. (2008). *The Shaping of Western Civilization: From Antiquity to the Enlightenment*. Peterborough, ON: Broadview Press.

Burns, T. S. (1991). *A History of the Ostrogoths*. Bloomington, IN: Indiana University Press.

Bury, J. B. (1920). Review of Peisker, J. Die Abkunft der Rumdnen wirtschaftsgeschichtlich untersucht. *The English Historical Review, 35*(140).

Cancatuzino, C. (1997). *Istoria Tarii Romanesti*. Chişinău: Litera International.

Cantemir, D. (1997). *Descrierea Moldovei* (P. Pandrea, Trans.). Bucharest, Romania: Litera International.

Chappell, L. S. (2005). *Romanization in Dacia*. Los Angeles, CA: University of California Los Angeles.

Chirol, I. V. (1881). *'Twixt Greek and Turk, or, Jottings during a journey through Thessaly, Macedonia, and Epirus*. London, UK; Edinburgh, UK: William Blackwood and Sons.

Chiţoran, I. (2001). *The Phonology of Romanian: a constraint-based approach*. Hawthorne, NY: Mouton de Gruyter.

Choniates, N. (1984). *O City of Byzantium: annals of Nicetas Choniates* (H. J. Magoulias, Trans.). Detroit: Wayne State University Press.

Christich, E. (1923). Dacians of To-Day. *New Blackfriars, 4*(42), 1070-1076.

Chronicon Pictum Vindobonense. Lipsiae: 1883.

Chrysostom, D. *Oratores*.

Cicero. *De Haruspicum responsis*.

Cioban, Ş. (1989). *Istoria literaturii române vechi [The History of Old Romanian Literature]*. Bucharest, Romania: Editura Eminescu.

Ciolan, I. N., Voicu, C., & Racoviţan, M. (1993). *Transylvania: Romanian history and perpetuation, or, what official Hungarian documents say*. Bucharest, Romania: Military Pub. House.

Clark, C. U. (1932). *United Roumania*. New York, NY: Dodd, Mead and Company.

Clark, H. (2000). *Civil Resistance in Kosovo*. London, UK; Sterling, VA: Pluto Press.

Cornwall, M. (2004). Great Britain and the Splintering of Greater Hungary: 1914-1918. In L. Péter & M. C. Rady (Eds.), *Proceedings to the conference on British-Hungarian Relations Since 1848*. London, UK: University College London; Hungarian Cultural Centre.

Costin, M. *Letopiseţul Ţării Moldovei*.

Crişan, I. H. (1978). *Burebista and His Time*. Bucharest, Romania: Editura Academiei Republicii Socialiste România.

Cunliffe, B. (2001). *The Oxford illustrated history of prehistoric Europe*. Oxford, UK: Oxford University Press.

Curta, F. (2001a). *The Making of the Slavs*. New York, NY: Cambridge University Press.

Curta, F. (2001b). Pots, Slavs, and Imagined Communities. *European Journal of Archaeology, 4*(3), 367-384.

Curta, F. (2001c). Transylvania around A.D. 1000. In P. Urbanczyk (Ed.), *Europe Around the Year 1000*. Warsaw, Poland: Wydawnictwo DIG.

Curta, F. (2004). The Slavic Lingua Franca: (linguistic notes of an archaeologist turned historian). *East Centra Eurpe, 31*(1), 125-148.

Curta, F. (2005a). Before Cyril and Methodius: Christianity and the Seventh-Century Danube Frontier. In F. Curta (Ed.), *East Central & Eastern Europe in the Early Middle Ages*. Ann Arbor, MI: University of Michigan Press.

Curta, F. (2005b). Frontier Ethnogenesis in Late Antiquity: The Danube, the Tervingi, and the Slavs. In F. Curta (Ed.), *Borders, barriers, and ethnogenesis: frontiers in late Antiquity and the Middle Ages* (pp. 449-471). Turnhout: Brepols.

Curta, F. (2005c). Review of Cumans and Tatars: Oriental Military in the Pre-Ottoman Balkans, 1185-1365 by István Vásáry (Cambridge, 2005). *Canadian Journal of History, 40*.

Curta, F. (2006a). Response to István Vásáry's Response to Curta's review of Cumans and Tatars. Oriental Military in the Pre-Ottoman Balkans (1185-1365) (Cambridge: Cambridge University Press, 2005). *The Medieval Review, 06.04.03*.

Curta, F. (2006b). *Southeastern Europe in the Middle Ages: 500-1250*. Cambridge, UK: Cambridge University Press.

Curtius, E. R., & Trask, W. R. (1990). *European Literature and the Latin Middle Ages*. Princeton, NJ: Princeton University Press.

Cusack, C. M. (1998). *Conversion among the Germanic Peoples*. London, UK: Cassell.

d'Ohsson, C. (1852). *Histoire des Mongols, depuis Tchinguiz-Khan jusqu'a Timour Beyou Tamerlan*. Amsterdam: Frederik Muller.

Deletant, D. (1980). Slavonic Letters in Moldova, Wallachia and Transylvania from the Tenth to the Seventeenth Centuries. *The Slavonic and East European Review, 58*(1-21).

Deletant, D. (1986). Moldova Between Hungary and Poland 1347-1412. *The Slavonic and East European Review, 64*(2), 189-211.

Densusianu, O. (1901). *Histoire de la Langue Roumaine* (Vol. I). Paris, France: Macon & PRotat.

Diaconescu, A. (2004). The towns of Roman Dacia: an overview of recent research. In W. S. Hanson & I. P. Haynes (Eds.), *Roman Dacia: the Making of a Provincial Society*. Portsmouth, RI: Journal of Roman Archaeology.

Diaconescu, T. (2000). Historia Augusta: Una Nuova Lezione dei Testi di Vopisco. *Studia Antiqua et Archaeologica, VII*, 155-170.

Dillon, S. (2006). Women on the Column of Trajan and Marcus Aurelius. In S. Dillon & K. Welch (Eds.), *Representations of War in Ancient Rome*. New York, NY: Cambridge University Press.

Dio, C. (2004). *Roman History* (E. Cary, Trans. Vol. LXVII). Cambridge, MA: Harvard University Press.

Diodorus. (2004). *Library of History* (Vol. I). Cambridge, MA; London, UK: Harvard University Press.

Djakonov, I. M. (1991). *Early Antiquity*. Chicago, IL: University of Chicago.

Djuvara, N. (2007). *Thocomerius-Negru Vodă. Un voivod de origine cumană la începuturile Ţării Româneşti*. Bucharest, Romania: Humanitas.

Drace-Francis, A. (2006). *The making of modern Romanian culture: literacy and the development of national identity*. London, UK: Tauris.

Dragan, I. (2008). The Romanian Nobility of Transylvania in the Time of the Hunyadis *Matthias Corvinus' Personality and Time*. Cluj-Napoca, Romania: Babeş-Bolyai University Press.

Drummond, S. K., & Nelson, L. H. (1994). *The Western Frontiers of Imperial Rome*. Armonk, NY; London, UK: Sharpe.

Dumitraşcu, S., & Sfrengeu, F. (2006). Relaţiile interetnice în Dacia Occidentală in secolele IV-VI. In I. M. Ţiplic (Ed.), *Bibliotheca Septamcastrensis: Relaţii interetnice în Spatiul Românesc (secolele VI-XIII)* (Vol. XXI). Bucharest: Departamentul pentru Relaţii Interetnice; Altip.

el-Maqdisî, M. b. T. (1907). *Le Livre de la Création et de l'Histoire*. Paris: Cl. Huart.

Ellis, L. (1998). Dacia Terra Deserta: Populations, Politics, and the [de]colonization of Dacia. *World Archaeology, 30*(2).

Endrey, A. (1986). *The Other Hungary: the history of Transylvania*. Melbourne: The Hungarian Institute.

Engel, P. (2001). *The Realm of Saint Stephen: A History of Medieval Hungary, 895-1526*. London, UK: Tauris.

Epure, V.-A. (2011). Invazia Mongolă în Ungaria şi in spaţiul românesc [The Mongol Invasion in Hungary and the Romanian space]. *ROCSIR Revista RomâROCSIR Revista Româna de Studii Culturale (pe Internet)*.

Eutropius. *Breviary*.

Evans, R. J. (2006). *Austria, Hungary, and the Habsburgs: essays on Central Europe, c. 1683-1867*. Oxford, UK; New York, NY: Oxford University Press.

Everitt, A. (2009). *Hadrian and the Triumph of Rome*. New York, NY: Random House.

Fejér, G. (1830). *Codex Diplomaticus*. Budae: Regiae Universistatis Ungaricae.

Fejér, G. (1844). *Genus et incunabula Joannis, regni Hungariae Gubernatoris*. Buda: Magyar Orszagos Leveltar.

Ferencz, I. V. (2006). Settlements and Necropoles: few considerations on the archaeological discoveries on the middle course of the Mureş River belonging to the La Tene B2-C1. *Acta Terrae Septemcastrensis, V*(1).

Fiedler, U. (2008). Bulgars in the Lower Danube Region: a survey of the archaeological evidence and of the state of current research. In F. Curta & R. Kovalev (Eds.), *The Other Europe in the Middle Ages: Avars, Bulgars, Khazars, and Cumans*. Leiden, Netherlands; Boston, MA: Brill.

Fine, J. v. A. (2000). *The Early Medieval Balkans: a critical survey from the sixth to the late twelfth century*. Ann Arbor, MI: University of Michigan Press.

Firică, C. (2008). Slav influence upon the Romanian language - direct references to Croatian. *Rustvena Istrazivanja, 19*(3), 511-523.

Fletcher, R. A. (1999). *The Barbarian Conversion: from Paganism to Christianity*. Berkeley, CA: University of California Press.

Florescu, R. R. (1999). *Essays on Romanian History*. Iasi, Romania; Oxford, UK; Portland, OR: Center for Romanian Studies.

Franckenstein, V. F. v. (1696). *Breviculus origines nationum et praecipue Saxonicae in Transylvania*. Sibiu: Cibinii Transylvanorum.

Friedman, V. A. (1986). Linguistics, Nationalism, and Literary Languages: A Balkan Perspective. In P. C. Bjrakman & V. Raskin (Eds.), *The Real-World Linguist: Linguistic Applications in the 1980's*. Norwood, NJ: ABLEX.

Friedman, V. A. (2000). After 170 years of Balkan Linguistics: Whither the Millennium? *Mediterranean Language Review, 12*, 1-15.

Friedman, V. A. (2001). *The Vlah Minority in Macedonia: Language, Identity, Dialectology, and Standardization*. Helsinki, Finland: University of Helsinki Press.

Frontinus, S. J. *Stratagems*.

Fronto, C. (1988). *Principia Historiae* (C. R. Haines, Trans. Vol. II). Cambridge, MA: Harvard University Press.

Fryde, E. B. (1983). *Humanism and Renaissance Historiography*. London, UK: Hambledon Press.

Gallagher, T. (2001). *Outcast Europe: the Balkans, 1789-1989, from the Ottomans to Milošević*. London, UK; New York, NY: Routledge.

Gândilă, A. (2009). Face value or Bullion value? Early Byzantine coins beyond the lower Danube border. In M. Woloszyn (Ed.), *Polish Academy of Arts and Sciences* (Vol. III). Krakow, Poland.

Găzdac, C. (1998). Coins and the abandonment of Dacia. *Acta Musei Napocensis, 35*(I).

Georgescu, V. (1991). *The Romanians: a history* (A. Bley-Vroman, Trans.). Columbus, OH: Ohio State University Press.

Georgiev, V. (1966). The Genesis of the Balkan Peoples. *The Slavonic and East European Review, 44*(103), 285-297.

Gibbon, E. (2004). *The history of the decline and fall of the Roman Empire* (Vol. I). Holicong, PA: Wildside Press.

Giurescu, C. C. (1969). *Transylvania in the History of Romania: an historical outline*. London, UK: Garnstone.

Glodariu, I. (1976). *Dacian Trade with the Hellenistic and Roman World*. Oxford, UK: British Archaeological Reports.

Goldsworthy, A. (2006). *Caesar: Life of a Colossus*. New Haven, CT: Yale University PRess.

Goldsworthy, A. (2009). *How Rome Fell: Death of a Superpower*. New Haven, CT: Yale University Press.

Gönczöl-Davies, R., & Deletant, D. (2002). *Colloquial Romanian: the complete course for beginners*. London, UK; New York, NY: Routledge.

Green, D. H. (2000). *Language and History in the Early Germanic World*. Cambridge, UK: Cambridge University Press.

Grzesik, R. (2003). Sources of a story about the murdered Croatian king in the Hungarian-Polish Chronicle. *Izlaganje sa znanstvenog skupa, 30*.

Gusztáv, W. (1862). *Monumenta Hungariae Historica*. Pest, Hungary: Magyar Tudomanyos Akademia.

Haarmann, H. (1996). *Early civilization and literacy in Europe: an inquiry into the cultural continuity in the Mediterranean world*. Berlin: Mouton de Gruyter.

Halmos, M. (1982). *The Truth about Transylvania*. Youngstown, OH: The Author.

Halsall, G. (2007). *Barbarian Migrations and the Roman West, 376-568*. Cambridge, UK: Cambridge University Press.

Haraszti, E. (1971). *The Ethnic History of Transylvania*. Astor Park, FL: Danubian Press.

Haraszti, E. (1979). Origin of the Rumanians. In A. F. Sannborn & G. W. de Czege (Eds.), *Transylvania and the Hungarian-Rumanian Problem*. Astor Park: Danubian Press.

Haynes, I. P., & Hanson, W. S. (2004). An Introduction to Roman Dacia *Roman Dacia: the making of a provincial society*. Portsmouth, RI: Journal of Roman Archaeology.

Hazzard-Cross, S. (1929). Yaroslav the Wize in Norse Tradition. *Speculum, 4*(2), 177-197.

Heather, D. B. (2004). *A History of Education for Citizenship*. London, UK; New York, NY: Routledge.

Heather, P. (1996). *The Goths*. Cambridge, MA: Blackwell.

Herodotus. *The Histories*.

Historia Augusta.

Hitchins, K. (1996). *The Romanians, 1774-1866*. Oxford, UK: Claredon Press.

Hitchins, K. (2001). *The Idea of Nation among the Romanians of Transylvania, 1700-1849*. Paper presented at the Nation and National Ideology: Past, Present, and PRospects, Bucharest, Romania.

Hitchins, K. (2002). Romanian Intellectuals and the Enlightenment in Transylvania. *Annales Universitatis Apulensis Series Historica, 6*(I), 99-105.

Holló, L. (2007). Thinking God in National and Religious Conflicts: The Case of Romania. In N. Nintersteiner (Ed.), *Naming and Thinking God in Europe Today: theology in global dialogue*. Amsterdam, Netherlands; New Yor, NY: Rodopi.

Honig, B. (2001). *Democracy and the Foreigner*. Princeton, NJ: Princeton University Press.

Hügel, P. (2003). *Ulitemele decenii ale stăpânirii romane in Dacia (Traianus Decius - Aurelian)*. Cluj-Napoca: Nereamia Napocae.

Hupchick, D. P. (1995). *Conflict and chaos in Eastern Europe*. New York: Palgrave.

Hupchick, D. P. (2001). *The Balkans : From Constantinople to Communism*. New York, NY: Palgrave Macmillan.

Hurmuzaki, E. (1887). *Documente Privitoare la istoria românilor [Documents relevant to the history of the Romanians]*. Bucharest, Romania: Academia Româna.

Husar, A. (2002). *Din Istoria Daciei Romane*. Cluj-Napoca, Romania: Presa Universitară Clujeană.

Huszti, A. (1791). *Ó és újj Dácia*: Diénes.

Illyés, E. (1992). *Ethnic Continuity in the Carpatho-Danubian Area*. Hamilton, Canada: Struktura Press.

Imber, C. (2006). *The Crusade of Varna, 1443-45*. Aldershot, UK Burlington, VA: Ashgate.

Ionescu, P. (2002). Interferențe culturale germano-române în epoca iluministă: Franz Joseph Sulzer. *Annales Universitatis Apulensis Series Historica, 6*(I).

Jansson, S. B. F., & Foote, P. (1987). *Runes in Sweden*. Stockholm, Sweden: Royal Academy of Letters, History, and Antiques.

Jelavich, B. (1989). *History of the Balkans: Eighteenth and Nineteenth Centuries* (Vol. I). Cambridge, UK: Cambridge University Press.

Jesch, J. (2001). *Ships and Men in the Lakte Viking Age: the Vocabulary of Runic Inscriptions*. Woodridge: Boydell & Brewer.

Jones, T., & Ereira, A. (2007). *Barbarians: an Alternative Roman History*. London, UK: BBC Books.

Jordan-Bychkov, T. G., & Jordan-Bychkov, B. (2002). *The European Culture Area: a systematic geography*. Lanham, MD: Rowman & Littlefield.

Jordan, P. (1998). Romania. In C. B. Paulston & D. Peckham (Eds.), *Linguistic Minorities in Central and Eastern Europe*. Clevedon: Multilingual Matters.

Jordanes. *Getica* (Vol. XI).

Julian. *The works of the emperor Julian* (W. C. Wright, Trans. Vol. II).

Jung, J. (1878). *Römer und Romanen in der Donaulandern*. Innsbruck, Germany: Historisch-ethnographische Studien.

Justinus. *Epitome of the Philippic history of Pompeius Trogus* (Vol. XXXII; XXXI; XXXII).

Juvenal. *The Satires*.

Kahl, T. (2002). The Ethnicity of the Aromanians after 1990: the Identity of a Minority that BEhaves like a Majority. *Ethnologia Balkanica, 6*, 145-169.

Kaldellis, A. (2007). *Hellenism in Byzantium: the transformations of Greek identity and the reception of the classical tradition*. Cambridge, UK: Cambridge University Press.

Karácsonyi, J. (1912). *Die Ansiedlung der Rumänen auf dem linken Donauufer*. Kolozsvar.

Karpat, K. H. (2002). *Studies on Ottoman Social and Political History: selected articles and essays*. Leiden, Netherlands: Brill.

Kazar, L., & Makai, J. (2001). *Transylvania, in search of facts*. Linfield, Australia: Trianon Forum.

Kellogg, F. (1990). *A History of Romanian Historical Writing*. Bakersfield, CA: C. Schlacks.

Kersken, N. (2003). High and Late Medieval National Historiography. In D. M. Deliyannis (Ed.), *Historiography in the Middle Ages*. Leiden, Netherlands: Brill.

Kéza, S. d. (1999). *Gesta Hungarorum*. Budapest: ADU Press.

Koch, J. (2006). *Celticu Culture: a Historical Encyclopedia*. Santa Barbara, CA; Oxford, UK: ABC-CLIO.

Kogălniceanu, M. (1967). *Texte social-politice alese*. Bucharest, Romania: Editura Politică.

Kohl, P. L. (2007). *The Making of Bronze Age Eurasia*. Cambridge, UK: Cambridge University Press.

Komnena, A. Alexiad.

Köpeczi, B. (2002). History of Transylvania: from 1606 to 1830. In B. Köpeczi, L. Makkai & A. Mocsy (Eds.), *History of Transylvania, vol II: from the beginnings to 1606*. Boulder, CO; New York, NY: Social Science Monographs.

Kostovicova, D. (2005). *Kosovo: the politics of identity*. Abingdon, UK; New York, NY: Routledge.

Kosztin, Á. (1997). *The Daco-Roman Legend*. Hamilton-Buffalo: Matthias Corvinus Publishing.

Kosztin, Á. (2006). *Chronicle of Cruelties: Romanian mistreatment of the Hungarian minority in Transylvania*. Toronto, Canada: Corvinus Library.

Krapivina, V. (2005). Problems of the Chronology of the Late Hellenistic Strata of Olbia. In V. Stolba & L. Hannestad (Eds.), *Black Sea Studies: Chronologies of the Black Sea Area in the Period c. 400-100 BC*. Aarhus, Denmark: Aarhus University Press.

Kristó, G. (1996). *Hungarian History in the Ninth Century*. Szeged, Hungary: Szegedi Kòzèpkorász Mùhely.

Kristó, G. (2003). *Early Transylvania (895-1324)*. Budapest, Hungary: Lucidus.

Kulikowski, M. (2007). *Rome's Gothic Wars*. Cambridge, UK: Cambridge University Press.

Kunstmann, H. (1996). *Die Slaven : ihr Name, ihre Wanderung nach Europa und die Anfänge der russischen Geschichte in historisch-onomastischer Sicht*. Stuttgart, Germany: Steiner.

Lazar, I. (1997). *Transylvania: a short history*. Safely Harbor, FL: Simon Publications.

Lenski, N. E. (2002). *Failure of Empire: Valens and the Roman state in the fourth century AD*. Los Angeles, CA: University of California Press.

Leskien, A. (1872). Review of Romanian Studies. *The Academy and Literature, 3*(40).

Lewis, B., Jurmain, R., & Kilgore, L. (2010). *Understanding Humans: an introduction to physical anthropology and archaeology*. Belmont, CA: Wadsworth Cengage Learning.

Lewis, J. (2010). *Nothing LEss than Victory: decisive wars and the lessons of history*. Princeton: Princeton University Press.

Lica, V. (2000). *The Coming of Rome in the Dacian World*. Konstanz: University of Konstanz Press.

Life of Constantine. (1983). Ann Arbor, MI: University of Michigan.

Lind, J. H. (2001). Scandinavian nemtsy and Repaganized Russians. The expansion of the Latin West During the Baltic Crusades and its Confessional Repercussions. In S. Hunyadi & J. Lászlóvszky (Eds.), *The Crusades and the Military Order: Expanding the Frontiers of Medieval Latin Christianity*. Budapest, Hungary: ADU Press.

Lipcsey, I. (2006). *Romania and Transylvania in the 20th Century*. Budapest, Hungary: Corvinus Library.

Liutprand. Antapodosis.

Livezeanu, I. (1995). *Cultural Politics in Greater Romania: Regionalism, Nation Building, & Ethnic Struggle*. Ithaca, NY: Cornell University Press.

Lockyear, K. (2004). *The Late Iron Age Background to Roman Dacia*. Portsmouth: Journal for Roman Archaeology.

Löte, L. L. (1980). *Transylvania and the theory of Daco-Roman-Rumanian continuity*. Rochester, NY: Committee of Transylvania.

Louthan, H. (1997). *The quest for compromise: peacemakers in counter-Reformation Vienna*. Cambridge, UK: Cambridge University Press.

Ludescu, S. (1998). *Letopisețul Cantacuzinesc*. Chișinău, Moldova: Litera.

Luttwak, E. N. (1979). *The Grand Strategy of the Roman Empire from the First Century A.D. to the Third*. Baltimore, MD: John Hopkins University Press.

MacArtney, C. A. (2009). *The medieval Hungarian historians: a critical and analytical guide*. Cambridge, UK: Cambridge University Press.

MacKendrick, P. (1975). *The Dacian Stones Speak*. Chapel Hill, NC: University of North Carolina Press.

MacKenzie, A. (1986). *Archaeology in Romania: the mystery of the Roman occupation*. London, UK: Hale.

Macko, N., & Blair, J. (1999). Glimpsing Romania. *Frontiers: A Journal of Women Studies, 20*(3), 36-41.

Madgearu, A. (1997). *Continuitate si discontinuitate la Dunarea de Jos in secolele VII-VIII*. Bucharest, Romania: University of Bucharest.

Madgearu, A. (2001). *Rolul Crestinismului in Formarea Poporului român*. Bucharest, Romania: BIC ALL.

Madgearu, A. (2004). Voievodatul lui Menumorout în lumina cercetărilor recente" (The Duchy of Menumorout in the light of the recent researches). *Analele Universităţii din Oradea. Istorie-arheologie, 11*.

Madgearu, A. (2005a). Români şi pecenegi în sudul Transilvaniei [Romanians and Pechenegs in Southern Transylvania. In Z. K. Pinter, I. M. Ţiplic & M. E. Ţiplic (Eds.), *Relatii interetnice in Transilvania (secolele VI-XIII)*. Bucharest: Departmentul pentru Relaţii Interetnice.

Madgearu, A. (2005b). *The Romanians in the Anonymous Gesta Hungarorum*. Cluj-Napoca: Center for Transylvania Studies.

Madgearu, A. (2005c). Salt Trade and Warfare: the rise of the Romanian-Slavic military organization in Early Medieval Transylvania. In F. Curta (Ed.), *East Central & Eastern Europe in the Early Middle Ages*. Ann Arbor, MI: University of Michigan Press.

Madgearu, A. (2008a). *Istoria Militara a Daciei Post-Romane, 275-376*. Targoviste, Romania: Cetatea de Scaun.

Madgearu, A. (2008b). The mission of Hierotheos: location and significance. *Byzantinoslavica*(1-2), 119-138.

Madgearu, A. (2010). *Istoria Militară a Daciei Post-Romane*. Târgoviste, Romania: Cetatea de Scaun.

Magocsi, P. R. (1996). *A History of Ukraine*. Toronto, Canada: University of Toronto Press.

Makkai, L. (2002). Transylvania in the medieval Hungarian kingdom (896-1526). In B. Köpeczi, L. Makkai & A. Mocsy (Eds.), *History of Transylvania, vol I: from the beginnings to 1606*. Boulder, CO; New York, NY: Social Science Monographs.

Malcolm, N. (1996). *Bosnia: a short history*. Washington Square, NY: New York University Press.

Mallory, J. P. (1997). *Encyclopedia of Indo-European Culture*. Chicago, IL: Fitzroy Dearborn.

Maracz, L. s. K. r. (1996). *Hungarian Revival: Political Reflections on Central Europe*. Nieuwegein: Aspekt.

Marcellinus, A. Rerum Gestarum.

Marler, J. (2003). *The Iconography and Social Structure of Old Europe: The Archaeomythological Research of Marija Gimbutas*. Paper presented at the World Congress on Matriarchal Studies, Luxemburg.

Maurice. *Strategicon*.

McLynn, F. (2009). *Marcus Aurelius: A Life*. Boston, MA: Da Capo Press.

Micle, D. (2008). *Digital Cartography and Spatial Analysis of Elements of the Dacian-Roman Rural Habitat in South-Western Dacia between the 2nd and the 5th century A.D*. Sibiu: Lucian Blaga University.

Migne, J. P. (1862). Patrologiae Latina. *CCXV*.

Miracles of Saint Demetrius.

Mócsy, A. (1974). *Pannonia and Upper Moesia: a history of the middle Danube provinces of the Roman Empire*. London, UK Boston, MA: Routledge & K. Paul.

Moga, I. (1994). *Les Roumains de Transylvanie au Moyen âge*. Sibiu: Centrul de Studii şi Cercetări Privitoare la Transilvania.

Molnár, M. (2001). *A Concise History of Hungary*. Cambridge, UK: Cambridge University Press.

Murgescu, B. (2001). *Istoria României în Texte*. Bucharest, Romania: Corint.

Muşat, M., & Ardeleanu, I. (1985). *From Ancient Dacia to Modern Romania*. Bucharest, Romania: Editura Ştiinţifică şi Enciclopedică.

Nandriş, G. (1939). The Earliest Contacts between Slavs and Roumanians. *The Slavonic and East European Review, 18*(52), 142-154.

Nandriş, G. (1946). The Beginnings of Slavonic Culture in the Roumanian Countries. *The Slavonic and East European Review, 24*(63), 160-171.

Năsturel, P. S. (1969). *Les Journal des Visites Canoniques de Metropolite de Hongrovalachie Néophyte le Crétois*. Athens, Greece: Pepragmena Philologikos Syllogos.

Nay, A. D. (1980). The Daco-Rumanian Theory of Continuity: Origins of the Rumanian Nation and Language. In L. L. Lőte (Ed.), *Transylvania and the theory of Daco-Roman-Rumanian Continuity*. Rochester, NY: Committeee of Transylvania.

Nay, A. D. (1996). *The Origins of the Romanians*. Toronto, Canada: Corvinus Library.

Nay, A. D., Nay, A. D., & Kosztin, A. r. d. (1997). *Transylvania and the Rumanians*. Hamilton, Canada; Buffalo, NY: Matthias Corvinus Library.

Neamţu, G., & Cordoş, N. (1994). *The Hungarian Policy of Magyarization in Transylvania: 1867-1918*. Cluj-Napoca, Romania: Center for Transylvanian Studies and the Romanian Cultural Foundation.

Németh, G. (2003). The Origins of the Tale of the Blood-drinking Hungarians. In C. Levai & V. Vese (Eds.), *Tolerance and intolerance in historical perspective*. Pisa, Italy: Clioh's Workshop.

Nestor. (1884). *Chronique de Nestor* (L. Leger, Trans.). Paris, France: L'Ecole des Langues Orientales Vivantes.

Nestor. (1953). *Russian Primary Chronicle, Laurentian Text* (S. Hazzard-Cross & O. Sherbowitz-Wetzor, Trans.). Cambridge, MA: The Medieval Academy of America.

Nestor. (2003). *Nestors krønike: beretningen om de svundne* (G. O. Svane, Trans.). Højbjerg, Denmark: Wormianum.

Nicolle, D., & McBridge, A. (2004). *Hungary and the Fall of Eastern Europe, 1000-1568*. Oxford, UK: Osprey.

Niculescu, G. (2007). Archaeology and Nationalism in the History of the Romanians. In P. L. Kohl (Ed.), *Selective Remembrances: archaeology in the construction, commemoration, and consecration of national pasts* (pp. 139-141). Chicaco, IL: Chicago University Press.

Olmsted, G. S. (2001). *Celtic art in transition during the first century BC : an examination of the creation of mint masters and metal smiths, and a analysis of stylistic development during the phase between La Tene and Provincial Roman*. Innsbruck: Inst. für Sprachen u. Literatur.

Oltean, I. (2007). *Dacia: Landscape, Colonisation and Romanisation*. New York, NY: Routledge.

Opreanu, C. H. (2006). The North Danube Regions from the Roman Province of Dacia to the Emergence of the Romanian Language. In I.-A. Pop, I. Bolovan & A. Susana (Eds.), *History of Romania: Compendium*. Cluj-Napoca, Romania: Romanian Cultural Institute.

Ovidius. (2005). *Tristia* (P. Green, Trans. Vol. V). Berkeley, CA: University of California Press.

Păcurariu, M. (2007). Romanian Christianity. In K. Parry (Ed.), *The Blackwell Companion to Eastern Christianity*. Maiden, MA: Blackwell.

Paliga, S. (2006). *Etymological Lexicon of Indigenous (Thracian) Elements in Romanian*. Bucharest, Romania: Centrul Mass Media Evenimentul.

Papacostea, Ş. (1993). *Românii in Secolul al XIII-lea: între Cruciată şi Imperiul Mongol [The Romanians in the 13th Century: between the Crusade and the Mongol Empire]*. Bucharest, Romania: Editura Enciclopedică.

Părăuşanu, T. (2008). *Instituţiile juridice în procesul de formare a poporului român*. PhD., Universitatea de Stat din Moldova, Chişinău, Moldova.

Parchami, A. (2009). *Hegemonic Peace and Empire: the Pax Romana, Britannica and Americana*. Abingdon, UK; New York, NY: Routledge.

Pascu, Ş. (1982). *A History of Transylvania*. New York, NY: Dorset Press.

Pausanias. *Description of Greece* (Vol. I).

Peachin, M. (1989). *Roman imperial titulature and chronology, 235-284*. Leiden, Netherlands: Brill.

Pearson, R. (1996). Hungary: a state truncated, a nation dismembered. In S. Dunn (Ed.), *Europe and Ethnicity: World War I and contemporary ethnic conflict*. Florence, KY: Routledge.

Pei, M. (1976). *The Story of Latin and the Romance Languages*. New York, NY: Harper & Row.

Petculescu, L. (2006). The Roman Army as a Factor of Romanisation in the North-Eastern Part of Moesia Inferior. In T. Bekker-Nielsen (Ed.), *Rome and the Black Sea Region: Domination, Romanisation, Resistance*. Aarhus, Denmark: Aarhus University Press.

Péter, L. (1992). *Historians and the history of Transylvania*. Boulder, CO: East European Monographs.

Petrovics, I. (2009). Foreign Ethnic Groups in the Towns of Southern Hungary in the Middle Ages. In D. Keene & B. Nagy (Eds.), *Segregation – Integration – Assimilation*. Farnham, England; Burlington, VA: Ashgate.

Phang, S. E. (2001). *The marriage of Roman soldiers (13 B.C. - A.D. 235): law and family in the imperial army*. Leiden, Netherlands: Brill.

Pinter, Z. K., & Tiplic, I. M. (2006). Scurta istorie a Transilvaniei - perspective arheologice. In A. Dragota & I. M. Tiplic (Eds.), *Piese de Podoaba si Vestimentatie la Grupurile Ethnice din Transilvania (sec. 7-12)*. Alba Iulia: Departamentul pentru Relatii Interetnice.

Plato. *Charmides*.

Pliny. *Natural History*.

Polomé, E. C. (1987). Tradition and Development in Indo-European Studies. *The Journal of Indo-European Studies, 15*(3), 225.

Polyaenus. Stratagems.

Pop, I.-A. (1996). *Românii şi maghiarii în secolele IX-XIV: Geneza statului medieval în Transilvania [The Romanians and Magyars in the 9th-14th centuries: the genesis of the medieval state in Transylvania]*. Cluj-Napoca, Romania: Centrul de Studii Transilvane.

Pop, I.-A. (1997). *Istoria Transilvaniei medievale: De la etnogeneza românilor pînă la Mihai Viteazul [The History of Medieval Transylvania: from the ethnogenesis of the Romanians to Michael the Brave]*. Cluj-Napoca, Romania: Cluj University Press.

Pop, I.-A. (2002). Unele urmări în plan confesional ale cruciadei a IV-a (1204) în Centrul şi Sud-Estul Europei. In M. Dobre (Ed.), *Istorie şi Ideologie: omagiu profesorului Stelian Brezeanu la 60 de ani*. Bucharest, Romania: Editura Universitară Bucureşti.

Pop, I.-A. (2003). Nations and Denominations in Transylvania (13th-16th Century). In C. Levai & V. Vese (Eds.), *Tolerance and intolerance in historical perspective*. Pisa, Italy: Clioh's Workshop.

Pop, I.-A., Barbulescu, M., & Nägler, T. (2005). *The History of Transylvania, I (up to 1541)*. Cluj-Napoca: CTS, Romanian Cultural Institute.

Popescu, R. (1963). *Istoriile domnilor Ţării Româneşti*. Bucharest, Romania: Editura Academiei Republicii Populare Romîne.

Porphyrgenitus, C. (1967). *De Administrando Imperio* (G. Moravcsik, Trans.). Washington: Dumbarton Oaks Center for Byzantine Studies.

Poruciuc, A. (2008). An Opening to Remember: Meyer-Lübke's Outlook on the Old Germanisms in Romanian. In T. Khan (Ed.), *Das rumänische und seine Nachbarn*. Berlin, Germany: Frank & Timme.

Posner, R. (1996). *The Romance Languages*. Cambridge, UK; New York, NY: Cambridge University Press.

Pounds, N. J. G. (1973). *An historical geography of Europe, 450 B.C.-A.D. 1330*. Cambridge, UK: Cambridge University Press.

Price, G. (2000). *Encyclopedia of the Languages of Europe*. Malden, MA: Blackwell.

Procopius. Buildings.

Procopius. History of Wars.

Prodan, D. (1996). *Transylvania and Again Transylvania: a historical expose.* Cluj-Napoca, Romania: Centrul de Studii Transilvane, Fundația Culturala Română

Prodan, D., & Lăzărescu, M. (1971). *Supplex Libellus Valachorum: or, the political struggle of the Romanians in Transylvania during the 18th century.* Bucharest, Romania: Editura Academiei Republicii Socialiste România.

Psellus, M. *Chronographia.*

Quiles, C., & López-Menchero, F. (2009). *A Grammar of Modern Indo-European.* Badajoz, Spain: Indo-European Association (DNGHU).

Rădvan, L. (2009). Considerations Regarding the Urbanization Process in Wallachia (13th-15th Centuries). In L. Pilat (Ed.), *Medieval and Early Modern Studies for Central and Eastern Europe.* Iasi, Romania: Alexandru Ioan Cuza University.

Rădvan, L. (2010). *At Europe's Borders: Medieval Towns in the Romanian Principalities.* Leiden, Netherlands; Boston, MA: Brill.

Rady, M. C. (1988). Review of Köpeczi, Béla (ed.), Erdely tortenete. 3 vols. Akademiai kiad6, Budapest, I986. *The Slavonic and East European Review, 66*(3).

Rady, M. C. (2000). *Nobility, Land and Service in Medieval Hungary.* Basingstoke; New York: Palgrave.

Rankin, D. (1996). *Celts and the Classical World.* New York, NY: Routledge.

Rásonyi, L. (1979). Bulaqs and Oguzs in Medieval Transylvania. *Acta Orientalia Academiae Scientiarum Hungaricae, 33,* 129-151.

Reiffenberg, A. F. d. (1838). *Chronique Rimée de Philippe Mouskes* (Vol. II). Brussels, Belgium: Commission Royale d'Histoire.

The Resources and Future of Austria. (1863). *The Quarterly Review, 114,* 34.

Réthy, L. (1884). *Daco-Roumains ou Italo-Roumains? Études historiques et philologiques.* Budapest: Impr. "Magyar Nyomda, 1897.

Roca, I. M. (1999). Stress in the Romance Languages. In H. v. d. Hulst (Ed.), *Word Prosodic Systems in the Languages of Europe.* Berlin: Mouton de Gruyter.

Rodewald, C. (1976). *Money in the Age of Tiberius.* Totowa, NJ: Rowman and Littlefield.

Roe, P. (2005). *Ethnic Violence and the Social Security Dilemma.* London, UK; New York, NY: Routledge.

Rogerius. (1938). Carmen Miserabile. In E. Szentpetery (Ed.), *Scriptores Rerum Hungarorum* (Vol. II). Budapest: Academia Litter. Hungarica atque Societate Histor. Hungarica.

Romocea, C. G. (2004). Reconciliation in the ethnic conflict in Transylvania: theological, political and social aspects. *Religion, State and Society, 32*(2), 159-176.

Róna-Tas, A. (1999). *Hungarians and Europe in the Early Middle Ages: an introduction to early Hungarian history.* Budapest: Central European University Press.

Rösler, R. (1871). *Rumänische Studien: Untersuchungen zur älteren Geschichte Rumäniens.* Leipzig.

Rossi, L. (1971). *Trajan's Column and the Dacian wars.* Ithica, NY: Cornell University Press.

Rothschild, J. (1992). *East Central Europe between the two World Wars.* Seattle, WA: Univ. of Washington Press.

Ruhlen, M. (1991). *A Guide to the World's Languages: Classification.* Stanford, CA: Stanford University Press.

Ruscu, D. (2004). The Supposed Extermination of the Dacians: the literary tradition. In W. S. Hanson & I. P. Haynes (Eds.), *Roman Dacia: the making of a provincial society.* Portsmouth: Journal for Roman Archaeology.

Rusu, M. (1997). Continuitatea Daco-Romana in Perioada 275-568 *Istoria Romaniei. Transilvania.* (Vol. I). Cluj-Napoca, Romania: George Baritiu.

Sala, M. (2005). *From Latin to Romanian: the historical development of Romanian in a comparative Romance context.* Oxford, MS: University of Mississippi Press.

Sălăgean, T. (2005). Dextram Dantes, Notes on the Specificity of the Relations Between the Hungarian Conquerors and the Local Population in Northern Transylvania in the 10th-14th Centuries. In Z. K. Pinter, I. M. Țiplic & M. E. Țiplic (Eds.), *Relatii interetnice in Transilvania (secolele VI-XIII).* Bucharest: Departamentul pentru Relații Interetnice.

Sassu, C. (1973). *Rumanians and Hungarians: historical premises*. Bucharest, Romania: P. Georgescu-Delafras.

Schmitz, M. (2005). *The Dacian Threat: 101-106 AD*. Armidale, Australia: Caeros Publishing.

Schulte, K. (2009). Loandowrds in Romanian. In M. Haspelmath & U. Tadmor (Eds.), *Loanwords in the World's Languages: A Comparative Handbook*. Berlin: De Gruyter Mouton.

Schwandner-Sievers, S. (2004). Times Past: References for the Construction of Local Order in Present-Day Albania. In M. Todorova (Ed.), *Balkan Identities: nation and memory*. New York, NY: New York University Press.

Sedlar, J. W. (1993). *East Central Europe in the Middle Ages, 1000-1500*. Seattle, WA: University of Washington Press.

Seton-Watson, R. W. (1922). Transylvania (I). *The Slavonic Review, 1*(2), 306-322.

Seton-Watson, R. W. (1925). Transylvania (IV) Transylvania since 1867. *The Slavonic Review, 4*(10), 101-123.

Seton-Watson, R. W. (1934). *A History of the Roumanians*. Cambridge, UK: Cambridge University Press.

Simocatta, T. History.

Sisa, S. (1990). *The Spirit of Hungary: a panorama of Hungarian history and culture*. Toronto, Canada: Rákóczi Foundation.

Skylitzes, J. (2010). *Synopsis of Histories* (J. Wortley, Trans.). Cambridge, UK: Cambridge University Press.

Southern, P. (2001). *The Roman Empire from Severus to Constantine*. London, UK; New York, NY: Routledge.

Sozan, M. (1997). *Ethnocide in Romania*. Safely Harbor, FL: Simon Publications.

Spinei, V. (1986). *Modlova in the 11th-14th Centuries*. Bucharest, Romania: Editura Academiei Republicii Socialiste România.

Spinei, V. (2006). *The Great Migrations in the East and South East of Europe from the Ninth to the Thirteenth Century*. Amsterdam: Hakkert.

Spinei, V. (2008). The Cuman Bishopric: genesis and evolution. In F. Curta & R. Kovalev (Eds.), *The Other Europe in the Middle Ages: Avars, Bulgars, Khazars, and Cumans*. Leiden, Netherlands; Boston, MA: Brill.

Spinei, V. (2009). *The Romanians and the Turkic Nomads North of teh Danube Delta from the Tenth to the Mid-Thirteenth Century*. Leiden, Netherlands: Brill.

Steed, H. W. (1914). *The Habsburg Monarchy*. London, UK: Constable & Company.

Stefanescu-Draganesti, V. (1986). *Romanian Continuity in Roman Dacia: linguistic evidence*. Miami Beach, FL: Romanian History Studies.

Stephenson, P. (2000). *Byzantium's Balkan Frontier: A Political Study of the Norhtern Balkans, 900–1204*. Cambridge, UK; New York, NY: Cambridge University Press.

Stoianovich, T. (1994). *The Balkans: the first and last Europe*. Armonk, NY: Sharpe.

Stoicescu, N. (1980). *Constituirea Statelor Feudale Românesti*. Bucharest, Romania: Editura Academiei Republicii Socialiste România.

Stoicescu, N. (1993). *O falsă problemă istorică: discontinuitatea poporului român pe teritoriul strămoşesc*. Bucharest, Romania: Editura Fundatiei Culturale Romane.

Stokes, A. D. (1961). The Background and Chronology of the Balkan Campaigns of Svyatoslav Iogrevich. *The Slavonic and East European Review, 40*(94), 44-57.

Strabo. (1924). *The Geography* (J. R. S. Sterrett & H. L. Jones, Trans. Vol. VII).

Stratilescu, T. (1906). *From Carpathian to Pindus*. London, UK: T. Fisher Unwin.

Sturluson, S. (1964). *Heimskringla*. Austin, TX: University of Texas Press.

Sugar, P. F. (1977). *Southeastern Europe under Ottoman Rule: 1354-1804*. Seattle, WA: University of Washington Press.

Sugar, P. F., Hanák, P. t., & Frank, T. (1990). *A History of Hungary*. Bloomington: Indiana University Press.

Tanaşoca, N.-Ş. (2001). Aperçus of the History of Balkan Romanity. In R. Theodorescu & L. C. Barrows (Eds.), *Politics and Culture in Southeastern Europe*. Bucharest, Romania: UNESCO.

Taylor, T. (2001). Thracians, Scythians, and Dacians, 800BC-AD 300. In B. Cunliffe (Ed.), *The Oxford Illustrated History of Prehistoric Europe*. Oxford, UK; New York, NY: Oxford University Press.

Themistius. Oration.

Thompson, E. A. (1982). Zosimus 6. 10. 2 and the Letters of Honorius. *The Classical Quarterly, 32*, 445-462.

Thucydides. *The Landmark of Thucydides: a comprehensive guide to the Peloponnesian War* (R. B. Strassler, Trans. Vol. II).

Thunmann, J. (1774). *Untersuchungen über die Geschichte der östlichen europäischen Völker*. Leipzig.

Thuroczy, J. d. (1766). *Chronica Hungarorum*. Vienna.

Todorov, B. (2010). The value of empire: tenth-century Bulgaria between the Magyars, Pechenegs and Byzantium. *Journal of Medieval History, 36*(4), 312-326.

Toncilescu, P. L. (1996). *Cronica Notarului Anonymus*. Bucharest, Romania: Miracol.

Tóth, E. (2002). The Roman Province of Dacia. In B. Köpeczi, L. Makkai & A. Mocsy (Eds.), *History of Transylvania* (Vol. I). Boulder, CO; New York, NY: Social Science Monographs.

Tóth, Z. n. (1998). *Az erdélyi román nacionalizmus elso"szazada*. Csíkszereda: Pro-Print könyvk.

Trencsényi, B., & Kopeček, M. (2006). *Discourses of Collective Identity in Central and Southeast Europe (1770-1945)*. Budapest, Hungary: Central European University Press.

Treptow, K. W., & Bolovan, I. (1995). *A History of Romania*. Iasi, Romania: Center for Romanian Studies.

Tudela, B. o. (1888). *Itinerary of Benjamin of Tudela*. London, UK: Henry G. Bohn.

Tuetsch, G. D., & Fimhaber, F. (1857). *Urkundenbuch zur Geschichte Siebenbürgens*. Vienna.

Turnock, D. (2007). *Aspects of Independent Romania's Economic History with Particular Reference to the Transition for EU Accession*. Burlington, VT: Ashgate.

Varga, R. (2008). The Peregrine Names from Dacia. *Acta Musei Napocensis, 43-44*(I), 244-245.

Varzari, A., Stephan, W., Stepanov, V., Raicu, F., Cojocaru, R., Roschin, Y., . . . Weiss, E. (2007). Population history of the Dniester-Carpathians: evidence from Alu markers. *Journal of Human Genetics, 52*(4), 308-316.

Vásáry, I. (2005). *Cumans and Tatars: Oriental military in the pre-Ottoman Balkans, 1185-1365*. Cambridge, UK: Cambridge University Press.

Vasiliev, A. (1958). *History of the Byzantine Empire, 324-1453* (Vol. 2). Wisconsin: University of Wisconsin Press.

Vegetius. *Epitome rei militaris*.

Vékony, G. (2000). *Dacians, Romans, Romanians*. Budapest, Hungary: Corvinus Library.

Verantius, A. (1857). *Expeditionis Solymani in Moldaviam et Transsylvaniam libri duo. De situ Transsylvaniae, Moldaviae et Transalpinae liber tertius*. Pest: Eggenberger Ferdinand Akademiai.

Verdery, K. (1995). *National Ideology Under Socialism: identity and cultural politics in Ceausescu's Romania*. Berkeley, CA; Los Angeles, CA: University of California Press.

Victor, A. *De Caesaribus*.

Vida, T. (2008a). Conflict and Coexistence: the local population in the Carpathian Basin under Avar Rule (sixth to seventh century). In F. Curta & R. Kovalev (Eds.), *The Other Europe: Avars, Bulgars, Khazars and Cumans*. Leiden, Netherlands; Boston, MA: Brill.

Vida, T. (2008b). Conflict and Coexistence: the local population of the Carpathian Basin under Avar rule (sixth to seventh century). In F. Curta & R. Kovalev (Eds.), *The Other Europe in the Middle Ages: Avars, Bulgars, Khazars, and Cumans*. Leiden, Netherlands; Boston, MA: Brill.

Villehardouin, G. d. (1908). *Memoirs of the Fourth Crusade and the Conquest of Constantinople* (F. Marzials, Trans.). London, UK: J. M. Dent.

Wanner, R. (2010). *Forts, fields, and towns: communities in Northwest Transylvania from the first century BC to the fifth century AD*. Leicester, UK: University of Leicester.

Wass, A. d. (1977). *Documented facts and figures on Transylvania*. Astor, FL: Danubian Press.

Watson, A. (1999). *Aurelian and the Third Century*. London, UK: Routledge.

190

Wawro, G. (2000). *Warfare and Society in Europe: 1792-1914*. London, UK; New York, nY: Routledge.

Wieczorek, A., & Hinz, H.-M. (2000). *Europe's Center Around 1000: Contributions to History, Art and Archaeology*. Stuttgart: Konrad Theiss Verlag.

Wilkes, J. (1995). *The Illyrians*. Oxford, UK; Cambridge, MA: Blackwell.

Williams, S. (1999). *Rome that did not Fall: the Survival of the East in the Fifth Century*. Florence, KY: Routledge.

Windisch, R. (1981). Teza lui Robert Roesler – o sută de ani mai târziu. In W. d. Gruyter (Ed.), *Logos Semantikos. Studia in honorem Eugenio Coseriu* (Vol. I). Madrid, Spain; Berlin, Germany: Gredos/Walter de Gruyter.

Winnifirth, T. J. (1987). *The Vlachs: the History of a Balkan People*. New York, NY: St. Martin's Press.

Wolff, R. L. (1949). The Second Bulgarian Empire: its origin and history to 1204. *Speculum, 24*(2), 167-206.

Wolff, S. (2004). *Disputed Territories: the transnational dynamics of ethnic conflict settlement*. New York, NY; Oxford, UK: Berghahn.

Wolfram, H., & Dunlap, T. J. (1988). *History of the Goths*. Berkeley, CA: University of California Press.

Wollman, A. (1993). Early Latin loan-words in Old English. In M. Lapidge (Ed.), *Anglo-Saxon England*. Cambridge, UK: Cambridge University Press.

Woodard, R. D. (2008). *The Ancient Languages of Europe*. Cambridge, UK: Cambridge University Press.

Wright, R. (2008). Romance Languages. In K. Brown & S. Ogilvie (Eds.), *Concise Encyclopedia of Languages of the World*. Oxford, UK: Elsevier Science.

Xenopol, A. D. (1913). *Istoria Românilor din Dacia Traiană [The History of the Romanians from Trajan's Dacia]* (Vol. I). Bucharest, Romania: Librariei Şcoalelor.

Xenopol, A. D. (1914). *Istoria Românilor*. Bucharest, Romania: Institutul de Arte Grafice si Editura "LIBRARIEI SCOALELOR" C. SFETEA.

Xenopol, A. D. ((1884) 1998). *Teoria lui Rösler: Studii asupra stăruinţei Românilor în Dacia Traiană*. Bucharest, Romania: Albatros.

Zamosius, S. (1598). *Analecta lapidum vestutorum et nonullarum in Dacia antiquatorum*. Francofurit ad Moenum.

Zosimus. *New History*.

INDEX

Made in the USA
Coppell, TX
28 September 2020